Noor-un-

Noor-un-nisa Inayat Khan
(MADELEINE)

George Cross, M.B.E, Croix de Guerre with Gold Star

JEAN OVERTON FULLER

with a foreword by

THE LATE BARONESS WARD
OF NORTH TYNESIDE C.H., D.B.E.

EAST-WEST PUBLICATIONS
LONDON AND THE HAGUE

PRINTING HISTORY

First published as **Madeleine** by Victor Gollancz, London,
on September 29th, 1952
Second impression before publication
Third impression October 1952
Fourth impression November 1952
Fifth impression December 1952
Sixth impression January 1953
Republished, revised as Noor-un Nisa Inayat Khan
by East-West Publications Fonds N.V., 1971
This edition reprinted, with revisions, by East-West
Publications (U.K.) Ltd., 1988

All enquiries regarding this book should be addressed to:
East-West Publications Fonds B.V.
P.O. Box 85617, 2508 CH,
The Hague, Holland

Printed and bound in Great Britain by
Biddles Ltd, Guildford and King's Lynn

CONTENTS

ILLUSTRATIONS

Frontispiece Noor-un-nisa Inayat Khan,
oil-painting by Violet Overton Fuller

Photographs
Between pages 16 and 17
Tipu Sultan
Moula Bakhsh
Hazrat Inayat Khan
Begum Inayat Khan
Family group, Inayat Khan, the Begum, the children and the uncles

Between pages 80 and 81
Fazal Manzil
The four children
Concert in Fazal Manzil
Noor on horseback
Vilayat on horseback
Noor playing the vina
Noor sitting among the sand-dunes near a beach in Holland
Noor playing the harp
Noor with dog whose broken leg she had set in splints
By the Van Tuyll's lily-pond
Detail of Sufi group
Noor in coat with big collar

Between pages 240 and 241
Noor
Noor in WAAF uniform
84 Avenue Foch
The FANY memorial at St. Paul's Church, Knightsbridge
Memorial plaque in Suresnes to Noor
RAF Memorial at Runnymead

OTHER ILLUSTRATIONS

FOREWORD BY THE LATE BARONESS WARD
OF NORTH TYNESIDE C.H., D.B.E.

The pleasure Jean Overton Fuller will give to many people by telling us so much more of NOOR-UN-NISA INAYAT KHAN'S early life is immense. Noor for her service in SOE has a special place of her own in the history of the Second World War which will never be forgotten by her contemporaries. Her war service makes wonderful reading.

I like to think, however, that to-day's youth, anxious as it is apparently to forget history, will be curious in human terms to read about the real characters and background of those who served the free world with such gallantry before many of them were born. This to me is the especial fascination of this book.

Irene Ward.
House of Commons.
January 25th, 1971

AUTHOR'S FOREWORD

This book was first published, in 1952, by Victor Gollancz Ltd. This was not the first firm to which I had submitted it; it was a case of 'seventh time lucky' for I had submitted it to six others. The chief reason given by the six who had turned it down was the division of interest between Noor's Indian background and the war. Readers who wanted a story of the Resistance would not be interested in her Sufi background, and *vice versa*. Messrs. Gollancz felt that to some extent too and their editor, deciding that more people would be interested in it as a war story than as a Sufi one, greatly cut down the parts relating to Noor's family background and the nature of her father's teaching.

The book went into six printings in the original hard-bound edition, then into a paperback, in which it enjoyed mass sales. It was translated into French, serialised in various papers; I was invited to give two talks about it on the B.B.C. and it was made the subject, in 1955, of a television play produced by Duncan Ross. In other words, it was a success. But even successful books come to an end; at least for a time. It went out of print. Over the years, I have received many pathetic letters from people asking where they could buy copies, and had to tell them it had now become a rare book. People were advertising for it.

In 1970, Mr. Wite Carp, of East-West Publications, Rotterdam, offered to republish it. But Mr. Wite Carp was a Sufi, and for him the greatest interest lay precisely in those parts which had been cut out. Moreover, though Messrs. Gollancz were certainly right from their point of view, it occurs to me that, now that the war is receding from people's minds, it may be the integration of Noor's mission in a more fully rounded picture of her life, with its overtones of awareness of her father's teaching, which will give the book its lasting interest. Even after I had restored Gollancz's cuts, Mr. Carp's appetite for more concerning Noor's father remained unassuaged; until I thought at last of two introductory chapters concerning the ancestors of Noor, which I myself had shorn off—considering them too much for the balance of the book — before ever Messrs. Gollancz saw it. I found them at the bottom of a trunk. I had not looked at them in twenty years; but when I submitted them to Mr. Wite Carp, he pronounced unhesitatingly for their inclusion.

For my part, I could not let the book go into a new edition without inserting in the war section certain facts touching her story which only became known to me when the book was out of print in all editions. And since it was for a different sort of publisher this time, there were appendices I wanted to add: a horoscope of Noor, and a poem telling of the effect she had had upon one human being, the German who took her prisoner and conducted her interrogation, as he told it to me.

I have been able to add to the present edition the testimony of Monsieur Rémy Clément, French pilot, during the war assistant to Déricourt. I traced him in 1973, when researching for a further book on Déricourt, which never appeared because the publisher who commissioned it went bankrupt. I met M. Clément at Easter, 1973, just before and just after visiting the birth-place of Déricourt (which I had managed to discover) and meeting the people of that village who had known him as a child in his parents' home. All this being quite unknown to M. Clément, to whom the origins of his friend had always been a mystery, he was much moved, and proposed to me that I should come again to Paris some time when there was a full moon, and he would drive me to all the fields on which, in 1943, he had assisted Déricourt to receive and despatch clandestine aircraft, Pocé-sur-Cisse, St. Martin-le-Beau, Azay-sur-Cher, Soucelles and to Le Vieux Briollay, where they had received "Madeleine". Thus it was that a missing detail in the story of Noor was unexpectedly filled in, for I had never known where she was set down, except vaguely that it was somewhere in the Angers district. On 12 September, 1973, he met me at Orly and we made this tour, arriving in Angers as the shadows were gathering. "No Lysander will come, but otherwise everything will be the same," promised M. Clément himself becoming affected by finding the old scenes. Thus it was that just as the setting sun turned the scene golden, he stopped the car by a field that was unexpectedly small and closely encompassed by hedges, moreover set on quite a steep slope. "That's it!" he said. "That is where we set out the lights for the Lysander that night. That is where she stepped down".

JEAN OVERTON FULLER, 1984

THE ANCESTORS OF NOOR-UN-NISA

THE TIGER OF MYSORE [1]

Noor was the great-great-great-granddaughter of Tipu Sultan, 'The Tiger of Mysore', last Moghul Emperor of Southern India; the story of her antecedents is this.

In the eighteenth century, a weak and internally disrupting Hindu dynasty, in the state of Mysore, found itself briefly displaced by a Muslim rule. If the star of this Muslim dynasty burned only for a short time, yet it was with a bright light. The two rulers, a father, and after him a son, left names which are still meaningful in history — less happily resonant in England than elsewhere, since it was in their warfare against the British that they were mainly distinguished.

Haidar Ali Khan (1722—82), a warrior chieftain who, in 1761, usurped the supreme power, was a man of able brain and vigorous temperament.

The Hindu in Mysore had been a quiet neighbour to the East India Company, politically and militarily somewhat negligible. The usurpation of Haidar brought into being, quickly, a very different situation. By a historical process which it is not the purpose of this book to examine, Haidar and the British came before long to be engaged in armed hostilities. (Haidar had at his back some support from the French.)

At first the advantage was with Haidar. In 1780, he swept through the Carnatic with 20,000 men, scoring over Colonels Braithwaite and Baillie victories so annihilating as to imperil the very existence of the East India Company.

Subsequently the British recuperated, stood, and after about a year's defensive warfare, advanced under Sir Eyre Coote, and

[1] It was mainly during the summer of 1949 that I did the research concerning Tipu Sultan which has gone into this chapter, and wrote it, later to discard it because I thought it inessential to Noor's story. Though both Vilayat and Noor spoke to me of Tipu, I obtained most of the factual information here given from a very handsome book which, by one of those strange accidents which providence seems to place in one's way, I found on a secondhand bookstall: **A View of the Origin and Conduct of the War with Tippoo Sultaun; comprising a narrative of the operations of the army under the command of Lieutenant-General George Harris, and of the Siege of Seringapatam,** by Lieutenant-Colonel Alexander Beatson, late aide-de-camp to the Marquis of Wellesley, Governor-General of India and Surveyor-General to the Army in the Field; printed by W. Bulmer and Co. Cleveland Row, St. James; and sold by C. and W. Nicol, Booksellers to His Majesty, Pall Mall, 1800. (pp. 265 with clxxii of Appendices; illustrations and diagrams.)

I also visited Windsor Castle and the India Office Library to see the relics of Tipu kept there. His Grace the Duke of Wellington had the kindness to reply to an enquiry I addressed to him on some point it was found impossible to resolve.

secured two signal victories over Haidar, at Porto Novo, on the Madras coast, and at Pollilore.

Haidar always felt that the sea had been his worst enemy. "The defeat of many Braithwaites and Baillies will not destroy them," he said on his death-bed. "I can ruin their resources by land, but I cannot dry up the sea."

So saying, he bequeathed the conduct of the war to Tipu, his son, and died.

Tipu Sultan (1749—99) was a genius rather different in nature from his father. Whereas, according to the British, Haidar's attitude was frankly secular, and he cared not at all what a man's religion might be, so long only as he were a good soldier, Tipu was before everything devout. It has, however, been claimed that Haidar was of the Sunni or orthodox Islamic faith, in which case the difference between them may rather have been that where his religion was of the conventional order, Tipu was a mystic, with a mystic's fervour. Traces of the Shi'ite, intensely individualistic, thinking (or, to the Sunnis, heresy) are evident in many of his pronouncements; he regarded himself as a Defender of the Faith. More especially, he believed himself to be inspired by the direct tutelage of Ali, the son-in-law of Mohammed.

His mother, Fakhr-un-nisa, the beautiful and pious sister of Abdul-ul-Hakim, the Nawab of Kalapa, had been, on the eve of his birth, to visit the ascetic, Tipu Mastan Aulia, to ask for his blessing on her first-born, and some indication concerning his future. That he ascribed some spiritual character to the child appears in that he told the Begum Fakhr-un-nisa she should give it his own name.

Concerning the origin of the name Tipu, there is some controversy, but on grounds other than linguistic, the thesis which would make it a derivation from the Kanarese word for 'tiger' recommends itself.

From the first, Tipu took this beast as his personal symbol, and upon his accession to the throne in 1782, he made it the official emblem of the state of Mysore. The tiger's head figured as his armorial bearing, and the word *Sher* ('tiger') or its initial letter, appeared stamped, embroidered or engraved upon every article of his use. Throughout India, he was known as 'The Tiger of Mysore'. Even the stripes upon his clothing, and upon the upholstery of his throne and the cushions of his chamber, represented the stripes of the tiger. His throne had eight corners, surmounted by eight tigers' heads [1], and the whole was set as though across the back of a tiger, whose huge gold head [2] projected in front. Live tigers upon chains guarded the great doors of

[1] Op. cit. p. 154
[2] Now in the Queen's Gold Pantry at Windsor

12

his palace on the fortified island of Seringapatam, and inside the palace more tigers were kept, some in cages, and some upon chains — and it is said that two of his Ministers, having incurred his gross displeasure, were thrown to them alive. The proud words for which he was best known were, 'Better two days as a tiger, than two hundred years as a sheep!' [1]

The mystical value which he saw in this symbol appeared, however, in a cypher which he had engraved upon most of his arms, in which the words *The Lion of God is the Conqueror,* written in the cursive Persian script, were so interwoven and arranged as to form the semblance of a tiger's face.

This inscription certainly had reference to the son-in-law of Mohammed, Hazrat Ali, whom the Prophet formally styled as 'The Lion of God' and whom Tipu regarded as his tutelary saint. (There being no lions in India, but tigers, Tipu seems to have taken the terms as synonymous.)

His sense of a spiritual connection with the son-in-law of Mohammed seems to have been very deep. He was accustomed to keep, in his own hand, a record [2] of such dreams as seemed to him important. This manuscript, which he considered particularly private, he kept normally in a drawer of an escritoire in his chamber and his servant told how the Sultan would always put it away if he was writing it when the servant entered. [3] On one page he records a dream that Hazrat Ali himself appeared to him, and said, "I will not place my foot in Paradise without thee. I will wait for thee, and enter Paradise with thee." Tipu was accustomed to write his own comments beneath each dream, in which he attempted its interpretation; beneath this, he wrote simply, "It sufficeth." [4]

Tipu Sultan inherited the war with England in an hour when it was going badly. He was unable ever to make up his father's losses, and in 1792, the eleventh year of his reign, he was obliged to sign a treaty with Britain by which he lost nearly half his dominions. He signed with a bad will, and never ceased to scheme for their recovery.

His dearest ambition, however, was not merely the restoration of the former boundaries of the Sultanate, but nothing less than the total expulsion of the British from India. For its accomplishment, he knew that he must be dependent upon a French alliance, and he was content to bide his time.

His first embassy to France, in 1778, had been disappointing in its results. His delegates had been, indeed, courteously and

[1] **The War with Tippoo Sultaun**, pp. 153—54.
[2] Now in the possession of the India Office Library, where I was given permission to have it photostated entirely.
[3] **The War with Tippoo Sultaun**, pp. 196—97.
[4] Op. cit. Appendix XXXV, p.cxi.

lavishly entertained by the king, Louis XVI, but had returned without concrete guarantees. Under the growing shadow of popular discontent, Louis hestitated, understandably, in sending to Tipu arms and supplies which he might need at home.

The French Revolution, coming in the same year that Tipu lost half his dominions, was a source of peculiar embarrassment to the Sultan. A monarch himself, profoundly convinced of the divine consecration, inspiration and right of kings, he could not feel sympathy toward a popular government which had arrived by the decapitation of the consecrated head.

Nevertheless, France and Mysore were natural allies. He did nothing precipitate. A little time passed. The Republic, when it took to considering affairs in the East, expressed itself desirous of maintaining those relations of amity which had always obtained between France and Mysore. Tipu broached the question of a supply of men and arms.

Gradually both began to find their way into the Sultanate. On May 14th, 1797, the Tricolor was formally hoisted in the city of Mysore, and François Ripaud proposed a toast to 'Citizen Tipu!'

The presence of French troops on his soil, though very welcome, was not entirely without embarrassment to the Sultan. A devout observer of the prescriptions of the Koran, he had early in his reign issued an edict forbidding the sale and consumption of spirituous liquors in his dominions, and had followed this up by sending his officials out to require from every previous distiller or vendor an engagement to turn to another occupation. To a Minister who had represented to him the loss of revenue which must be consequent, he had retorted that a *king should be inflexible in his orders, and God had forbidden the use of wine.*

Tipu was in his way a moralist and a puritan; two other things particularly excited his abomination: polyandry and the appearance in the street of women bare to the waist. Following his conquests in Southern India, he forbade both by edict. One of his secretaries assured Lt. Col. Wilkes he had seen the draft of an edict in the Sultan's hand forbidding the faithful to eat meat or embrace their wives except on the evening of Thursday in every week. [1]

Now, a Monsieur Lally made representations to him that the French stationed in his capital must absolutely have the possibility of drinking wines. Considering that he was not responsible for the souls of the Infidel, he consented in the end to the esta-

[1] In so far at any rate as concerns the women naked to the waist in Southern India his efforts to make them cover were shortlived. As late as 1913 my mother tells me she saw them — the Naya's — on the coast of Malabar, but she formed the impression that despite their nakedness they had a natural modesty. See my **Shelley** note on p. 319.

14

blishment of premises where French persons might consume wines, on the condition that it should be set up in the desert, and at a sufficient distance from the boundaries of the city to ensure that the Faithful should not suffer contamination.

At the end of January, 1798, the Governor of Mauritius had a proclamation posted in the island, by which he made known to the citizens an invitation extended to them by Tipu Sultan to come to Mysore and serve under his flag in a war to expel the British from India.

In February 1798 the young General Napoleon Bonaparte, having just arrived in Egypt, wrote a letter to Tipu Sultan. [1]

FRENCH REPUBLIC

Liberty   Equality

BONAPARTE, Member of the National Convention, General in Chief, to the most Magnificent Sultaun, our greatest Friend, TIPPOO SAIB.

Headquarters at Cairo, 7th Pluviose, 7th year of the Republic, One and Indivisible

You have been informed of my arrival on the borders of the Red Sea, with an innumerable and invincible army, full of the desire of delivering you from the iron yoke of England.

I eagerly embrace this opportunity of testifying to you the desire I have of being informed by you, by way of Muscat and Mocha, as to your political situation.

I would even wish you could send some intelligent person to Suez or Cairo, possessing your confidence, with whom I may confer.

May the Almighty increase your power and destroy your enemies.

(Signed) BONAPARTE
True Translation from the French,
(Signed) Francis Woppers, Translator.

(Seal)

This letter Bonaparte enclosed in one addressed to the Sheriff of Mecca, begging him to forward it to Mysore — but the Secretary and First Vizier of the Sheriff had copies made of both documents, and gave these to a Captain Wilson of the British Army, whilst sending on the originals

That Tipu and Bonaparte were natural allies, had been from the first obvious; yet notwithstanding this intelligence of their

[1] **The War with Tippoo Sultaun,** Appendix VII, pp. XXXI—XXXII

15

intercourse, it was not until the news of Lord Nelson's victory in the Nile reached Calcutta on October 31st, that the Governor-General felt in a position strong enough to reveal to Tipu his knowledge of his relations with the French and evident intent to violate the terms of his treaty of 1792.

A correspondence ensued. Tipu's replies to Lord Mornington's letters were manifestly 'unsatisfactory' and of a delaying nature.

On February 3rd, 1799, the Governor-General signified that he now considered England to be at war with Tipu Sultan.

In March, Colonel Wellesley was appointed to the command of the British Forces serving with the Nizam of Hyderabad; and in the same month, the army marched.

After some manoeuvres and skirmishing, the Sultan found himself obliged to a defensive action, and fell back upon his island fortress of Seringapatam, in the Cauvery river, a few miles to the North of the city of Mysore.

The fortress was formidable. It was entirely surrounded by double rows of ramparts, varying in height from twenty to thirty-five feet. A wide, deep ditch, cut in the solid rock, ran at the back of each wall. On the North side was a sloping stone glacis, and the facing shore of the mainland was covered, mile after mile, with an apparently impenetrable forest of thorn trees.

Tipu seems to have been under the impression that the place was impregnable. Blithe and debonaire, he remarked to his commander, Badr-ul-Zeman Khan, "In the course of my life, I have been present at many actions, but never at the defence of a fort. I have no idea of the proper method of defending this fort; and after the present siege, by God's favour, I will make myself a master of this part of the art of war."

With him, he had at this time only 120 French, of whom 20 were officers.

From the British point of view, it was crucial to reduce the fort before the bursting of the rains. The river, then, must swell to a torrent, but comprised, now, only a few streams gliding over the wide bed in the rock.

On the evening of May 3rd, British guns breached the ramparts, and at half past one on the following afternoon, General Baird led forward the storming party.

The fighting was fierce. The Sultan himself stood with those who were attempting to hold the breach, firing with his own hand.

When it became evident they could not stem the invasion, he turned abruptly, and attempted to force his way through the press, on horseback, toward the Zenana. According to Rajah Khan, the only person to have been at his side the whole afternoon, the thought of the ladies of his household had been in his

16

Tipu Sultan

Moula Bakhsh

Inayat Khan

Ora Ray
a picture taken
soon after her
marriage to
Inayat Khan

Family Group
At the back standing left Maheboob Khan,
on the right Musharaff Moulamia Khan
Centre Inayat Khan and the Begum
In front Noor, Claire, Hidayat, Vilayat

mind since the moment when he realised the fort was going to fall, and he had considered it his duty to put them to the sword with his own hand, lest they be exposed to outrage in the tumult.

The great gateway, when the Sultan and Rajah Khan reached it, presented already a scene of carnage. Trying to push his way through a mêlée, in which British soldiers and his own were closely mingled, the Sultan was wounded, first in his breast, then in his right side. Rajah Khan, seeing how heavily he was afflicted, cried out to him that he should make his identity known to the British soldiers, who would surely treat his person with respect.

"Are you mad?" shouted Tipu. "Be silent!"

Rajah Khan attempted to disengage him from the saddle and they both fell to earth together.

Rajah Khan, wounded in the leg himself, was yet able to drag the Sultan a little to one side, and so prop him up under the relative shelter of the arch of the great gate. An English soldier, catching sight of the rich gold buckle with which the Sultan's belt was fastened, stooped and tried to take it off him. Tipu, however, was not dead yet. So many bodies had fallen across his own that he could not get to his feet, being pinned amongst the dead and dying; but he reached out with his hand, laterally, plucked a sword from one of those who had fallen, and struck upwards, slashing the grenadier across the knee. The grenadier, incensed, raised his musket, put it straight to the Sultan's temple, not knowing who he was, and shot him.

Only Rajah Khan knew what had happened. When in the later afternoon, he led General Baird to the spot where 'The Tiger' had fallen, so deeply was the gateway piled with dead that a long task was still ahead of the searchers. One by one, the bodies were lifted and brought out from the shadow of the arch for examination; and when the daylight faded, torches had to be brought out to enable Rajah Khan to continue to scrutinise them. At last the body was brought out which he at once identified. [1] The Sultan had lost his turban and his sword; but his eyes were open, and his features in no way disfigured or contorted.

Even in death, wrote one present, he carried such a vivacity of hatred that Arthur Wellesley, standing over him in the flickering torchlight, could not believe him dead till he had felt the heart and pulse.

He was dressed in a white linen jacket, and loose drawers of flowered chintz, with a crimson cloth of silk and cotton round the waist. He was of small stature, a trifle corpulent, very dark

[1] Op. cit. pp. 136—37.

17

of complexion, with aquiline nose, bold eyes and prominent chin. His brows were finely arched, and his hands and feet remarkably small and delicately shaped.

The following day, four companies of Europeans marched with his bier. It was borne by his personal attendants, and accompanied by the Kazi, chanting verses from the Koran. Thousands of the faithful prostrated themselves as the Sultan passed on his last journey through the streets toward Lal Bang, where they laid him with his father; the occasion of the last obsequies being rendered more awful by the bursting of an almighty thunderstorm. [1]

THE HOUSE OF MOULA BAKHSH

I

The Secret Princess

The British considered that it would be folly to permit the heir of Tipu accession to the throne, and therefore decided to restore the Hindu dynasty in the person of the five year old son of the last Rajah. The state of Mysore was first reduced in size. A strip neighbouring upon Hyderabad was awarded to the Nizam, in recognition of his assistance in the war against Tipu Sultan; a smaller strip adjoining the Mahrattas' dominions was given to the Mahrattas; two strips, one along the West coast, and one along the Southern and Eastern boundaries, the British kept for themselves; and what remained in the middle — a territory about two-thirds of the size of England — they offered as a free gift to the infant Hindu prince, Krishnaraj, on the condition that an annual subsidy be paid to the British Government, that a general control over the affairs be exercised by a British Resident at his court, and that the island of Seringapatam be ceded to the British Government in perpetuity.

These terms, so unexpectedly restoring the fortunes of their family, were gratefully accepted on behalf of the young prince, by the widows of his two grandfathers, in a document dated June 24th, 1799.

The surviving sons of the Sultan, who fell into British hands, together with their entire households, were pensioned and transported, under the escort of the Marquis of Wellesley, to the town of Vellore in Madras. Here they resided until 1806 when, being charged with the instigation of the Sepoy mutiny of that year, they were further removed to Calcutta.

[1] Op. cit. pp. 148—49

18

According to Mahmood Khan: [1]

"Those of the Tipu clan and household not transferred to Calcutta were, and continued to be, treated generously by the succeeding Hindu rulers. They were installed honourably and comfortably in a palace built for them, in recognition of the Tipu dynasty and clan's position as 'national' figures who had given the state of Mysore its largest extent and greatest international position, and in spite of dynastic rivalries.

The Tipu family and household were now headed by the Nawab of Kalapa. In the absence of Tipu's sons, it was he who then reassumed Haidar Ali's erstwhile rank of premier Muslim noble of Mysore state. Not only that but he, and after him each eldest son or senior heir succeeding as head of the family group, continued to be recognised and ceremoniously received by the ruling Maharajas as the Tipu-sultan or Tipu-sahib of his time, there thus being a Tipu, numbered like the successors in a dynasty, in each generation."

The further history of the antecedents of Noor-un-nisa has to be picked up from the oral tradition of her family. Her brother, Vilayat, made it very clear to me that they held no documentary evidence of their descent from Tipu, and that he could tell me only what he had understood from his father, as his father had understood it from the older generations; the uncles of Noor-un-nisa and Vilayat also laid stress upon this lack of anything which could be shown as evidence, and made the point that they were not claiming anything, only repeating what had been passed down to them, believing it to be true.

One of the sons of Tipu, who was known as Tipu II, participated in the Indian Mutiny of 1857, and died in the fighting, apparently during the British siege of Delhi (which had been captured by the Mutineers), and it was his orphaned daughter, a girl of about fourteen named Casime-bi, who was stolen to safety by two faithful servants of her father's. Brothers, known as Sultan Khan Sharif[2] and Pir Khan Sharif, they were sons of an officer who had served 'the Tiger'. The assumption of responsibility for Casime-bi placed them in considerable danger, both from the British, who were issuing manifestoes requiring that any members of Tipu's family discovered still alive should be handed over to them, and even from the males of the Tipu dynasty who might be still at large, since they might not view in the best light the action of the two faithful servants in taking care of a lady of their house. In an uncertainty what to do, they conducted her secretly to

---

[1] Mahmood Khan, a younger cousin of Pir Zadi Noor-un-nisa, the son of the late Shaikh-ul-Mashaikh Maheboob Khan, who lived in The Hague.

[2] Khan is a title signifying royal, noble or gentle birth.

19

Mysore, and after hiding with her there for a while, took the step of making their presence known to a young Muslim nobleman, Moula Bakhsh, and telling him of the secret jewel they guarded. Moula Bakhsh Khan, who was born in 1833, in Delhi, of a Zamindar family, had devoted his life to music. He trained in the first place as a singer, but later became impassioned for the ancient, sacred music of southern India, the well from which he drew to revive the stylised music of the north. His work received quick recognition in many courts, and whilst still only twenty-four he was widely hailed as "The Morning Star" or the hope for a revival of the profound mystical music of India.

His sweet nature was as renowned as his gifts, and he seemed a young man destined to enjoy the light of a bright and radiant celebrity. Nevertheless, being by birth of the minor nobility only, he was not of such a station that he could, in the normal way, have been married to the Princess. She, as the grand-daughter of the Tiger, could only be married to a royal Prince.

What happened next is a little curious. The Hindu ruler, the Maharajah Krishnaraj, raised him to the princely rank, which enabled the grand-daughter of Tipu to find in him a husband of her own degree.

Vilayat put it to me that it seemed to him that the Hindu rajah understood what he did; for his generosity and kindness in making it possible for the grand-daughter of Tipu to have in Moula Bakhsh a husband with whom she could live in dignity and happiness, made it forever impossible that her descendants should bear arms against his House.

II

Baroda

Shortly after their marriage, Moula Bakhsh Khan and the Begum received an invitation from the Maharajah Gaekwar of Baroda to spend some time at his Court.

They accepted, taking with them the two officers who had so faithfully served their mistress from the beginning. Finding the state of Baroda congenial, they decided to settle; and took up residence, all together, in the mansion known as Moula Bakhsh House, which remains with the family to the present day.

In Baroda, Moula Bakhsh founded under the patronage of the Maharajah Gaekwar a musical academy, the Gayan Shala, now the University Faculty of Indian Music, and a department of Western Music.

He rendered also a great service to Indian music in that he

20

worked out a feasible system of notation by which it might be recorded.

To Moula Bakhsh and the Begum Casime-bi were born four children, a son Murtuza Khan Moula Bakhsh [1] and three daughters Fatima-Khanim, Khatija-Bibi and Inayat-Bibi. It is from the second daughter, Khatija-Bibi[2], that Noor-un-nisa is descended. Moula Bakhsh (a Muslim) married two more wives, taking a Brahmin as well as a Rajput wife. By marriage with his second wife he had a son, Dr. A. M. Pathan.

Khatija-Bibi (1867—1902) was a gracious and serious minded girl, and although she was quiet and reserved in her manner, her children tell that her disposition was both sunny and exceedingly sweet. She was bright, and as a child developed with extraordinary rapidity. She was taught to read whilst very small, acquired classical Persian and Arabic almost simultaneously with her mother tongue,. Urdu. Khatija-Bibi continued during the whole of her life to extend her literary culture. She read, in particular, much Persian poetry, and was interested in questions of religious philosophy.

Musharaff Moulamia Khan (1895—1967), her youngest son, writes in his book, *Pages from the Life of a Sufi*[3], 'She had an equal interest in the religion of Islam — this word, it must be remembered, means peace — and in the religion of the Hindus. She loved specially the happy view of life, and in this she resembled her father, Moula Bax[4], who looked always on the happy side of things. And so she loved the manner in which the Hindus express the many happy aspects of God, in symbolical figures of gods and goddesses which represent delight, prosperity, benevolence, such as the many-armed one who represents the manifold help perpetually offered by Divinity. Also the symbolical figure of Ganesh was loved by her, the elephant-headed, who represents the quiet-pacing majesty, the strength, the patience of God.'

She married Rahmat Khan (1843—1910), a northerner fair skinned as a European, the son of Bahadour Khan, of the Mash-

---

1 Who later succeeded his father in his rank and positions.
2 -Bi, or -Bibi, like -un-nisa, is a termination added to the names of Muslim ladies of a certain elevation. Amongst friends, the names can be used without these terminations.
3 Rider, 1932, pp. 32—33.
4 This name, like most Indian names, has suffered various transcription into Roman characters. The spelling I use is I believe the more phonetic. The name means Gifted One and was bestowed on him by a dervish to whom he had rendered a service. Before this, he had been called Shole Khan.

21

aikh [1] family of the Punjab, and a direct descendant of Juma Shah Mashaikh, the Sufi saint whose tomb is still visited every year by pilgrims from all parts. They were of Turkestani origin. Rahmat Khan too was a musician, and had particularly absorbed himself in the study of *dhrupad,* the ancient, sacred music which had matured in India in the epoch of the Moguls. He was therefore pursuing a line of research parallel to that initiated by Moula Bakhsh but in the Northern, Rajput tradition rather than in the Southern, Brahmin one.

The way in which he came to Baroda was rather remarkable. He never considered himself to be a mystic, yet he told that it occurred whilst he was visiting the tomb of the Sufi saint, Khwaja Moin-ud-Din Chisti [2] that his state of consciousness became a little changed, and he saw the figure of the saint rise from the ground and signal to him that he should take the road to Baroda. This he did — not knowing what should await him there.

He had no connections in this town, but when he arrived in it, he made quite by chance an acquaintance who brought him to the house of Moula Bakhsh. Here a musical evening gave him the opportunity to perform. Moula Bakhsh, as a musician, recognised at once that he had in his guest a singer and player of some quality; and when he learned from the young man that his chief interest lay in just that branch of musical study to which he had devoted his own life, it seemed to him as if he must have been 'sent.'

After studying him for some time, and coming to form a good impression of his character, he invited him more intimately into his household, and a marriage was arranged with his daughter, Fatima-Khanim. But she died young after giving birth to a daughter.

Rahmat Khan married Khatija-Bibi as his second wife. Yielding to the earnest wish of Moula Bakhsh, the young couple remained with him at Moula Bakhsh House, and so the generations grew together under the shadow of the ancestral roof.

Khatija-Bibi had naturally been brought up in conditions of strict Purdah — in which she continued to live during the whole of her life. However, the seclusion of Indian ladies need not be taken to imply isolation. Moula Bakhsh House, comprehending the vassal and servant families, as well as the married sons' families and other relatives, was in itself a veritable community. The ladies of the House of Moula Bakhsh indeed followed the Begum Moula Bakhsh in maintaining the Purdah in the com-

---

[1] Mashaikh means Grand Sheikh, and is a title, not a name. Vilayat says he was told that Rahmat Khan was descended on his mother's side from the Royal Family of Khairpur.

[2] The founder of the Chistia line of Sufis, died at Ajmer 1036.

22

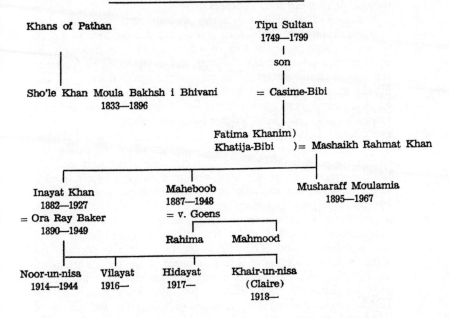

pletest possible way, in accordance with their ideals of dignity and refinement, but one should not think they were without opportunity for cultured intercourse and developing their lives according to their aptitudes.

Again, though it rested with the father of Khatija-Bibi to find a man whom it would be suitable for her to marry, if she had disliked him when he was presented, her feeling would certainly have been respected.

On July 5th, 1882, a son was born to Khatija-Bibi and Rahmat Khan; this was Hazrat Inayat[1] Khan, the father of Noor-un-nisa. After him came two more boys, Maheboob Khan ((1887-1948), the father of Mahmood, and Musharaff Moulamia Khan (1895-1967)[2]. To this family of three boys, there became added later a cousin, on the side of Moula Bakhsh, Mohammed Ali Khan (1881-1959) whose parents had died. Family ties being very close in

1 Inayat means 'Favour'. He received this name after an aunt, Inayat-Bibi, who wished that her name should be perpetuated in him.
2 Muslims have no surnames. They are known simply by their personal names, together with any titles they may bear. They may, however, add a patronymic, and when living in the West usually do this, and so create a sort of surname. Thus the four children of Inayat all use Inayat Khan for identification whereas Mahmood uses Youskine. In Indian custom the patronymics are not necessary.

23

India, he grew up with the other three, and it was effectively as though there were four brothers. [1]

Khatija-Bibi, though a lettered woman, was none the less a devoted mother. Musharaff Moulamia Khan, her youngest, writes in *Pages from the Life of a Sufi*, p. 33 ' my mother's life was indeed given up to her children, and in educating her children she was specially interested in the psychological teaching of the Hindu religion, too often with us debased into forms that have become meaningless superstitions. But under these external forms lie deep truths and knowledge of human nature. Impression is everything. This is the underlying motive of so many Hindu observances. It was our mother's endeavour in educating her children and in building their characters, to avoid ugly and unhealthy suggestions of any kind, and to encourage happy impressions. Children are specially susceptible to impression. They are like sensitive photographic plates. They quickly pick up a gesture, a movement, an inflection of voice, and the impressions that are unconsciously received make sometimes an even deeper mark in the childish mind. The Hindu thinks it even important, for instance, to consider what is the character of the people attending an infant . . . All such details interested our mother, who wished only happiness for her children. She also knew much of the Hindu teaching about the qualities of character, and habits of mind and manner, which bring happiness and prosperity in life. For the Hindu religion, when understood, shows itself deeply scientific in its analysis of human types and in its comprehension of human character and life.'

The children were brought up with the two cultures, Hindu and Muslim, equally at their disposition, and in an acquaintance with Sufi [2] ideas, their father, Rahmat Khan, coming of a Sufi lineage. Moula Bakhsh, as patriarchal head of the whole family, kept practically open house. Men of learning and refinement were always welcome beneath his roof, and at his receptions the philosopher, the scholar, the faqir, the mystic, the poet and the

[1] For convenience I have throughout comprehended him in the term 'the brothers' or when speaking from the point of view of Pir-Zadi Noor-un-nisa, 'the uncles'.

[2] Sufism, generally described as the mystical tradition within Islam — though many of the Sufis would claim that it is older than Islam — has relations with Hinduism, Buddhism, Judaism, Zoroastrianism, Neo-Platonism and Gnostic-Christianity. The name is believed by most scholars to be connected with Arab Saf, 'wool' with reference to woollen garments widely worn by Sufis, but according to some interpretations means purity, as the Sufi teachings are directed to achieving purity of body, mind, heart and soul. Sufism is to be found in all the lands to which the Islamic faith has spread, and has inspired nearly all the great poets in Persia (Rumi, Hafiz, Saadi). There are many different orders of Sufis having slightly differing customs and beliefs. The Sufi traditions are still much alive in North Africa, the Middle East, Pakistan, India and the Far East.

musician, whatever their communal allegiance, might find themselves in company. The children, growing up in this household, took for granted this ease and naturalness of contact between persons of every order, and it was not until they had seen something of the world outside that they realised that the atmosphere of Moula Bakhsh House was something rather special — and which proceeded from the personality of Moula Bakhsh.

INAYAT KHAN

I

In India

Inayat Khan (1882—1927) was from the first a studious and reflective child, given to the love of poetry, music and philosophy. These passions he shared chiefly with his grandfather, Moula Bakhsh, whose company, he tells, was always dearer to him than that of boys of his own age.

He tells: "I was sent to school when quite young, but I fear that I was more inclined to play than to study. I preferred punishment to paying attention to those subjects in which I had no interest. I enjoyed religion, poetry, morals, logic and music more than all other learning, and I took music as a special subject at the Academy of Baroda and repeatedly won the first prize there.

I had so much curiosity about strangers, fortune-tellers, faqirs, dervishes, spiritualists, and mystics, that I would very often absent myself from my meals to seek them out. My taste for music, poetry and philosophy increased daily, and I loved my grandfather's company more than a game with boys of my own age. In silent fascination I observed his every movement and listened to his musical interpretations, his methods of study, his discussions and his conversation." [1]

His father, Rahmat Khan, was a little disturbed by what seemed to him the premature dedication of his eldest son to contemplation. He was always pleased to entertain ascetics and dervishes; but he was also the descendant of warriors, and hoped that his boys would grow up to enjoy what he felt to be a fuller and more balanced view of life. To inspire them, he used to tell them

---

[1] **The Sufi Message of Hazrat Inayat Khan**, Vol XII, p. 130. Barrie & Rockliff, London, 1967. (The English has been slightly altered from that of the original edition published by The Sufi Publishing Society, 1915, pp 8—9, which was itself an adaptation into the first person of an earlier narrative in the third).

25

stories of the prowess of Hazrat Ali, the warrior son-in-law of Mohammed, and also of his own father, Bahadour Khan, a giant man, whose chivalry was well known in the Punjab. He would tell them how once in a solitary place, Bahadour Khan had come across the caravan of a Hindu lady which was at that moment being attacked by thieves, and how he single-handed put them all to flight.

When Inayat was still young, there came a crisis in his development. He had always been of a devotional temperament; but one evening whilst he was standing on the roof, offering up his *nimaz,* or evening prayers, the thought came to him suddenly that he did not know to Whom he was talking, or even if it was to anybody at all.

He hurried downstairs and went to find his grandfather in his study. Although he felt impelled to communicate this doubt which had come to him, he was half afraid lest the elderly man should be shocked, and even angry.

But Moula Bakhsh was not angry. For some moments he sat very still and did not reply. It seemed he was thinking how he should answer. Then he leaned forward and took his copy of the Koran, and opened it at random, looking to see what he should find.

Then he read out the words, *We will show them our signs in the world and in themselves, that the truth may be manifested unto them.*

Then he turned to the boy and explained the text, saying, "You see, the signs of God are seen in the world, and the world is seen in yourself."

For Inayat these words revealed an entirely new point of view. From this time on, it was the thought of the Divine *Immanence* that was the starting point of all his meditations, and which gave the direction to his whole life.

Inayat was educated at the Gayan Shala of his grandfather, developing his great gifts as a singer and player of the vina. In these two arts he developed such excellency that he became known over all India as an artist of outstanding qualities and great promise.

The death of his grandfather in 1896, when he was about fourteen, left him feeling profoundly bereaved, and with this bereavement came a restlessness and a desire to pursue the researches which Moula Bakhsh had initiated, and to give back to India the old, traditional sacred music which had been superseded.

Just now, Providence helped him. His father, who had received an invitation to the court of the Maharaja of Nepal, yielded to the boy's entreaties and took him with him. Inayat was entranced by the grandeur of the Himalayas, and also by the splend-id martial life of Nepal. Whilst his father was teaching music in the palace, the day was his own and he would go out and wander about, exploring the country.

One day, whilst he was following a track through one of the wilder parts of the mountains, he came suddenly upon an ascetic, in a cave. Inayat, having discovered him seated in meditation, was at first abashed by the thought that he had intruded upon a Mahatma in his retreat. The ascetic, however, did not mind being disturbed, and allowed Inayat to sing to him; and after this time Inayat came often to this place, sometimes with his vina, and the ascetic would teach him concerning some of the mysteries of sound.

In 1897, after a year's stay in Nepal, Inayat and his father returned to Baroda, where Inayat was most affected by the reunion with his mother. There had been an incident while he was in Nepal when he had slipped on a mountain path and hurt his leg; he had dreamed that his mother comforted him, and Khatija-Bibi was able to tell him she had dreamed he had come to her and showed her the injured knee. The link between them became increasingly deep; they loved to be together and to talk — and then quite suddenly, in 1902, she died, after a brief illness. Inayat was overwhelmed by this loss, even more than by that of his grandfather.

After this, he decided to travel. He went first, alone, to Madras, where he found himself without money. Whilst he was here he received an invitation from the State of Mysore to attend the Maharajah Krishna Raja Wadyar. He was very willing to visit Mysore, the state which held such tremendous associations for his family, but he had only just the money to take the train. He was standing on the platform of a railway junction, hungry because he had not been able to afford a meal, after buying his ticket, and feeling a little anxious, also, as to the shift he would make when he arrived, when he was suddenly addressed by a person who looked like a beggar, who invited him to eat from the bowl of food he was holding. Whilst Inayat Khan hesitated, not seeing any instrument with which he could serve himself out of this bowl, the man put his dirty hand into it, and held out to him some of the hot mixture on his palm. Inayat Khan, realising the insult he would offer if he were to refuse, took the food in his own hand and ate it. To his surprise, the beggar said, "Do not be worried. You are going to a place where you will be received with open arms and a warm heart. You will be honoured at the court of the Maharajah, and from the moment you set foot on the soil of Mysore you will be received as a royal guest." Inayat Khan was considerably startled at being addressed in these words by a person who could have known nothing of his affairs; but it turned out as the seer had said.

From Mysore he returned to Baroda, then set out again and visited first Bombay and then Hyderabad.

Here he knew no one when he first arrived, but after a time he received an introduction to the Prime Minister, the Maharajah Kishan Pershad, who received him in a place where he was camping for some festival. Whilst he was there, word came that the Nizam was to visit the camp that evening, an announcement which caused the very greatest excitement. The Maharajah suggested to Inayat Khan that he must stay. No one knew for certain at what time to expect His Highness, and all through the evening reports concerning the Nizam's movements kept arriving at intervals. The atmosphere of intense expectation and suspense was almost palpable. Midnight passed and he did not come; and people began to be uneasy, fearing perhaps he had changed his plans. Then at two o'clock in the morning there came a great sound of bugles and of drums, and at last the Nizam himself appeared, seated on an elephant gloriously accoutred, surrounded by Arabs singing and performing sword-dances all around him, the whole procession moving in the light of thousands of torches.

The great elephant came up to the Maharajah's gate, led by the A.D.C., and the Nizam dismounted amidst tremendous ceremony, and was brought inside, followed by his courtiers. Now a ceremony of presentation began according to the old custom of Hyderabad. When the Maharajah brought Inayat Khan forward, he spoke of him with enthusiasm. After a few words, the Nizam said he would like to hear him sing, and asked him to be seated. He himself remained, however, standing, whilst he listened to him. During this time, the whole court had to remain standing also.

Less than six hours after he had gone, a word was sent back from the Nizam that he felt Inayat Khan's music had for him a message and he wished to receive it in private. He invited him to his residence.

When he arrived, His Highness received him in his private apartment, and Inayat Khan saw that he was wearing completely plain dress, without a single one of his orders or decorations. The meaning of this gesture seemed to be that he wished the meeting to take place upon a plane where the insignia of his worldly rank had no meaning. He sat with Inayat Khan, very simply, on the floor, neither courtiers nor any other kind of persons appearing. Again Inayat Khan sang to him, and they talked far into the night till it grew pale. The Nizam, who was a Sufi, wished to know what mystery was in his music. Before they parted, he called

28

him "Tansen," after the great singer, and took off his own finger the huge emerald ring, the only jewel he had kept, and placed it upon the finger of Inayat.

It was whilst he was in Hyderabad that he met at the house of Khairul Mumineen Sahib, the Sheikh-ul-Mashaikh, or Chief of the Sufis, the man whom he always felt to be his real Master.

Khwaja Syed Mohammed Abu Hashim Madani, a lineal descendant of the Prophet Mohammed, a gracious and radiant figure, unbelievably dignified, seemed to Inayat, in the very moment when he saw him as he came in at the door, the teacher for whom he had been searching.

The recognition was mutual; and the Murshid asked their host almost immediately, "Who is this young man? He makes a good impression on me."

After this, Inayat Khan became his pupil, and passed through the various grades of Sufi teaching, yet in the presence of his teacher, it was rather the privilege of being in his atmosphere which he received than any concrete instruction. The Murshid would invite him to take tea, or walk with him in his garden; he would talk about quite ordinary things, and his illumination shone through, as it were, obliquely.

Once only, after Inayat Khan had stayed six months at his master's house, he began to speak about some question of a metaphysical order. His eager pupil immediately brought out a pencil and paper to write his words down — but the Murshid, seeing this preparation, ceased his discourse and reverted to everyday topics. Inayat Khan understood this as an indication he should not attempt to trap the spirit in the letter.

The Murshid seemed to have an intuition of his death before it came; [1] for although he appeared in perfect health he summoned, one after another, all his pupils and bade them goodbye. When Inayat Khan came to him the last time, he appointed him his successor in the Chain of the Sufis, and told him he should go to the Western World to "Unite East and West through the harmony of his music."

So saying, he gave him his blessing.

After the death of his Murshid, Inayat Khan set out on a pilgrimage, visiting the holy men of India, and the tombs of her saints.

In the forests near Ajmer, he came across a group of dervishes chattering on the grass; they were shoeless and utterly ragged — one wore a coat with only one sleeve and one a hat without a crown. Later their Murshid approached, even more scantily clad than the others, a group of them circling round and round

[1] In 1907.

29

him shouting holy verses. The rest sat lost in contemplation or reciting charms. Later in the evening, when they all began to sing, Inayat Khan was so affected by their ecstasy that he was tempted to join their company and live on alms as they did, for it seemed to him they had a complete freedom from the world; but soon he realised it was not his path, and tore himself away.

Afterwards he went again to Southern India, passing once more through Mysore, and then to Tanjore — where he spent three days as the guest of the old royal house, kindly entertained by the young Rajah Shivaji Rao and the Queen Mother — and thence via Malabar, Cochin and Travancore to Ceylon. From here he took ship to Burma; thence back to Calcutta, where he came to know Rabindranath Tagore, and so eventually home.

The death of his father in 1910 cut his last remaining link with India, and on September 13th, 1910, he sailed from Bombay for New York, the Western World and the fulfilment of his mission. He was now twenty-eight.

II

In the West

At this time the mother of Noor-un-nisa, then Miss Ora Ray Baker, born in Albuquerque, New Mexico, on May 8th, 1890, was still a young girl, living in the house of her family in America. She was the niece of a Senator O'Brien, [1] and the granddaughter of a certain Judge Baker. Her father Erastus Warner Baker [2] was a solicitor, and most of the men of her family were either of the legal profession or doctors. Her family were very wealthy, and possessed considerable properties. At the time when she enters the story, her parents were both dead and she, being still in her minority, was the legal ward of her half-brother, a doctor.

She was of entirely British stock, her father being half English and half Irish, and her mother Scottish, of the Wyatt family [3]. She had light, golden hair, with a hint of red; blue eyes, and the very delicate complexion which sometimes goes with this colouring. Her build was fragile, and her general appearance somewhat ethereal.

She was not a committed Orientalist, but had been brought up

[1] According to Madame Mignon Nevada, see next chapter.
[2] It is from her marriage certificate, a copy of which I obtained from Somerset House, that I take the name of her father. Noor and Vilayat believed their mother was a distant cousin of Mary Baker Eddy, the evangelist, but I have been unable to establish this.
[3] This is from Vilayat.

30

to a certain acquaintance with mystical doctrines, because her brother used to run a discussion group where speakers of different religions used to be invited to lecture. From childhood she had always been fascinated by India, and had read all that she could find about it. She had probably heard Swami Vivekananda when he adressed her brother's group, and when she heard Professor Inayat Khan[1] was to speak in a hall in the neigbourhood she attended.

He spoke saying that through all the different religions of men there shone everywhere one light: only it was a pure light, which became diversely coloured as it was filtered through the diversely coloured minds of men; when one transcended this local colour, one found always the same light.

After the discussion which followed the address, she approached him and asked if she might have an interview privately. A little surprised, he accorded naturally to her request. They fell in love.

Yet, reflecting on the uncertainty of his fortunes and the sacrifice in their home-life his mission would demand, he felt constrained to say, "I am a dervish. Today I eat dry bread, tomorrow perhaps none. If you come with me, this will be your life also."[2]

All the members of her family disapproved of the match; and her brother, although he had been the means of introducing the pair, refused his consent to it. Conversely, Inayat Khan's three brothers were politely but profoundly reserved towards it as well.

Inayat Khan did not wish to snatch her from her legal guardian. He had come to the town only to give this address, and would not linger. He said they would write to one another, and later she could join him, when she had won her guardian's consent or when she came of age.

Inayat Khan sailed for Europe. A Sufi Order in France was founded, with Albert Caillet as the head. Lady Churchill and Edmond Bailly introduced him to the musical world of Paris; he came to know Lucien Guitry, Sarah Bernhard, Gabriele D'Annunzio, Isadora Duncan and Walter Rummel, who introduced him to Debussy.

As money was needed to live on, Inayat Khan and his brothers accepted stage engagements and so it came about that they were engaged by Mata Hari, who referred to them as "mon orchestre" and had herself photographed with them, in 1912, in the gardens

1 Professor of Music in the Royal Academy of Baroda, founded by Moula Bakhsh. Since his arrival in the U.S.A., Inayat Khan had had a certain success, and had given lectures on Indian music in the Universities of Berkeley, California and at Columbia, New York, with demonstrations in which he was assisted by his brothers, who had now all come out to join him. In San Francisco he had opened a Sufi centre, and he had founded already a Sufi Order in America, of which he left a Mrs. Ada Martin as representative.

2 These words are exactly as given me by Musharaff Khan.

of her home at Neuilly. She was then at the height of her fame as a dancer; nobody could then have foreseen that within a few years, "The Eye of the morning" was to face, one dawn, the firing-squad, in the Bois de Vincennes. For some months Inayat Khan and Ora Ray corresponded. Miss Baker hoped that she would win her brother's good-will, but he remained firmly against the marriage. When she realised this she wrote to Inayat Khan that she was coming to France to join him. Ora Ray's boat brought her into Antwerp, (Memory of Mignon Nevada), where Inayat Khan met her, and together, they took another boat, to London, meeting aboard it an Indian who undertook to perform a religious rite to solemnise their union.

Inayat Khan and Ora Ray Baker were married at the civil register office of St. Giles, London, on March 20th, 1913. From the marriage certificate, it appears that they were staying at the time, at 4, Torrington Square, Bloomsbury. Her brother was very annoyed, and she never had any further relations with her family. The Begum Inayat Khan now adopted Indian dress, wearing a golden sari of the same colour as her husband's robe, and taking the veil. This was her own idea. Inayat Khan had no wish she should forsake the customs in which she had been brought up, in order to follow those of his own people. The desire proceeded entirely from herself. She explained that she had always envied the women of the East their secluded lives, and felt that in the street the veil offered a protection against the casual glance. Indeed she wrote an article which explains her attitude in the matter, which starts as follows: [1]

WOMAN'S SECLUSION IN THE EAST

by Begum Inayat Khan

God is hidden in the vision, truth in the world unseen, the soul is hidden in the body, and love's tender feeling in the heart; so is woman, for all that is most precious is protected by nature from the sight of man.

It sounds strange to us in the West when we hear of the Purdah women who still observe the Zenana customs in this civilized age. After giving the question further thought we find that seclusion originated amongst mystics, who not only close their lips from speech, but also seclude themselves in grass-huts, forests and caves in the mountains.

The Khalifs and leaders of ancient times veiled their faces in order to preserve their magnetism and a commanding personality. Even until the present day the royalties of both East and

[1] This article appeared in "The Sufi", No. 3 Vol. I, Sept. 1915.

West, as well as the more important personages throughout the world, expose themselves much less than people in general.

Another benefit of the Zenana is the consideration of motherhood and its responsibilities. The mother being the moulder of the child's character and form, it is most necessary for her to be away from the world, avoiding all undesirable impressions, worries and anxieties of life, in order for her thoughts to dwell upon naught else but love, harmony and beauty. She must also at such times avoid all excitements and irritabilities. This is really the most important reason for which seclusion was adopted.

In 1913, Inayat Khan decided to visit Russia. His brothers came with him, naturally, as well as the Begum, and also a young Hindu, Rama Swami, whom they had met in America, and who had attached himself to their little group as a tabla-player.

December 1913 found them in Moscow, where Count Serge Tolstoy, the son of the great Russian author, invited them to his house.

The Mashaikh brothers were happy in Moscow, feeling themselves in this semi-oriental city of towers, domes and cupolas, more than half-way home. The temperament of the people was sympathetic to them; they were extremely well received everywhere and felt themselves to be in a kindly element. When Inayat Khan gave an address at the Conservatoire, the enthusiastic students drew his carriage from the courtyard. He founded a Sufi Order in Russia, and his first book[1] was translated into Russian. All the time they received invitations; the Russians were captivated by their Indian music and their personalities, and wanted them everywhere. They received introductions to all the most brilliant men of letters and artists, as well as to the highest aristocracy in the land. It was in this crescendo of lustre and brilliance that the time drew near for the Begum to bear her child.

[1] The Sufi Message of Religious Liberty.

33

BOOK I

BABULY

With gentle yet prevailing force,
Intent upon her destined course;
Graceful and useful all she does,
Blessing and blest where'er she goes.

W. COWPER

CHILDHOOD

I

Noor-un-nisa was born in Moscow at 10.15 in the evening on December 20th 1913 by the calendar then used in Russia, or (allowing the thirteen days' interval between the Julian and Gregorian calendars) Friday, January 2nd, 1914, by that in general use throughout the world today.

Her name meant 'Light of Womanhood', Noor being 'Light' and un-nisa simply a polite feminine suffix. As the eldest child of her father she had the title Pir Zadi, 'Daughter of the Pir'. Her full name and style were, therefore, Pir Zadi Noor-un-nisa Inayat Khan.

She was tended by the nurse who looked after the Imperial family. This aged Tartar lady horrified the Begum by administering to the baby strong black coffee, when she was supposed still to be fed at the breast, and by brushing her whole body every day with a brush with stiff bristles. More serious, she betrayed a Mongol ancestry in binding the baby Noor-un-nisa's feet, much in the same way as children's feet used to be bound in China, to keep them small.

The storm-clouds of the revolution were gathering fast, and a short time afterwards one of the Czar's officers came to tell Inayat Khan confidentially that a major conflict of the European powers had become imminent and he ought to leave. The Emir of Bukhara invited him to his Court, and it was suggested they should travel with his Ambassador, who was returning from Moscow. But they had decided to go West again, and left in May.

Tolstoy lent them a sledge; but there were riots in the city on the day they left, and they found the gates closed by a barricade.

An angry crowd gathered round them. Inayat Khan took the baby Noor-un-nisa from his wife's arms, and stood up, holding her out for them to see. Every eye travelled from the dark-skinned, priestly figure in the golden robe to the white baby in his arms. It seemed as though this extraordinary tableau found a response in every heart. There was a scraping sound. They were drawing back the barricade, and the little party left for St. Petersburg.

The whole family arrived back in Paris in the summer after the outbreak of war. Inayat Khan then proceeded to London where he founded the Sufi Order in England, the symbol of his Movement being a winged heart with the star and the crescent inscribed.

The Begum now dropped the veil, because she found it excited attention and many people believed she had adopted it under the influence of her husband. Yet she regretted it, because, she said, it gave her some protection from the gaze of strangers in the street.

On June 19th, 1916, the first son was born at 86 Ladbroke Road, London. He was called Vilayat, meaning 'Chief', and had the title Pir Zade, 'Son of the Pir'. [1] In the next few years two more children came to complete the family, another boy, Hidayat, and the youngest, again a girl, Khair-un-nisa, 'Peace-of-Womanhood'. After she grew up she was known as Claire, by her wish.

In the family Noor-un-nisa was known as Babuly, 'Father's Daughter', because he felt that she was in some way specially his child, and Khair-un-nisa as Mamuly, 'Mother's Daughter'. Vilayat was Bhaijan ('Brother dear') to Noor all his life. Noor mothered them all.

From the beginning the children were brought up in an atmosphere of music. Noor and Vilayat could remember being carried up and down in their father's arms whilst he sang them sacred Sufi songs. Sometimes, when they could not sleep at nights, he would sit down beside the bed and sing to them — but they loved his music so deeply that they would force themselves to keep awake in order to detain him longer. To his disciples Inayat Khan said that the consciousness of children of this age being so very sensitive, the vibrations of this music which he sang to them now would affect them through their whole lives. He would never allow them to be wakened abruptly and, if necessary, would sit down by the pillow and sing them out of their sleep.

Indeed, music was part of their whole life. Madame Mignon Nevada, the singer, tells how one afternoon she called with some fellow-artistes. None of the grown-ups were at home, but Babuly, a small tot with her dark hair scraped back — she could not have

[1] As a young man, Vilayat used the title Pir Zade; now that he feels mature he uses the title Pir, and is called Pir by members of the Sufi Order.

36

been more than three or four — received them gravely and asked, "Would you like me to sing to you?"

"Why yes, dear!" they exclaimed.

Babuly assumed an attitude, as best she could, by the piano and began to sing in a small, high, wandering and indeed quite tuneless voice, an unforgettable little song:

"Do you like mice?
I like mice.
Do you like them in the house or in the garden?
If you don't like them in the house,
Pick them up and put them in the garden."

To these days belongs a story which assumed in the family almost the status of a legend. Babuly started asking continually for chocolates. As she was not normally a child to ask for things, her elders began to watch her. They noticed that when she obtained one she always left the room with it in her hand. A search of the nursery revealed an empty chocolate-box in the process of being refilled, and she explained that she had heard the grownups say the children in Russia had not enough to eat, so she was getting together something to send them.

But the great preoccupation of her childhood was with the existence of fairies. When very small she talked as though she actually saw them, in Gordon Square. Nobody in the family challenged this, but when she found that other children laughed at her she was profoundly upset — the more so because the shock disorganized the faculty that had been at work and she could not see them any longer.

It was another child who told Babuly and Vilayat that there was no such person as Father Christmas. As they had been told about him by their mother they were very troubled and went together to ask their father.

Inayat Khan said slowly, "children . . . when something exists in the imagination of anybody you can be sure there is a plane on which it has real existence."

It was perhaps too metaphysical an answer to have satisfied most children. Babuly and Vilayat were not sure whether they understood what it meant, but they felt they had been told something very profound, and went away together silently.

About this time, through a number of misfortunes, the family became so poor as not to be able to afford even adequate food and shoe repairs. The Begum, with four children to feed, was distracted when mealtimes arrived and there would be almost nothing to put on the table, except a bit of bread. An additional source of untold suffering and humiliation to her lay in the prejudice of English people against mixed marriages. In addition, although Inayat Khan always tried to keep out of politics, he had met Gandhi, and felt that he was, perhaps in consequence, suspected of pressing the cause of Indian liberty; and that Indians, altogether, were not very popular in England at that time. He felt the only thing to do was to move to another country, and in 1920, he took his family to France.

Names and styles of the four children in Inayat Khan's hand

Here he settled them in Tremblay, a small town to the North of Paris, in what Vilayat describes as 'a horrible house with no heat and no food', and, leaving them, proceeded to Geneva, where he was to establish the International Headquarters of the Sufi Movement in October 1923.

Early in 1921 he returned to Tremblay to collect the Begum and the children, who had huddled miserably through the winter, and took them to Wissous, another small town this time to the South of Paris. Here he left them again to make a tour of Belgium, Germany, and Holland; during the summer months he held a small summer school with some close disciples at Wissous.

His spiritual influence seemed to be approaching its zenith, while the material means remained at their nadir, when there came into his life, a Dutch widow, Madame Egeling, who offered to buy a house for his family.

In France once more, and walking with some of his disciples in the Bois de Boulogne, he crossed the river and went up the hill of Suresnes. Suddenly his eye was taken by a house standing back among the trees, and he exclaimed, "It must be here!" Approaching, they found it was indeed for sale. It was within a stone's-throw of Mont Valérien, of sacred associations, and yet hardly out of Paris, the centre of the crossways of Europe and, said Inayat Khan, 'the spiritual heart of the world.'

The house, which Inayat Khan called 'Fazal Manzil' (the 'House of Blessing') stood in a stoutly walled garden — chiefly remarkable for a most productive quince tree — and gave on to the rue de la Tuilerie. The district had, at this time, hardly been built up, and it enjoyed near-isolation and leafy quiet. From

38

this position, high on the hill, there was an uninterrupted panorama of the metropolis spread out beneath, the Eiffel Tower the one giant vertical in an otherwise horizontal perspective. Past its base one could trace the winding, shining course of the Seine under its many bridges down to the Ile de la Cité and the Cathedral of Nôtre Dame, whilst in the north the white Eglise du Sacré Coeur looked remarkably small.

In this quiet French suburb the arrival of so colourful a family could hardly fail to attract attention. Inayat Khan in his golden robe is a figure remembered to this day. The Suresnois used to call him *Le Grand Seigneur*.

At 'Fazal Manzil' he instituted the ritual of the Universal Worship. This was a form of service in which the scriptures of the major religions were laid together upon an altar, and each evoked in turn by the lighting of a candle, with the words, 'To the glory of the Omnipresent God we kindle the light symbolically representing the Hindu religion ... the Buddhist religion ... the Zoroastrian religion ... the Hebrew religion ... the Christian religion ... the religion of Islam'. The room would be filled with incense, and there would be no light except what came from the candles.

The Universal Worship was then held in the sitting-room of Fazal Manzil. There were the three cherags (persons taking the service), and Inayat Khan gave only the blessing.

Later when the land opposite Fazal Manzil was acquired, the lectures and the Universal Worship were held in the hall at the end of the land. Hidayat remembers going with his father into Paris to buy the yellow curtains for the hall, in the Galeries de Lafayette. During the Universal Worship, Inayat Khan used always to sit at the back, in a particular chair, which nobody else would take. He would come in last, and would leave first.

From 1922 to '26, Inayat Khan held three months' Summer Schools at Suresnes. Then, on warm summer evenings he would often give talks out in the garden beneath a pear tree he was fond of. At the back of all his teaching was the idea of the fundamental unity of all people's ideals, whatever the form in which they were dressed. He would never say of any person's idea of a thing that it was wrong; he would rather say that such a person looked at it from a different point of view, and from that point of view it looked different. He would not say that any man's ideal was false; if it seemed to him limited and therefore likely to bring him into conflict with others he would still say he should follow it, loyally, and in the increase of experience his outlook would become widened. If you killed a man's ideal, very often he could not find another, and became spiritless. His teaching was based essentially on the text *Resist not evil*. That is to say, he was aware that to oppose a particular tendency in a person, or to tell him to oppose it in himself, caused the repressed part to redouble its energy. This difficulty is known to all great spiritual teachers, but with Inayat Khan it was very much to the forefront of his mind. Therefore, rather than tell a person not to do something which it would be better he should cease to do, which might only make him want to do it more, even if the desire was for the moment checked, he would always try to find some other channel into which the person could put his energy, and so lead the energy away from the channel in which it was doing harm. If, for instance, he had to do with a gambler, who was ruining himself and his family, he would try to avoid saying, "Do not go to the Casino." Instead, he would seek to find what were the man's own deeper interests, the interests of his better self, and develop those. If, for instance, he found that the man had at any time tried to paint or to sing, or to study some learned subject, he would encourage him to renew his efforts to paint or sing, or to take up again that subject, knowing that if the man responded, his new pursuit would occupy his time to such an extent he would hardly notice he was no longer going to the Casino. The harmful tendency would have been overcome, without opposition and without violence: creatively. Working in this way, with the positive instead of against the negative tendencies, he helped very many people to redeem themselves from what had been, in some cases, serious obstacles to their own unfoldment; the stories of some of these cases became legends that grew in poetry with the years. These legends became a heritage to the children, though some came to have a dream-like quality to the children, who later became uncertain as to which were genuine memories of their father and which the exaggerated stories of his disciples. Vilayat feels sure his father told him of meeting Rasputin in Russia, although no other source confirms this story.

Vilayat describes his father as like "a luminous being around whom people from all parts of the world came to seek enlightenment and peace. His slow majestic walk, like a prophet of old amongst the fruit trees and flowers of the garden facing our home, surrounded by his disciples, was the centre of gravity of our world. All else was peripheral".

He told them whilst very young of their descent from 'The Tiger of Mysore', though he said they should not speak of this outside the family. "You are royal," he said, "and have that in your veins which nothing in the world can take away. You need not be afraid to hold up your heads in any court in the world." But he stressed very much, after the Oriental manner, the spiritual responsibilities which nobility conferred.

A Dutch disciple, Mrs. Kafia Blaauw-Robertson, told Mr. Wite Carp of an amusing incident. Some of the children had been naughty. Inayat Khan called Noor to him, and asked if she had been naughty too. She replied, "I wanted to, but my goodness prevented me."

Inayat Khan used to teach the children something of Indian music, and would illustrate upon his vina various traditional *ragas*. Afterwards he would ask them questions, which Noor always answered well and intelligently. Hidayat recalls that Noor would sometimes take down the notes and words of the songs their father sang to them, in the Western as well as the Eastern manner. Often he would invite the children to sing or play to him, to tell him a story or act a little play, to bring out their creativity.

II

When Noor was eight or nine she was sent to school for the first time, the Collège Moderne de Filles, Suresnes. Here she met another little girl, Raymonde Prénat, who was to be her friend all her life. They were practically the same age, Raymonde being six weeks younger. Neither of them was a child to make numbers of friends, both being reserved; yet a steady confidence grew between them. Her other friend was Geneviève Vanlaère, who lived almost next door. At this time Noor was full of sensibility, delicacy, and poetry. She chattered, like the other children, of exams and the interests of school, and played with her schoolfellows; yet at the same time she always had a certain reserve and a seriousness beyond that of a normal child of her age. No doubt some of this came from the atmosphere of her home, which had a certain remote and fairy-tale quality.

With most of the girls, her quietness was a drawback. They did not dislike her — she even won a Good-Comradeship prize — but because she was so very abstracted, and seemed to be living in an interior world of her own thoughts and dreams, they did not draw her very much into their games. She used to smile and try to play her part, but she had been brought up to a different rhythm and did not quite know how to join in.

To many of her classmates she appeared as timid, and indeed she was not remarkable for boldness. One day, as they came out of school, they were followed by an unpleasant-looking man, and all ran away. It was Raymonde who turned, stood her ground, and asked him what he wanted. Abashed, he retreated.

When she returned in triumph to the party, Noor, who was waiting wide-eyed with stupefaction, could only exclaim in a small, high voice, tremulous with awe, "Oh, Raymonde! Oh, Raymonde! Oh, Raymonde!"

The friendship between the two girls was very affectionate. They used to visit each other's homes, and on each other's birthdays would every year bring round a cake set with the appropriate number of candles. Noor always brought with her cake a little card, painted by herself and inscribed with a verse of her own composition.

From her earliest years Noor was creative. She learned musical notation and used to make up little pieces of music which she would play on the piano, and composed poems and stories. These she generally told in the first place, extempore, for the family circle, and would spin out as long as required, seeming to have an inexhaustibly fertile-imagination.

Raymonde still keeps a poem which Noor gave her when they were twelve years old:

LES MYSTERES DE LA NATURE

Que dis tu, joli ruisseau,
Dans ce vallon paisible et doux?
— J'écoute le roman de l'eau;
Qui de sa source coule jusqu'au bout.

Que fais tu, joli nuage,
Dans l'azure frais que tu traverse?
— Je cours, et dans le rivage
Je me mire après une averse.

Oh! Charmant bouton de rose,
Que gardes tu ce jour d'été?
— Mes belles mains à peine écloses
Gardent le secret de ma beauté.

Dis moi, petite pensée,
A quoi penses tu, dans cette verdure?
— Je songe à mon cher passé,
Je rêve de mon joyeux future.

(What do you say, pretty stream,
In this valley peaceful and sweet?
— I listen to the song of the water;
Which runs from its source to the end.

What do you do, pretty cloud,
In the fresh blue sky you traverse?
— I run, and after a shower,
Reflect myself in the shore.

Oh! Charming rose-bud,
What keep you this summer's day?
— My beautiful hands, half open,
Hold the secret of my beauty.

Tell me, little pansy,
What think you in this green bank,
— I muse on my dear past,
And dream of my joyous future.)

Naturally the children were steeped in their father's books
— which were actually his talks, as taken down by his three
secretaries in turn, and amounted to more than thirty volumes,
of which one of the most important was *The Unity of Religious
Ideals* — as well as in the stories from the Koran and the Hindu
epics he used to tell them.

Among the more slender volumes of their father's books probably none made more impression on the children than his *Diwan*
or poems with coloured frontispiece of a figure in the orange-
golden robe and turban of the Sufi. In after years it was this
painting of their father which they remembered[1] as him they had
known; and the winged heart, which appeared on all his works,
and which he wore on his breast, was engraved on their consciousness. Even before they could read, these images impressed themselves, as did also the stories he told them verbally, before they
found them in his pages. Such was the story of the elephant in the
dark. In the pitch-black night, several people all got hold of something; one, who had his arms round it, said it was like a pillar,
stout, leathery and rough. Another insisted that it was a sinuous,
twisting thing; a third declared that it was but the merest little
whisp, while the fourth was sure that they were all wrong; for
whereas they all agreed in describing it as leathery, though differing in its proportions, he found it to be exceedingly smooth, but
very hard.

What they had in fact got hold of, respectively, was one of
the legs, the trunk, the tail and a tusk of an elephant. As it was
dark, none of them saw the whole elephant; so each of them
thought the others were wrong though each was right, concerning the part that he had grasped. The elephant, of course,
was religious truth; and the men grasping in the dark, religious

[1] It was a reproduction of a painting by M. H. Thurburn of Inayat Khan
done in the style of a Moghul primitive, the original of which is still at
Fazal Manzil. It also bore Inayat Khan's signature in the Urdu-Arabic
alphabet, an unusual feature, as in their private correspondence he and
his brothers invariably wrote Urdu in the Gujarati script, with only the
occasional exception of Mohammed Ali Khan, whose early years had
been spent in Rajputana where the Urdu-Arabic script was the rule.

43

sects. He would tell them that most often it was like this with matters of opinion. Where difference occurred, usually each was right on his point, but did not see the other's; and so he told them they should not contradict, but bear with another who saw things differently. The impression made on them by his teachings was indelible, even though the amount of time they were actually with him was not very great.

At thirteen, Noor wrote another poem:

NOCTURNE

Déjà sont tirés les voiles nocturnes,
Sous les caresses argentés du clair de lune
Le rossignol chante sa charmante berceuse,
La nuit expire sa plainte silencieuse.
Comme de frêles fleurettes, d'innombrables diamants
Scintillent dans un vaste et sombre océan
Nuancées de vert, argent, violet bleutés,
Les feuilles frémissent d'un frissonnement léger
La nature est plongée dans une rêverie,
La forêt mystérieuse est une féerie.
Dans le sein du ruisseau qui murmure doucement
Sont tombées des étoiles du bleu firmament.
Oh! fascinant mystère de la nuit lyrique,
Souffle, à moi, tout bas, ton secret mystique.

(Already the veils of night are drawn,
Beneath its caresses silver in the moonlight
The nightingale sings her charming lullaby.
The night exhales her silent plaint.
As pale flowers, innumerable diamonds
Sparkle in a vast and sombre ocean
Shot with green, silver and bluish violet.
The leaves tremble with a light fluttering,
Nature is plunged in a reverie,
The mysterious forest, faery.
In the bosom of the stream murmuring quietly
Have fallen the stars from the blue firmament
O! fascinating mystery of the lyric night,
Breathe to me, low, your mystic secret.)

Presumably at about the same age, she wrote in English,

SWEET PEAS

Oh! flowers of my sweetest dream
In you alone does beauty gleam.
Fairies of an enchanting sphere,

44

Whisper your secret in my ear.
Sweet peas, who has, with so much skill,
Painted your wings that shiver still.
Such sweet perfume as you exhale,
To produce it, who would not fail?
Treasure of love and purity,
You move my soul to ecstasy.
Like butterflies of distant lands,
What do you hold between your hands?
When morn comes with pure white laces,
Pearls adorn your blushing faces.
Oh! flowers of my sweetest dream,
In you alone does beauty gleam.

During these years Inayat Khan made wide tours, visiting and founding Sufi centres in England, Germany, Switzerland, Italy, Belgium, Holland, Norway, Denmark, Sweden, and the United States; so that the Begum and her children were very much alone, except during the months of the Summer School which he held annually in Suresnes, when the little suburb would be overflowing with visitors. Even then, as Inayat Khan was always at the disposal of his disciples, the children did not have much of their father. The house was continually invaded by people who had travelled from far to see him. His children were taught that he belonged to the world, and that they should not press their claims upon him. He was a Dervish, and could know no attachments. They felt it was a great privilege to be his children, but at the same time were acutely conscious that it was one upon which they must not presume. As they grew in an understanding beyond their years, so they effaced themselves with a kind of instinctive tact.

It was not that they had not feelings like ordinary children; but they learned to suppress them. All their lives they had been accustomed to hear discourse upon the spiritual life, and the idea of self-abnegation was inherent in their philosophy. They felt their part was to carry their burdens as inconspicuously as possible and not to be a charge on him. In this restraint — so foreign and so strange to Western conceptions of family relationship — lay the foundations of a discipline of renunciation that was to leave a lasting trace in their characters.

When Noor was only twelve, she fell in love. The man according to Hidayat, was quite well known, not only to her own family, but to some members of the Sufi Movement. Inayat Khan feared that the attachment could be detrimental to her, and discouraged it; and she was very sad.

In the summer of 1926, Pir-o-Murshid Inayat Khan began to

make preparations to go to India. The more sensitive of those about him realized that this was not for an ordinary tour, and that they would not see him again. He even said, privately, "I shall not come back."

During the last weeks of the Summer School the tension at 'Fazal Manzil' gradually increased. The children were all sensitive to it. Sometimes when the disciples collected in the garden, watching whilst Pir-o-Murshid walked slowly up and down the paths before a lecture, the silence would become so palpitating that they could hardly contain their emotion.

A few nights before he was due to go Noor dreamed the baker was flying away in an aeroplane. She tried to call him back, but the plane diminished in the sky and she knew she would never see him again. This seemed a terrible thing, and she woke up crying like one forsaken.

In the morning she told her father about the dream. Inayat Khan sat quite still, and they looked into each other's eyes until each knew what the other knew. Then he said, with great emotion, "Yes, Babuly, the bringer of the bread will not return."

On September 13th, a ceremony was held in the garden. The foundation stone was laid of a temple to be called *L'Universelle* and some manuscripts and coins representing many countries buried beneath it. After the consecration a procession of the disciples passed before Pir-o-Murshid, headed by Vilayat — now ten years old — whom he designated as the Head of a new Order to be called the Confraternity. He had wished him to be dressed in a golden robe, in replica of his own; but the Begum, overwhelmed, and seeing in this gesture a foreboding presage, failed to produce the robe.

Both Noor and Vilayat understood quite well what this ceremony meant and the trust which now reposed in them.

When on the following morning their father said goodbye they knew it was for the last time; yet although they felt they were being profoundly bereaved they neither of them attempted to hold him back or ask him why he had to do so.

Hidayat says that on February 5th, 1927, Noor was in the kitchen when she heard her father's voice say, "Babuly, look after the little ones." On the following day, a cable arrived, saying that Inayat Khan had died. He was then aged forty-four. The Begum was plunged in unutterable desolation, and Noor, just thirteen, took upon herself the entire work of the household.

In the autumn of the next year, 1928, the Begum and her children went to India, together with the uncles, to pay homage at the tomb of Inayat Khan in Delhi.

For all of them it was a deeply moving experience, at once stranger and more stirring because they carried in their veins the blood of the people whom they were seeing for the first time in their own country. An early morning walk by the river Ganges, and, in the dawn light, the spectacle of cantering horses tracing circles on the grey sand; the harvest of oranges in the garden of their hotel; an evening ride in a *tonga* (horse-drawn cart) through the crowded and curiously colourful streets of Old Delhi — these were things the children remembered. They left a mark for ever on Noor's observant and impressionable mind.

From Delhi they made a tour, visiting the tomb of Moin-ud-Din Chisti at Ajmer, and other places of Sufi pilgrimage, making their way eventually to Baroda. Here they stayed at Moula Bakhsh House, from which Inayat Khan and his brothers had set out more than eighteen years before.

This visit to the ancestral house — rather neglected since the departure in turn of so many of the family — affected them deeply. With their Western upbringing, they were unaccustomed to the rapt, devotional attitude of Indian servants, and Noor was almost overwhelmed when a very old woman prostrated herself on the floor before her, pressing her knuckles against her temples and cracking her finger-bones, which in India signifies the very deepest respect — for she said she saw in Noor something of Inayat, whom she had nursed. Also, the extremely deferential attitude of the descendants of the retainers who had accompanied Tipu Sultan's granddaughter, and always remained with the family, made for them a living link with their ancestral history. It was interesting for them, too, to find how the house was organized into a men's and a women's section. Each married couple had its own apartment; but the unmarried ladies and widows had their rooms — boudoirs and a sitting-room — in a portion at the back of the house reserved exclusively for the women. In the front of the house, however, was a common sitting-room where the whole family met together. As it might be a long time before they were able to bring them out to India again, the uncles, anxious they should not lose the sense of the culture to which by right they belonged, made every effort to draw around them the elements of the world in which they themselves had been brought up.

The following year, 1929, just before the setting in of the hot weather, they sailed again for Europe. Noor was now fifteen.

She never really believed that her father was dead. All her life she clung to the thought — rightly or wrongly no one can know — that he had become one of the band of ascetics and holy men of India who lived in solitary, secret places in the hills and devoted their lives to perpetual contemplation. "We have all been to pay homage at my father's tomb," she told Raymonde when she was back in France, "but I don't think he's in it.". His work in the West was done, and he had nothing further to stay here for. "I think he is living in a cave in the Himalayas or a monastery in Tibet."

II

The passing of Inayat Khan profoundly changed the atmosphere in which his children grew up. The apricot tree under which he used to sit died. Everybody noticed this, as he had been accustomed to speak of the sympathy existing between a mystic and his tree, saying that very often such a tree did not survive the death of the one who had sat beneath it, but passed away with the life that had become mingled with its own and upon which it had come to depend. And so, as the children watched the fading of the apricot tree, which all their efforts could not arrest, it seemed to them the symbol of their desolation.

The Begum felt more deeply than words could tell the shock of losing her husband. For at least four years she was completely stunned.

In Vilayat's words "Very few can appreciate in its fullness the position that was the Begum's, first as the wife and now as the widow of a man whose life was consecrated to his mission and his followers, and who was regarded by them with supernatural awe. The periods of united family life had been brief and numbered; and most of the time she had been left to bear the brunt of domestic responsibilities — often under the most difficult conditions — alone. Although she had a strongly persevering character and an uncanny propensity for self-effacement and self-sacrifice, was most methodical, tidy, conscientious, and possessed of intuition where those near to her were concerned, yet even as the observer who is too near a great picture cannot see it fully, so the wife of the Master had difficulty in gauging his perspective. Nevertheless, when he passed from the world she felt herself profoundly bereft, and it seemed to her that her own life held nothing more."

She became seriously ill, and as she had always inclined towards the secluded life, she now retired from the world completely. She lived on the upper floor of 'Fazal Manzil', with the curtains of her rooms drawn, and maintained during the next several

48

years a purdah as complete as the strictest woman in India. She received nobody at all, except her children and her husband's brothers. Like Noor, she never became completely reconciled to her husband's death. She came in the end to believe that he must have died; yet, even so, in a sense she never really accepted it. During these dark years of her life she wrote a number of poems in this vein, some of them very beautiful.

She still interested herself in her children's education and in the progress they made at school, but she was unable to continue the normal duties of the household. The spectacle of her mother's desolation awoke all Noor's latent protective disposition, and notwithstanding her school work and her youth (she was still only fourteen) she held within her hands the entire government of the house, assuming full and sole responsibility for its management and maintenance, the buying of food and clothes and the care of the younger children.

This state of things at 'Fazal Manzil' was a source of amazement to all who knew the family, and the devotion with which Noor yielded herself to her responsibilities touched everybody.

One day, when she was at Raymonde's house, she told Madame Prénat that she had lain awake all night, very anxious, because Vilayat had a sore throat and she was not sure whether the remedy she had given him was appropriate.

"But surely your mother will look after him!" exclaimed Madame Prénat.

She shook her head: "I have the care of the younger ones."

Noor was now going to the Lycée Saint Cloud. She must have seemed an exciting and mysterious figure to her classmates. At this time she had a markedly Oriental appearance, and wore dark European clothes which did not suit her at all. She was always smiling, very timid, spoke very little, and did not talk about her romantic family, about which her class-mates were so curious. She made no close friendships, and always gave an impression of being 'elsewhere', though it was difficult to say whether this remoteness came from her own nature or from the fact that she belonged to a different race. Her 'difference' showed itself in many things: in her French compositions, for instance, which used to take the form of evocations or incantations, very poetic and totally different from the productions of the little Lycéens; and in the gymnastic exercise which she had to learn but at which she was always very awkward.

In 'Fazal Manzil' Madame Egeling took the services as usual throughout the year, and the uncles presided over the Summer School, which continued, as before, every year, from June to September.

To all the people who came, 'Murshid's children' were objects of intense interest, and there was a tendency to invest them with a kind of halo. On the other hand, they were continually observed and criticized for any failure to come up to the disciples' idealized picture. Their mother, of course, was never seen. Visitors strolling or sitting in the gardens surrounding at the back of the house would look up, and say respectfully, "The Begum's blinds!' But the children had no retreat, and felt the strain increasingly.

Vilayat ascribes much of his sisters' reticent manner — which many people noticed — to this over-exposure and the necessity of defending their privacy of mind. Noor retired to her room whenever she could and spent her time in writing and reading. She loved romantic tales of chivalry and sacrifice. Her hero was Roland, and her heroine Joan of Arc, to whom she remained faithful all her life.

She had always played the piano, but now she conceived a desire to learn the harp. She had seen medieval and pre-Raphaelite pictures showing women and angels bending gracefully over their strings, and felt it was 'more a woman's instrument'.

In 1931 she took her Baccalauréat Certificate and left the Lycée Saint Cloud, being now seventeen.

III

In April 1931 Noor became a student of the Ecole Normale de Musique de Paris, where she studied for the next six years. She undertook a comprehensive programme: harp, piano, solfeggio, harmonic analysis and harmony. The last she studied under the well-known pianist and conductor, Mademoiselle Nadia Boulanger, who remembers her as 'a charming pupil'.

As though this were not enough, she started in 1932, at the Sorbonne, Université de Paris, a course in the Psycho-Biology of the Child, with the purpose of taking a licence.

Despite this division of her energies, her musical studies progressed so that in the following year it was considered that she could profit from harp lessons with a private teacher. She now became a pupil of Mademoiselle Henriette Renié, and so entered upon a period of her life which was to be to her a source of great happiness.

Mademoiselle Renié, who taught her for two years, describes her as an affectionate, industrious pupil. "She loved the harp (and her teacher, which yielded her good returns!). She worked seriously, and I was able to present her at the Salle Erard, in the course of the second year, in one of my matinées. She played with taste, and was appreciated. She was at this time engaged to be married. I remember her as a very gentle girl, but she studied so hard that I thought she must have an inner fire which her quiet manner hid."

The engagement to which Mademoiselle Renié refers was to a young piano student whom Noor had met in her first year at the Ecole Normale. It was never recognized by her family, who considered the match unsuitable, but continued in a non-official form for about six years. The problems arising out of this relationship were frequently the source of deep distress to her, even to the point of affecting her health.

During these years she produced several musical compositions. When she was fifteen, she wrote a song called *Chant au Madzub,* a kind of Sufi holy-man. The words are:

> At thy Feet, o Madzub, I come to seek for rest,
> In the Fire of thy Glance, may this yearning soul be blessed.

> Thy footprints of Crushed Thorns are strewn
> with Pearls Divine,
> And Lo! Their Glory unveils, these dazzled eyes of mine.

> Thro' Life's Test, may this heart, O Thou Living Shrine,
> As a Lotus once bloom. Bloom in these Rays of Thine.

> At thy Feet, O Madzub, I come to seek for Rest,
> In the Fire of thy Glance, may this yearning Soul be blessed.

On the cover, she painted a seated figure in the glowing golden robe of the Sufis. Though she gave him a white beard and white hair, which he had not, her model for the Madzub was evidently her memory of her father. The imagery of the poem belongs, of course, to the received tradition of Oriental — specially Persian — mysticism. The style has certain resemblance to her father's, and she could, for instance, have found the image of the pearl in his *Diwan,* or in the lines he wrote to his own Murshid, at the time of becoming his pupil: [1]

> Thou art my salvation and freedom is mine,
> I am not, I melt as a pearl in sweet wine
> . . .

Nevertheless, the totality with which she had absorbed this tradition tells much about her at this time. Notice that she expects the footprints of the saint, in which she will tread, to be filled with thorns. There is here, already, germinally, the idea of martyrdom.

[1] **Confessions** of Inayat Khan, p. 39 of original edition; p. 148 of Vol XII of Barrie & Rockliff edition of his works.

Noor composed also a *Song to the Butterfly*, piano music for which was written by one of her father's pupils, a Jhr. van Ingen. But the harp was her instrument, and she wrote a *Prelude for harp*, and — her most important work — an Elegy for harp and piano, which was performed at a private concert in Fazal Manzil.

All the children were bi-instrumental, each playing the piano and a stringed instrument. In the composition of the 'home' orchestra, Noor played the harp, Vilayat the 'cello, Hidayat the violin and Khair-un-nisa the piano. All four composed; Vilayat (who studied under Stravinsky) in a rather modern style, and Claire (who studied, like her sister, under Nadia Boulanger) in a more classical one. But in fact it was Hidayat who was destined to become the main composer of the family, basing his music on Indian ragas written for Western orchestras. His haunting work *La Monotonia* is an orchestration and development of the bars of melody Noor wrote for her *Chant au Madzub*. Her friend Raymonde was also studying music very seriously, and was introduced by Noor to the orchestra.

Noor had a high opinion of her fiancé's playing, and lamented to Madame Prénat that her family did not recognize his qualities. "He is a man in a thousand!" she assured her.

Although she took Madame Prénat into her confidence, she never told Raymonde anything of this side of her life, perhaps because her friend grew up more slowly. Noor tried to give her courage by making her presents of toilet preparations — a scent-spray, a box of powder, a bottle of eau de Cologne — but Raymonde never used them.

Raymonde was probably the only person whom she ever brought to see her mother. Although the Begum did not normally receive, one evening after a concert at 'Fazal Manzil' Noor brought Raymonde up the stairs to her mother's room. Raymonde, who was a little awed, remembers the Begum as a very pale-faced, fragile-looking lady in a room dimmed by drawn curtains, who spoke in a faint, far-away voice. They remained only for a few minutes, and then Noor took her down again in case her mother should become over-fatigued. But after this, whenever there was a reception at 'Fazal Manzil', Noor would bring Raymonde upstairs for a few minutes to see her mother before she went.

Noor spent much of her time at her friend's house. "She made herself as much at home here," says Madame Prénat, "as if she had been in her mother's house."

Raymonde was the middle one of three sisters. The eldest had a very high regard for Noor. *"Elle avait une moralité!* You cannot think how high her moral standard was!" She realized better than most people the intensity, as well as the secrecy, of

Noor's nature. "Noor-un-nisa had a very complex inner life, and I doubt whether any of us had more than an occasional glimpse into the dramas which absorbed her. She was always a silent person, and it was to Mother that she talked most, probably because Mother is also very close."

Madame Prénat was pure Spanish by blood, and, like a certain Spanish type, reserved and deep. She had an absolute reliance on the word of Noor-un-nisa. "If Noor-un-nisa said she would do a thing, there was no further question. She would never let anybody down."

All this time Noor was becoming progressively Europeanized. The first fourteen years of her life had been lived under a predominantly Oriental influence, but this was now very much diminished. Only one uncle still had a house in Suresnes, and in her student life she continually met French people. She dressed — except on special occasions — entirely in European dress, and used light make-up. Vilayat, though generally seen in Suresnes in a black robe, used most often to change before going into Paris — the river dividing Suresnes from the Bois de Boulogne having an almost symbolical value. But it was Claire — even more silent and more reticent than Noor — who swung the most markedly to the West, which was the reason she preferred this French name, which preserved something of the sound of Khair.

To the uncles, this tendency to 'escape' from the Sufi background was the cause of some anxiety. They had never liked Noor's going every day alone to attend classes. They were pleased she should be educated in music, but would have preferred it if she could have had private lessons in her home. For them, as Orientals, a woman's dignity found its reflection in the protection afforded her by her family, and they were concerned that she should not lose the grace of personality of which they felt a sheltered condition to be the indispensable safeguard. When they heard she had attended an evening concert in Paris by herself they did not like it.

Yet the pull was not a simple one. There was much of her mother in Noor, much which responded to a pre-Raphaelite ultra-Romantic conception of woman which reciprocated in Western terms the model proposed by the uncles. The Begum's total dependence on her for all her material wants had thrown them very much together; Noor made it one of the prime ends of her life to cherish her mother, and there existed between them such a sympathy as to promote an almost unintentional communication of emotional states.

At the same time, Noor possessed a spring of boundless energy, a curiosity and full-blooded enthusiasm for life, which carried her irresistibly out into its main thoroughfares.

In relation to thoroughfares, Madame Hélène Bouvard has a recollection. A student at the Sorbonne at the same time as Inayat Khan's two elder children, she knew them both. When she thinks of Noor, there comes back into her mind, particularly, an occasion when they crossed the Avenue Matignon together on their way to see a ballet. Caught between streams of swiftly moving traffic, they were obliged to stand still for some moments. Noor-un-nisa, she avers, was petrified with terror. Some people, she comments, learning after Noor's death, the story which gained her posthumous fame, might suppose her to have been a person endowed with a natural and cool courage. The reverse was the case. "Noor-un-nisa was a being capable of every heroism" she said; but insisted that the heroism was of a kind which came only with an extremity of nervous tension. That day on the Avenue Matignon, she was the very image of terror; and fear was always in her nature, beneath the winding-up of her courage.

Madame Bouvard is a person with deep knowledge of philosophy and insight into human nature. She never became a Sufi — it is always the teachings of Krishnamurti which she has followed most closely — but her glimpse of Noor's emotional or nervous constitution may be worthy of respect.

Noor's occupation with children remained constant. A storyteller since childhood, she used to invite children of the suburb into the garden of 'Fazal Manzil' and weave them tales, sometimes quite of her own, sometimes from the Ramayana, the Mahabharata, the Jataka, with a little interpretation. The little Suresnois accepted quite naturally this cultivation in Oriental myth and philosophy. At one time she gave them a series of connected talks on Sufism.

When she was about twenty she had to have an operation on her stomach. The family physician, Dr. Jourdan, came frequently to visit her whilst she was in hospital. When she came out she presented him, in token of gratitude, with a pink climbing rose tree in a pot.

The doctor and his wife were charmed by this gift, and transplanted it to a bed against the side of their country house at Marly-le-Roi. They baptised it the *Noor Inayat* and it flourished exceedingly.

For their birthdays, Noor would sometimes write poems for her brothers and sister. One which she wrote for Vilayat, in 1935, has been preserved: [1]

---

[1] I leave untouched some small faults in French.

Toi, qui lui a tendu les bras en lui disant:
  "Viens près de ton aimé, viens donc, chère enfant,
Sur mon coeur reposer ta tête et tes pensées,
  Nous verrons ensemble succéder les années,
Qui devront faire l'image de nos destins unis.
  Tu seras pour moi la compagne et ma vie."

          ... Toi que Dieu m'a donnée,
Chère compagne, sois là pour toujours près de moi,
  Nous marcherons ainsi, Dieu n'abandonne pas
Ses enfants sur la terre que sa main a unis.
  Inclinons nos deux têtes et nous serons bénis.
Notre amour devant nous comme un astre radieux
  Nous donnera la force et nous serons heureux.

          ... Elle veut avec toi
Partager la vie, les tourments et la joie.
  Et toutes les richesses que ce monde procure
Ne pourront vous donner un bonheur aussi pur...
  Ta main guidera celle que Dieu t'a donnée,
Elle est ta vie, ta joie, elle est ta bien-aimée.
  Garde-la pour toujours protégée dans tes bras.

Vous marcherez ainsi par le monde pas à pas,
  Votre amour devant vous comme un astre radieux
Vous donnera la force et vous serez heureux.

Seigneur, sur Tes enfants verse un regard d'amour,
Entends leurs prières qui s'élèvent en ce jour,
Dieu de compassion, notre Dieu Eternel,
  Entoure ces deux enfants de Tes bras paternels.

(You who opened your arms to him saying:
  "Come to your beloved, come then, dear child,
Rest on my heart your head and your thoughts,
  Together we shall see the years succeed each other,
Which will make the image of our united destinies.
  You will be for me the companion and my life."

          ... You whom God has given me,
Dear companion, be there always near to me,
  We will walk side by side, God will not abandon
His children on the earth whom His hand has joined.
  Let us bow our two heads, and we shall be blessed.
Our life before us like a radiant star
  Will give us strength and we shall be happy.

... She wishes
To share life with you, its torments and joy.
And all the riches the world procures
Cannot give you a joy so pure ...   ˙
Your hand will guide her whom God has given you,
She is your life, your joy, she is your beloved.
Keep her always protected in your arms.

You will walk thus through the world side by side,
Your love before you like a radiant star
Will give you strength and you will be happy.

Lord, cast on your children a glance of love,
Hear their prayers which rise this day,
O God of compassion, our Eternal God,
Embrace your two children in your paternal arms.)

Translating this poem, one finds that the structure is rather strange. The alternation between the first, second and third persons leaves it not always clear who is speaking. In the first two verses, we have "my heart ... near to me", then in the third, "She", while in that following, "You will walk ..." seems to be written from the standpoint of another person, looking at the brother and sister, while the last verse is, like the first, an appeal to God. If the logical sequence is obscure, confused, nevertheless the total meaning is plain, and moving. Yet it is also surprising, to her brother, aged nineteen, from a girl aged twenty-one, who was engaged to be married; and gives one to wonder how much substance there was to her engagement, and whether it was more than conceptual. She writes here as though it were her brother with whom she accepted to walk side by side through life, the companion God had given her. This was perhaps the deeper relationship.[1]

To her mother, also, she wrote a poem each year for her birthday. In 1932, at eighteen, she had written:

Abba's own hand is o'er our head
Though far away to seek
And deep within our longing heart
His voice doth ever speak.

---

[1] Mahmood Khan comments:
"Note further the sense of loneliness or isolation, implicit in the sensitivity underlying the poem, which could not possibly be that of a girl in love; and that the expectant regard for her brother, equally was an element of their specific mental background: it was he who was regarded both in the family and by the Sufi following at large, as the eventual successor and continuator par excellence of his father's Sufi position, teaching and responsibilities, and hence a personality central in their interest, and in their expectations and hopes for the future."

"Abba" was the name by which the children called their father. Again, she wrote; as though she felt that he inspired her:

> This poem Abba has written
> to console your heart
> His thoughts to his dear children
> to you he doth impart.

The archaisms, "O'er", "doth" and the cliché betray that she could have had little acquaintance with contemporary poetry of the twenties and thirties.

For her fiancé she wrote, for his birthday:

> O! my Abba, on this birthday
> Put Thy hand on his head, I pray
> And may Thy music in his heart
> Unceasing streams of joy impart
> And with Thy love, throughout life's test,
> At every step, may he be blest.

One notices that it is to her father that the poem is address-ed. The "Thy . . . Thy . . . Thy . . ." are appeal of a prayer to him. Her fiancé is referred to in the third person "his . . . he . . ." Though she gave it to him (and it is to him its preservation is owed), it is not exactly a love-poem, in the ordinary sense, but the disclosure of a prayer she had prayed for him.

IV

About this time, the Baron and Baroness van Tuyll van Serooskerken, two of her father's oldest disciples, invited Noor to spend a holiday with them at their home at The Hague. At first she was reluctant to leave her mother, who was so very dependent on her, but in the end the Baroness persuaded her that Claire was now old enough to hold the reins for a little.

In the van Tuyll's home Noor found herself introduced to the quintessence of Dutch civilization. It was a house in which the stillness was almost palpable. Every room evinced that order and degree of upkeep which seems to remain the peculiar genius of the Netherlands. There was not an article of wood but gleamed with a soft light, whilst exquisitely fine and close Oriental carpets were used as table as well as floor coverings.

Above all, it was the quiet that was impressive and in keeping with the apparently age-long undisturbed ponds — their green-carpeted surface broken only by an occasional water-lily — of the little Dutch gardens she had passed in the train.

"It was a good place for study," says the Baroness. This thought had partly underlain her invitation, for she felt that·at 'Fazal Manzil' Noor was too largely absorbed in the duties of the house. It seemed to her quite wrong that a girl like Noor should have had to make the beds, for instance.

Noor spent much of her time in the Baron's library. Discovering on the shelves the *Vedas,* the *Puranas,* and the *Bhagavad Gita,* she settled down to many hours of reading.

She went to the museums of The Hague and Leiden, and also to see the dunes at Katwyk, where her father had once held a Summer School in 1922 and the fishermen still remembered him as 'a figure like John the Baptist'. Taken for a longer excursion, she saw the little towns of Volendam and Marken, on the Zuider-Zee, about the only places in Holland where the distinctive national dress is still worn by the ordinary people.

Most exciting of all, she learned to ride. The van Tuylls had their own horses, and the Baroness took her out regularly. They used to canter along the wide, flat beach at Scheveningen, where the low tide left the sand firm and the sea gave a tang to the air. Later she taught her to jump. The Baroness noticed that she had no physical fear, even on the first occasion when she took an obstacle. She fell off, but it did not worry her and she was willing to try again immediately.

A telegram brought her back to 'Fazal Manzil', where her management was missed. Nevertheless, a precedent had been set, and she went to The Hague again, accompanied at different times by Vilayat and Claire.

v

There was no doubt that Noor did too much. Concurrently with her programmes at the Ecole Normale and the University, she undertook a number of subsidiary studies, dictated by her interest or impulse of the moment, making progress in several modern languages, extending her general reading, and writing copiously. At the same time, if the gas leaked, it was she who telephoned the gas company, or if the drains were out of order, it was she who obtained the services of a plumber.

According to Hidayat, Madame Egeling gave Noor 3000 francs a month for the household; even bearing in mind that food in France used to be cheap, to maintain five people on this must have taught her a prudent use of money.

The only thing she did not do was sew. Vilayat remembers she was extraordinarily awkward at any form of needlework. Whilst all the children were very young she was obliged to cope as best she could, but very soon Claire relieved her of the darning-bag. She was devoted to Noor, and appreciating her transcendental, and so to speak governmental, gifts, silently undertook the upkeep of her wardrobe. She also laundered her sister's lingerie.

A great deal of Noor's trouble came from her readiness to place herself at the disposal of everybody they knew. Vilayat asked her sometimes, "Why do you carry all these people's burdens? It might be better for some of them to have to carry their own!" But he did not have any success with this line of argument.

She was extremely tender-hearted, and tended to 'collect' ineffectual people and to mother them, as she did sick animals. It was this which worried her brother; he felt they sapped her vitality, one or two of them feeding upon it in a parasitical manner and draining the energy she required for her intellectual and creative occupations.

Again, a natural champion of the under-dog, she could not bear to see anything in the nature of bullying, and before the spectacle of an unequal contest would become so passionately moved as to be unable to resist throwing in her weight upon the side of the weaker party—not always judiciously. This involved her in entanglements which could have been avoided, and which completely exhausted her. She was very emotional during these years, Vilayat recalls, and would sometimes burst into tears at the mere account of an injustice. At one time it even seemed as if she was heading for a breakdown. Yet she hung on, and if she was highly strung (as were also Vilayat and Claire) she did not lose her grip.

A brightening feature of the situation was that the Begum, after four or five years' complete seclusion, began gradually to recover her interest in life and to come out. At first she came only downstairs for short periods, then out into the garden. At last, with Noor and Claire one each side of her, she took timid steps into the street—in European clothes.

Once she began to take the air her health improved so rapidly that her children even considered she might benefit from a sojourn in the warmer and brighter climate of the South of France. In the summer of 1933 Noor, Claire, and Vilayat took her to the Massif Central, where they stayed at a small place called Royat, near Riom, in the Puy de Dôme.

Afterwards the Begum and Claire returned there together, whilst Noor and Vilayat—it was a tradition that these two did everything together—pushed their adventures southwards, crossed the Pyrenees and made a tour of Spain in 1934. Eventually they found their way to the little village of San Vincente, near Valencia, where they called at the home of Maurice Eisenberg, Vilayat's 'cello teacher. He was charmed that they had come to see him. Noor wrote home: [1]

Hier Eisenberg nous a fait rentrer chez lui et il nous a joué deux morceaux que Casals avait composés à 19 ans et qu'il vient de lui dédier. L'une est une "rêverie après une messe" et l'autre est une romance. Ce sont de vrais petits chefs-d'oeuvres de finesse et de musicalité. Eisenberg les a joués avec beaucoup de recueillement, accompagné par le pianiste de classe, le pauvre pianiste qui reçoit tant de coups sur l'épaule! Il a dit qu'il les jouera cette année en première audition à Paris. Et tu sais il a dit qu'il emmenera Vilayat et moi un de ces jours pour visiter Casals chez-lui.

(Yesterday Eisenberg asked us to his home and played us two pieces composed by Casals when he was 19 and which he had dedicated to him. One was a "dream after a mass" and the other a romance. They were masterpieces of finesse and musicality. Eisenberg played them with much reflection, accompanied by a good pianist, the poor pianist who received so many taps on the shoulder! He said he would play them for the first time this year in Paris. And do you know, he says he will take Vilayat and me to visit Casals one day at his home.)

In fact, he was good as his word, and took them to see the master, who lived close by. Casals also received them very kindly, and gave Vilayat some lessons himself.

After their return Noor kept up her Spanish with Madame Prénat.

The following year she learnt some Italian before going with Vilayat to Italy. They visited Padua, where they had friends, and Noor wrote describing a visit they made from there to Venice:

Nous sommes partis hier matin au lieu de samedi soir car la fête était hier soir. Le voyage d'ici à Venise était de 3/4 d'heure en train et à la sortie de la gare quelle était notre surprise à Vilayat et moi! C'était un monde nouveau absolument, un monde plein de charme, de paix et d'harmonie. Avec quelle tranquilité les gondoles se balancent sur l'eau et chaque maison qui borde l'eau est une pièce d'art, tous les petits ponts sont sculptés par des artistes. Nous sommes arrivés au palais ducale qui est une des plus grandes merveilles du monde tant la sculpture est fine.

[1] I have not been permitted to see the body of letters written by Noor from which this and the following extracts (all from places away from home while on holiday with her family) have been selected and copied and sent me for inclusion in this book. While I have no doubt the copying has been done in a faithful spirit, I cannot, therefore, assume editorial responsibility.

Puis nous sommes partis le soir pour retourner à Venise et nous avons écrit des cartes postales en attendant que la fête commence. Il faut t'imaginer la grande place de l'église San Marco transformée en salle de concert avec au moins 15.000 mille places. Là nous avons attendu à nos places et quand il a commencé à faire nuit toutes les places étaient occupées, toute la ville de Venise était là. Puis toutes les lumières se sont éteintes et seulement de petites bougies entourrées de papier de couleur scintillaient. Si tu voyais dans quel silence tous ces milliers sont venus à leurs places et ont attendu et tout à coup un grand cri d'admiration s'est élevé de la foule, sais tu pourquoi? Tout à coup l'église de San Marco qui restait invisible dans l'obscurité était illuminée par une douce lumière bleue et l'effet était tel que c'était comme si une oeuvre d'art, un beau tableau était sorti du ciel obscur, tu peux t'imaginer quelle impression cela a produit. Puis le concert a commencé.

L'orchestre avec des chanteurs Italiens ont joué des operas Italiens, puis il y a eu des feux d'artifice et le concert a fini avec une partie de la Walkyrie. L'orchestre était d'une telle perfection et les chanteurs étaient vraiment formidables. Et tu sais tout le public a crié pour demander à Mussolini de paraître sur un balcon, mais il faisait si obscur que nous n'avons pas su s'il a paru. Mais pendant la musique il y avait un silence complet et on sentait que tous comprenaient combien la musique était belle. A 1 h. nous étions de retour à Padova.

(We left yesterday morning instead of Saturday because the festival was yesterday evening. The journey from here to Venice took 3/4 of an hour in the train, and on leaving the station, what a surprise it was to Vilayat and me! We were in a different world absolutely, a world full of charm, peace and harmony. The gondolas balanced on the water with such tranquillity and each house on the water is a work of art, all the little bridges are sculpted by artists. We reached the ducal palace which is one of the wonders of the world, the sculpture is so fine.

We came back in the evening and wrote postcards while waiting for the festival to begin. You have to imagine the square in front of San Marco transformed into a concert hall with at least 15,000 seats. There we waited, and with the darkness all the seats were filled. Then the lights were extinguished and only little candles remained, surrounded with paper of scintillating colour.

Can you see in what a silence the thousands are waiting until suddenly the church of San Marco which had been invisible is illuminated by a blue light, and the effect is of a work of art; a picture has appeared out of the dark sky, you can imagine the impression it produced. Then the concert began. The orchestra with Italian singers played Italian operas, then there were fireworks and the concert finished with part of the Walkyrie. The or-

chestra was of such perfection and the singers so wonderful. And
do you know, the public called out for Mussolini to appear on the
balcony, but it was so dark we could not see whether he came
out. But during the music there was complete silence and one felt
everyone understood how good the music was. At 1 we returned
to Padua).

They made a stay, also, in Milan, from where she wrote:

Mais je vois que ce n'est pas pour rien que je suis restée ici. Tu
sais, j'ai appris tant de choses. J'ai voulu profiter autant que
possible de tout le temps que j'avais pour bien étudier les vestiges
de l'art du moyen-âge et de la Renaissance et beaucoup de choses
m'ont tellement émues. Aussi j'avais lu ensemble avec Madame
Guignard, le livre de mon père: *Yesterday, today and tomorrow*
et ce livre m'a tellement aidé à comprendre tant ce que j'ai vu.
C'est drôle qu'elle avait justement choisi ce livre, on aurait dit
que c'était une préparation avant de venir ici. Aussi dans ce livre
il y a un chapitre sur les pièces de theâtre et opéras et tu sais toute
cette semaine on a joué une série des plus celèbres opéras Italiens,
dans le même parc comme l'opéra d'Aida, et alors j'ai pu voir
encore: Rigoletto, Le Troubadour de Verdi et La Bohème de
Puccini. Maintenant j'ai un peu une idée des opéras Italiens, ce
n'est pas ce qu'il y a de plus profond, mais c'est tellement carac-
téristique de l'âme Italienne. Aussi ici des milliers courent aux
opéras comme à Paris aux courses. Il faut aussi que je te raconte
ce qui s'est passé durant l'opéra de Rigoletto. Tout à coup au
milieu d'une scène quelqu'un a reconnu le Duce et il a crié tant
haut "Il duce". Dans une seconde le public était tout en fièvre,
les acteurs sont presque tombés d'émotion, les musiciens ont
presque lâchés leurs violons et alors pour quelque temps il y avait
un silence absolu, c'était si impressionant, et après ce silence un
profond soupir de joie s'est élevé de toute la foule. Puis l'opéra
a repris son cours et on pourra dire que le duce était là comme un
simple spectateur parmi la foule.
Heureusement que c'était le tour du choeur de chanter après
toute cette émotion, car surement le pauvre Rigoletto n'aurait fait
qu'un trémolo.

(But I see it is not for nothing I have stayed on here. You
know, I have learned so many things. I wanted to profit as much
as possible from the time to study the vestiges of the art of the
middle ages and of the Renaissance and so many things have
moved me so much. Also I have been reading with Mme. Guignard my father's book, *Yesterday, Today and Tomorrow* and the
book has helped me to understand so much of what I have seen.
It is funny that she should have chosen just that book, one could

have said it was a preparation for coming here. There is a chapter in the book on plays and operas, too, and do you know this week they have been playing a series of all the most celebrated Italian operas, in the same park, such as *Aïda,* and I have been able to see *Rigoletto,* Verdi's *Trovatore* and Puccini's *Bohème.* Now I have a little bit of an idea of Italian operas, it is not that they are the most profound kind of thing, but they are so characteristic of the Italian soul. Also, thousands go to the operas, as in Paris to the races. I must tell you what happened during *Rigoletto.* Suddenly, in the middle of a scene someone recognised the Duce and cried out "Il Duce". In a second the public was in a fever, the actors almost falling over from emotion, and the musicians almost dropping their violins and for some time there was an absolute silence, it was very impressive and after the silence a profound sigh of joy rose from the whole crowd. Then the opera resumed and the Duce was there as a simple spectator amongst the crowd. [1]

Happily it was the turn of the chorus to sing after all that emotion, for the poor Rigoletto could not have managed a tremolo.)

Then in another letter:

J'ai lu à Milan le livre que j'ai avec moi de la vie de Mahomet et vraiment je ne crois pas qu'il peut exister un livre plus beau sur la vie.

Mais j'ai aussi pensé à ceux qui sont vraiment grands et qui ont toujours dû retenir en eux cet état d'âme, dans toutes les circonstances, pour pouvoir toujours donner le bonheur aux autres. Et dire que toute la réponse est dans ces paroles du 'Unity of Religious Ideals', "the soul that is tuned to God, begins to express God in all that it does."

(I have read while at Milan a book that I have with me on the life of Mahomet, and really I do not think there could exist a more beautiful book on life. But I think that those who are really great always retain something of that state of mind in all circumstances, to be able to give happiness to others. And to think that the whole response is in *The Unity of Religious Ideals,* "the soul that is tuned to God, begins to express God in all that it does.")

[1] Mussolini must have been fond of **Rigoletto.** A few years earlier than Noor, I was present at a very similar occurrence. It was at the open-air **Dopo Lavoro** in the Borghese Gardens in Rome, in the summer of 1931, that my mother and I were to taken to see—not the first—but the second night of **Rigoletto,** as it had got round 'on the grape vine' that the Duce would attend on the second night, though a booking of seats had not been made in his name. He was again late, but the square of empty seats in the middle of the stalls suggested a special booking, and the curtain was held until he came, when the whole crowd stood up and went mad, shouting "Viva!"

In the summer of 1937 Vilayat took his sister to Switzerland. They stayed for two or three months in a small place called Oberzug, high in the mountains, in a châlet perched above the lake of Zug, and Noor learned a little German. Vilayat particularly remembers this holiday, because his sister had not been very happy during the previous months, and he had arranged it largely to take her away from her troubles. They had brought bicycles—though bicycles might not seem very appropriate to Switzerland—and pushed them up the slopes and rode them down. She seemed very carefree and happy, and it was a period in their lives which he liked afterwards to recall.

Noor wrote further:

Veux-tu que je te raconte un peu notre vie ici. Vois-tu nous nous levons et couchons avec le soleil. Dès 6h¹/₂ tout le monde est debout. Puis j'arrange nos chambres jusqu'à 8 h. et alors nous prenons du bon lait tout frais. A 10 h. je prends le bain de soleil puis jusqu'à midi je m'occupe des enfants tandis que toute la matinée Vilayat travaille dans sa cabane. Puis après déjeuner je me repose sur le balcon jusqu'à 2h¹/₂. Et alors nous sortons soit dans les montagnes soit dans un petit bateau sur le lac, tu sais c'est si joli et si paisible. Je lis tout haut tandis que Vilayat rame et il n'y a pas de danger car le lac n'est pas très grand et tout autour sur les rivagers des bâteliers sont au travail et ils guettent sur le lac car même leurs tout petits enfants s'en vont seuls sur l'eau. Alors vers 4h. nous rentrons pour prendre du lait de nouveau. Puis nous travaillons à quelquechose jusqu'à 6h¹/₂ et puis nous allons dîner. Comme tu vas rire si je te raconte de quoi consiste notre dîner: Oh bien c'est tout à fait un repas paysan du pain, du beurre, du fromage, des fruits ou de la crème et c'est tout! Mais c'est si bon, c'est meilleur que tout un dîner!

(Shall I describe our life here? We get up and go to bed with the sun. By 6.30 everyone is up. I do the rooms until 8, and then we drink good milk, absolutely fresh. At 10 I take a sunbath, then at mid-day I take charge of the children; Vilayat works all the morning in his cabin. After lunch, I rest on the balcony until 2.30. Then we go out, either into the mountains or on the lake in a small boat, you know it is so pretty and peaceful. I read aloud while Vilayat rows, and it is not dangerous because the lake is not large, and there are boatmen working on the shores, and they watch the lake because their own small children go in the water. After 4 we come in and drink milk again. Then we work at something until 6.30, when we have dinner. How you will laugh if I

tell you what dinner consists of: it is a real peasants' meal, of
bread, butter, cheese, fruits and cream, and that is all! But it is
so good, it is better than a real dinner.)

Also from Switzerland, she wrote:

D'abord le matin j'ai fait une petite promenade seule et je me
suis arretée sous un arbre pour dire nos prières et juste douze
coups ont sonné de la petite chapelle, c'était comme une réponse,
puis un peu plus tard quand je suis entrée dans ma chambre il y
avait une colombe toute blanche qui m'attendait là.

(In the morning I took a short walk alone and stopped under
a tree to say our prayers and just twelve strokes sounded from the
little chapel, it was like a reply, and when I came to my room
a white dove was waiting for me...)

And again from Switzerland:

J'aide beaucoup Mme. Guignard avec les enfants, j'aide à les
lever, les coucher et j'aime tellement faire tout ce que je peux.
Je viens de donner une leçon de piano au garçon dont je t'ai parlé
et il apprend si vite, aussi à lire la musique que c'est incroyable
et il est si heureux quand j'improvise pour lui. Quand il commence à s'exciter, je lui joue cette prière que mon père avait com-
posé dans son rêve et il se calme tout de suite et je lui dis, ça
c'est une prière et il devient tout ému, et il m'embrasse après
chaque leçon. Mme. Guignard m'a dit que c'est la première fois
qu'il ressent de l'affection, il a été si renfermé. Vraiment la musique peut être un remède si merveilleux. Quant au petit qui
m'appelle mama on dirait qu'il n'est venu au monde que pour
donner la joie. Même à une distance rien qu'à entendre sa petite
voix toute éclatante de joie on devient tout heureux et ses yeux
sont si rayonnants de bonheur et d'affection.

(I help Mme. Guignard with the children. I help to get them
up and put them to bed and I so much enjoy doing everything I
can. I have just given lesson to the boy of whom I have already
spoken to you and he learns so quickly, also to read music, which
is incredible, and he is so happy when I improvise for him. When
he becomes excited I play for him that prayer my father composed
in a dream, and he calms at once, and I say to him, that's a prayer,
and he is moved, and kisses me after each lesson. Mme. Guignard
told me that it is the first time he has returned affection. He is
so closed within himself. Really, music can be a marvellous remedy. As to the little one who calls me Mama, one would say he
had come into the world to give joy. Even at a distance one feels

happy to hear his joyful voice, and his eyes shining with happiness and affection.)

As Switzerland was one of the countries in which Sufism had taken a certain root, and Vilayat and Noor met there a good many of her father's disciples, it was natural they should during this visit think about their father, and the time that he had spent in the places they were now seeing.

Noor wrote to her friend:

Hier après-midi nous sommes allés à Lausanne avec Mme. van Hogendorp chez les amis de qui je t'avais parlé. Nous sommes allés en bateau, et je pensais à combien de fois sur ce même lac mon père a voyagé et tu sais je crois que c'est ce lac qui a dû lui inspirer cette pensée: "When I look into the lake of my heart, I see thy image reflected."

. . . Une fois de plus dans ma vie j'ai vu mon père en rève. C'est si rare mais pour cette raison même c'est la plus grande bénédiction. Il semblait que nous étions tous agités, angoissés et il est venu et cette paix qu'il a apportée dans nos âmes était inexprimable en paroles.

. . . L'autre livre est une conférence que mon père a donné au Musée Guimet à Paris. Je me rappelle encore de cette conférence car bien que j'étais très petite encore, elle m'avait beaucoup impressionée et je me souviens comme je me suis faufilée après, parmi le public pour entendre ce qu'on en pensait et en revenant je racontais tout à mon père.

. . . Il me semblait entendre de nouveau résonner au fond de moi-même cette voix pleine d'amour, je me rappelais exactement le timbre de cette voix lorsque mon père me parlait et j'étais sur son lit ou sur ses genoux. Et ces mots me sont venus comme si lui parlait dans ce même language enfantin qu'il empruntait toujours pour parler à ses petits. "When Abba's love is there, what fear is there." Même je crois me souvenir qu'une fois il m'a dit ces mots, ils étaient imprimés profondément dans mon petit coeur et maintenant de nouveau je les entend comme une consolation qui ne vient que de lui.

. . . Et cette nuit je me suis reveillée et je sentais tellement le désir de dire nos prières. De toute mon âme je les ai dites et dans le silence de la nuit, il me semblait tellement que Dieu m'entendait. Et juste aux derniers mots la pendule a sonné c'était comme une réponse, trois coups qui tintaient au milieu du silence.

Mon père nous avait dit une fois cela veut dire que Dieu accorde nos prières. Et le coeur plein de joie et de confiance je me suis endormie.

(Yesterday afternoon we went to Lausanne with Mme. Hogendorp to the friends of whom I spoke to you. We went in a boat, and I thought how many times my father had crossed this lake in a boat, and you know I think it is this lake which must have inspired him with the thought: "When I look into the lake of my heart, I see Thy image reflected."

. . . Once again in my life, I have seen my father in a dream. It is so rare, and for that reason the greatest blessing. It seemed that we were very agitated, anguished, and that he came and that the peace he brought to our hearts was inexpressible in words.

. . . The other book is a talk my father gave at the Musée Guimet in Paris. I still remember that talk because although I was only very small it had impressed me very much, and I remember that afterwards I threaded my way through the crowd to hear what people were saying about it, and coming back recounted it all to my father.

. . . I seem to hear again in the depths of my being that voice full of love, I remember exactly the timbre of that voice when my father spoke to me and I was on his bed or on his knees. And his words came to me as though he spoke still the childish language he used to us when we were small. "When Abba's love is there, what fear is there?" Indeed, I think, I remember that he did once use these words to me, they were deeply printed on my little heart and now again I hear them like a consolation that comes only from him.

. . . And this night I woke and felt so strongly the desire to say my prayers. With all my soul I said them and in the silence of the night, it seemed so much that God heard me. And just at the last words the pendulum sounded, it was a reply, three knocks which rang through the silence. My father told us that meant God granted our prayers. And I fell asleep with my heart full of joy and confidence.)

She wrote of another occasion, when they were joined by Claire, whom some of her father's disciples now saw for the first time:

Cette fois de nouveau nous sommes allés à Zurich mais nous étions tous les trois et tous les mureeds étaient très enthousiastes dé voir Mamli. Cela nous a fait de la peine de quitter Mme. De Armas, celle dont les enfants et le mari sont aux Iles Canaries, elle va là aussi dans deux jours. Je lui dois beaucoup de choses, je lui dois de m'avoir montré par son exemple, à voir la vie d'une manière tellement plus profonde. Tu dois imaginer combien j'ai été émue de voir en une femme le conception de la vie qui j'ai tant recherchée et telle que j'ai tant voulu être, cette douceur vivante qui émane d'elle, prête à consoler chaque coeur qui vient à elle. Sa mère, notre grand'maman m'a dit qu'elle a beaucoup souffert. Et Dieu soit remercié si en souffrant je puis avoir cette même lumière en moi.

(We have been to Zurich again, but this time there were three of us and the mureeds [disciples] were enthusiastic at seeing Mam[u]li [Claire]. We were sorry to leave Mme. De Armas, whose children and husband are in the Canaries, she is going there in two days. I owe her many things. I owe her that she showed me by her example how to see life in a more profound manner. You can imagine how much I was moved to see in a woman the conception of life I have so much sought and [a being] such as I have so much wanted to be, that living softness which emanates from her, ready to console every heart which comes to her. Her mother, our "grandmama", told me she had suffered very much. And God be thanked if I, in suffering, could have the same light in me.)

Noor and Vilayat had known a certain amount of Hindustani as children, when they used to hear it spoken between their father and uncles. Now, however, they realized it was slipping away from them, and decided they must arrest this process. They took lessons together at the Berlitz School for some time; then, in 1937, Noor entered the Ecole des Langues Orientales, of the University of Paris, where she studied for two years.

I think it must have been while Noor was on holiday with her mother, during one of the Begum's later visits to the south of France, that Noor wrote to her friend a letter extracts from which lend themselves to the impression they were perhaps attending the Cannes film festival. The reference to the showing of English films to celebrate a coronation suggests an approximate date for the letter. King George VI was crowned King of England on May 12th, 1937.

Tu sais il faut pour sûr que tu voies trois merveilleux films que nous avons vu, s'ils se jouent aussi à Paris. Je crois pour sûr que l'on doit jouer au moins un ou deux parmi les trois maintenant à l'occasion du couronnement du roi, car tous les trois sont les plus beaux films anglais et le troisième est fait comme cadeau pour le couronnement, il est intitulé "Elephant Boy" d'après le livre de la jungle de Kipling. On voit la jungle et les chasseurs hindous sur leurs éléphants. Il y a une légende aux Indes que les éléphants sauvages dans la jungle se réunissent par centaines et la nuit au fond de la jungle ils dansent tous ensemble, et rares sont ceux qui ont vu cette danse en realité. Et il paraît que c'est vrai, on a trouvé leur cachette dans la jungle près de Mysore et on a pu filmer la danse.

Puis, il faut que tu voies ce magnifique film de "Romeo et Juliette" d'après Shakespeare. Sûrement on doit le jouer en ce moment à Paris. Combien les décors sont beaux et revèlent l'atmosphère de ce temps en Italie! Et les acteurs ne pourraient être mieux choisis, c'est de toute leur âme qu'ils le jouent. Sois sûr, d'aller le voir, c'est très triste mais c'est si beau. Sans doute connais-tu déjà l'histoire, ces deux familles qui, durant des générations se haïssaient si amèrement se sont unies par l'amour de leurs deux enfants.

Puis le plus profond de tous est intitulé "Berkeley Square". Peut-être est-ce moins probable qu'on le joue car il est moins connu. Le même acteur joue dans ce film, qui joue le rôle de Romeo. Maman était si profondément touchée par ce film, nous tous aussi, mais pour Maman c'était une consolation, cela ouvrait pour elle des pensées dont elle a besoin, et elle a dit, jamais de si profondes pensées n'ont été exprimées. Au fond ce devait être un vrai sufi qui l'a écrit, un vrai philosophe, c'est le point de vue de quelqu'un qui ne voit pas le monde comme lorsqu'il est au milieu du monde, mais, comme mon père a dit, à vol d'oiseau d'ou l'on voit avec une autre perspective, alors les choses qui importent beaucoup dans le monde prennent de petites proportions et l'horizon de vue devient immense. Aussi cette belle et profonde pensée y est exprimée qu'il y a des âmes qui sont faites l'une pour l'autre et qui s'aiment éternellement et se retrouvent dans l'éternité. Toute ces belles et profondes conceptions sont exprimées sous la forme d'une histoire et sûrement très peu comprennent ce film. Je suis sûre que tu aimerais tant le voir.

(You know you must see three marvellous films we have seen, if they are showing also in Paris. I think they are showing at least one or two now for the crowning of the king, for all three are beautiful English films, and the third was made to be a present for the coronation, and is entitled *Elephant Boy* after the jungle book by Kipling. One sees the jungle and the Hindu hunters on their elephants, and what is more marvellous, the dance of the elephants. There is an Indian legend that the wild elephants of the jungle dance in hundreds on certain nights in the depth of the jungle, and that few are those who have seen this dance in reality. And it seems that it is true, their hiding-place in the jungle near Mysore was found and the film made of the dance.

Then you must see the magnificent film made of Shakespeare's *Romeo and Juliet*. Surely they must be showing it now in Paris. The decor is so beautiful, and reveals, the atmosphere of the time in Italy! And the actors could not have been better chosen, they play with their whole soul. Make sure to go and see it, it is very sad but very beautiful. Doubtless you know the story, of the two families who hated each other and were united by the love of their two children.

But the most profound is the one called *Berkeley Square*. Perhaps that is less likely to be shown as it is less known. The same actor is in this film who played Romeo. Mother was so profoundly touched by this film, all of us, too, but for Mother it was a consolation, it opened for her thoughts of which she has need, and she said that never had such profound thoughts been expressed. It must have been a real sufi who wrote it, a real philosopher, it's from the point of view of someone who does not see the world as though he were in the middle of it, but as my father said, from a bird's eye point of view, which shows another perspective, in which things which seem important in the world take small proportions and the horizon visible becomes immense. Also, the beautiful and profound thought is expressed in it that there are souls that are made for each other and love each other eternally and re-find each other in eternity. All these beautiful and profound concepts are expressed in the form of a story and surely very few people understand the film. I am sure you would like to see it.)

Much of her life was still absorbed in the Sufi Movement. Every summer the usual influx would arrive. Readings were given of the teachings of Pir-o-Murshid Inayat Khan, and an occasional discourse delivered by one of the visiting Sufis, the uncles or Vilayat. Sometimes there was a turn of the unexpected. Mr. Basil Mitchell—the son of one of Inayat Khan's earliest disciples—an undergraduate at Queen's College, Oxford and a friend of Vilayat, was invited to give an address. He announced that his talk would be called "The Virtue of Tolerance", but after Vilayat, as Chairman, had presented him, said he hoped nobody would mind, but he had decided to speak on "The Virtue of Intolerance" instead. The Sufis were perhaps a little surprised, but showed themselves quite tolerant. This was on a day in 1937, the only time I ever attended the Summer School. I was not a Sufi, and it was in fact Basil Mitchell who brought me. In the garden afterwards I was introduced to Noor-un-nisa, but it was only for an ephemeral glimpse. She never spoke at these meetings, but seemed to be sensed by the visitors as a softly pervading presence.

Basil Mitchell (now Professor of the Philosophy of the Christian Religion, at Oriel College, Oxford) wrote for me,[1] "The lasting impression that remains with me of Noor-un-nisa is of a very gentle creature. Her determination and practical capacity were a matter for constant surprise. Perhaps someone who knew her better, or whose insight was deeper, might have guessed at her future career, but to me this was the culminating surprise. The surprise was not her fortitude, which could have been predicted, but her capacity to sustain an active role of tough, inventive, and deliberate daring. The one thing about her which was evident from the beginning and serves, perhaps, in retrospect to explain this odd combination of gentleness and efficiency was her freedom from any kind of selfishness or self-consciousness—her complete humility. I don't think it ever occurred to her to assess her own importance or wonder what impression she was making; and this gave her a peculiar objectivity and the power which that confers.

But the impression she made, and which remains, was not of any complication or mystery, but just of the gentleness I have spoken of, and which expressed itself most distinctly and quite unforgettably in her voice."

If there was not a meeting, then perhaps Noor would go for a walk in the afternoon with one of the visitors. Suresnes had now become largely built up as an industrial extension of Paris, but they were only a few minutes from the Parc de St. Cloud or the Bois de Boulogne.

After dinner she generally slipped away. Visitors continuing their discussions under the quince-tree, in the twilight of a warm evening, would sometimes hear the strains of a harp float out upon the air. Noor was playing in her room.

She renewed her friendship with Geneviève, from whom she had been separated for several years, and who remembers vividly the tiny figure sitting beside her great harp, with all her sweetness, her fidelity to her old friend, her tolerance and calmness. They made great plans to study together, but once again Geneviève had to go away.

Despite the appearance of the babyish word "Birdies", I quote in full the poem which in 1938 she wrote to her mother, for the way in which it shows her love for her, and because, indeed, it shows the kind of girl that she was, herself, still, at twenty-four

[1] In response to my request to write a paragraph for this book.

A little fairy told me why the flowers wake in May,
She said: It's for the birthday of a little "Ora Ray".
The Sun, they say, is jealous of her lovely golden hair,
The Flowers look their sweetest just to try and be as fair.
Ah! there is no other birthday half as sweet as this, you see,
The Birdies give a concert on a branch of every tree
I met some little sparrows as I skipped along the way,
"Her naughty little children are so proud
                                        — I heard her say —
Of course it is quite natural for they know as well as we,
There's not a sweeter mother over land and over sea.
You come and see us dancing on our bonny eighth of May,
You'll see the moon bend over just to watch
                                        us sing and play".
This secret little fairy came and whispered in my ear,
"And this is why the whole world wakes to greet our
                                        Mother Dear".

In the summer of 1938 Noor sat for her examination at the
University, and obtained her licence in the Psycho-biology of the
Child.

Almost immediately she was freed from this study she began
an engrossing literary work. All her life she had loved the Jakata
tales, a cycle of about five hundred legends symbolizing previous
incarnations of the Buddha. In each one he is represented as
some kind of animal which, by an act of sacrifice, furthered its
evolution. Now the Baroness van Tuyll wrote to her suggesting
a joint work. She had a fancy to illustrate some of these stories.
(Her professional name was H. Willebeek le Mair and she was
well known as an illustrator of children's books.) They existed
in an English translation, but not in a form which a child could
understand. Could not Noor adapt a few of the best to make a
children's book? They picked out twenty, and each set to work.

Noor used to rise at six in the morning, and begin work in her
room immediately, without taking breakfast. To use this early
part of the day was her only way of having a reasonable period
free from interruption. The family did not begin stirring till between eight and nine, so she was secure for nearly three hours.
Besides, she said, this was the time when she felt her freshest. The
cool, slightly damp air of the early morning had a magical quality
which it lost later.

The story she loved most was one she called *The Fairy and*

72

the Hare.[1] It seemed to her sublime, and there is no doubt that it affected her throughout her life.

THE FAIRY AND THE HARE

A young hare lived once in a small forest between a mountain, a village and a river. My children, many hares run through the heather and the moss, but none so sweet as he.

Three friends he had: a jackal, a water-weasel and a monkey.

After a long day's toil, searching for food, they came together at evening, all four, to talk and think. The handsome hare spoke to his three companions and taught them many things. And they listened to him, and learned to love all the creatures of the woods, and they were very happy.

"My friends," said the hare one day. "Let us not eat tomorrow, but the food we find in the day we will give to any poor creature we meet."

This they all agreed to. And the next day, as every day, they started out at dawn in search of food.

The jackal found in a hut in the village a piece of meat and a jar of curdled milk with a rope tied to each handle. Three times he cried aloud: "Whose is this meat? Whose is this curdled milk?" But the hut was empty, and hearing no answer, he put the piece of meat in his mouth, and the rope of the jar round his neck, and away he fled to the forest. And laying them at his side, he thought: "What a good jackal I am! Tomorrow I shall eat what I have found if nobody comes this way."

And what did the little water-weasel find on his rounds?

A fisherman had caught some sparkling golden fish, and after hiding them under the sand he returned to the river to catch more. But the water-weasel found the hiding-place, and after taking the fish out of the sand, he called three times: "Whose are these golden fish?"

But the fisherman heard only the rippling of the river and none answered his call! So he took the fish into the forest to his little home, and thought. "What a good water-weasel I am! The fish I shall not eat today, but perhaps another day."

Meanwhile the monkey-friend had climbed the mountain, and finding some ripe mangoes, he carried them down into the woods and hid them in a tree, and he thought: "What a good monkey I am!"

But the hare lay in the grass in the woods, and his beautiful eyes were moist with sadness. "What can I offer if any poor creature should pass this way?" he thought. "I cannot offer grass, and I have neither rice nor nuts to give."

1 Published by Harrap in a volume of stories entitled Twenty Jataka Tales, 1939.

But suddenly he leaped with joy. "If someone comes this way," he thought, "I shall give him myself to eat."

Now, in the sweet little wood lived a fairy with butterfly wings and long hair of moonlight rays. Her name was Sakka. She knew everything that took place in the wood. She knew if a small ant had stolen from another ant. She knew the thoughts of all the little creatures, even of the poor little flowers, trampled over in the grass. And she knew that day that the three friends in the wood were not eating, and that any food they might find was to be given to any poor creature they might meet.

And so Sakka changed herself into an old beggar man bent over, walking with a stick.

She went first to the jackal and said: "I have walked for days and weeks, and have had nothing to eat. I have no strength to search for food. Please give me something, O jackal!"

"Take this piece of meat, and the jar of curdled milk," said the jackal. "I stole it from a hut in the village, but it is all I have to give."

"I will see about it later," said the beggar, and she went on through the shady trees.

Then Sakka met the water-weasel, and asked, "What have you to give me, little one?"

"Take this fish, O beggar, and rest awhile beneath this tree," answered the water-weasel.

"Another time," the beggar replied, and passed on through the woods.

A little farther Sakka met the monkey, and said, "Give me of your fruits, I pray. I am poor and starved and weary."

"Take all these mangoes" said the monkey. I plucked them for you."

"Some other time," the beggar replied, and did not stay.

Then Sakka met the hare and said, "Sweet one of the mossy woods, tell me where can I find food? I am lost within the forest and far away from home."

"I will give you myself to eat," replied the hare. "Gather some wood and make a fire; I will jump into the flames and you shall have the flesh of a little hare."

Sakka caused magic flames to come from some logs of wood, and full of joy the hare jumped into the glowing fire. But the flames were cool as water, and did not burn his skin.

"Why is it," he said to Sakka. "I do not feel the flames? The sparks are as fresh as the dew of the dawn."

Sakka then changed herself into her fairy form again, and spoke to him in a voice sweeter than any he had ever heard.

"Dear one," she said, "I am the fairy Sakka. This fire is not real, and it is only a test. The kindness of your heart, O blessed one, shall be known throughout the world for ages to come. So

74

saying, Sakka struck the moon with her wand, and with the essence which gushed forth she drew the picture of the hare on the orb of the moon.

Next day the hare met the friends again, and all the creatures of the wood gathered round them. And the hare told them of all that had happened to him, and they rejoiced and all lived happily ever after.

At the same time, Noor—now twenty-four—was having an increasing success with the articles and stories she wrote as a freelance. Since the first had been accepted by the *Sunday Figaro* a year ago she had become an almost regular contributor to the Children's Page. One of her stories which was most appreciated was "*Ce qu'on entend quelquefois dans les bois*", published in *Le Figaro* the 13th August 1939.

CE QU'ON ENTEND QUELQUEFOIS DANS LES BOIS

Bien, bien des siècles passés vivaient des nymphes sur la cime d'une haute montagne.

Il y avait aussi des nymphes sur la terre, mais celles des montagnes étaient plus belles que toutes les autres, car elles buvaient le miel des jonquilles qui couvraient les pentes, et vivaient si près du ciel là-haut sur les rochers qu'elles en respiraient tous les parfums.

Aussi, recueillaient-elles tous ces parfums, les mélangeaient à ceux des pins, des branches de laurier, et lorsque Mistral. le roi des vents, passait par la montagne, elles les lui donnaient pour répandre sur la terre.

Parmi les nymphes, il en était une plus jeune que toutes les autres. On l'appelait Echo. C'était la plus petite, sa voix était plus douce, plus tendre que celle des autres, mais elle avait deux grands défauts.

D'abord, elle ne parlait jamais la première, c'était son habitude. Il fallut toujours qu'une autre lui dise d'abord bonjour.

Mais une fois la conversation commencée, elle ne cessait de babiller, car elle était bavarde, plus bavarde même que les pies et les cigales.

Un jour, une des nymphes allant porter à Mistral les parfums qu'elle avait recueillis, rencontra Echo sur le chemin.

— Bonsoir, Echo, ma petite soeur, lui dit-elle.

— Bonsoir! répondit Echo. Et aussitôt commencèrent les babillages. Et ils durèrent si longtemps que Mistral passa par la cime avant que la nymphe ait pu y arriver.

Si grande fut la colère de Mistral ce soir-là qu'il soufflat quatre fois plus fort, et les arbres se penchèrent, le sable des rochers s'envola, et sur toute la terre on n'entendit plus que soupirs.

Toutes les nymphes de la montagne étaient déjà rentrées dans les creux des rochers, mais la pauvre nymphe qu'Echo avait retardée courait éperdument, portant les baumes vers la cime.

Et Mistral, qui l'aperçut de loin, lui souffla du sable dans les yeux pour la punir.

Pauvre petite nymphe! Elle s'assit et sanglota jusqu'à que le grand soleil disparut et qu'elle s'endormît sous les sapins.

Mais le lendemain, en retrouvant Echo sur son chemin, la colère lui monta au gosier.

— Echo! méchante Echo! s'écria-t-elle, c'est toi qui m'as retardée par tes bavardages interminables! La terre n'a pas reçu les parfums du soir et Mistral m'a durement punie! Et tu crois que je vais oublier tout le mal que tu as causé! Non, désormais, tu ne pourras que répéter les derniers mots de ce qu'on te dira, et ainsi tu ne pourras plus retarder personne sur le chemin.

Aussitôt, la malheureuse Echo fut ravie de sa parole.

Elle se blottit sous les sapins tout au bord d'un sentier et se mit à sangloter amèrement.

— Tout parle, pensait elle, la source qui descend là-bas sur le rocher, le sapin qui ne cesse d'agiter ses branches... Que raconte-t-il? Les histoires interminables des nymphes, de Mistral, du grand soleil...

Et pendant qu'elle songeait ainsi à tout le bonheur qu'elle n'avait pas, un bruit de pas approchait doucement.

C'était Narcisse, le jeune berger.

— Un homme de la terre, si beau! pensait Echo, certes il est le fils de quelque nymphe car il est beau comme le lever du soleil.

A peine était-il passé à travers les sapins, qu'Echo suivit ses pas tout doucement.

— Qui est derrière moi? s'écria Narcisse.

— Moi! répondit Echo, qui se cachait derrière un sapin.

— Pourquoi fuis-tu? s'écria Narcisse.

— Pourquoi fuis-tu? répondit Echo.

— Attends que je te trouve... je viens! dit Narcisse.

— Je viens, répondit Echo.

Et à ces mots, elle fendit l'épais feuillage et parut devant Narcisse. Ses larmes étaient séchées et ses grands yeux brillaient comme des pervenches.

Mais Narcisse en la voyant tourna sur ses pas et s'enfuit.

Elle resta seule sous les sapins et pleura si longtemps qu'elle se transforma en rocher.

Il ne resta d'Echo que sa voix.

Et cette voix s'entend encore dans les montagnes et les bois.

Lorsqu'on appelle, elle répond et sa voix est encore toute triste, car elle pense à Narcisse qui la laissa seule un jour, sous les sapins.

Many, many centuries ago, nymphs lived on the top of a high mountain. There were also nymphs on the earth, but those of the mountain were more beautiful than any others, for they drank the honey of the jonquils which covered the slopes, and lived so near to the sky, among the rocks, that they breathed all its scents. Also, they gathered these scents, mixed them with those of pines and branches of laurel, and when Mistral, king of the winds, passed over the mountain, they gave them to him to spread over the earth.

Amongst the nymphs was one younger than the others. She was called Echo. She was the smallest, and her voice was softer and more tender than those of the others, but she had two great faults. She was never the first to speak; it always had to be another who said good morning. But once the conversation had begun, she never ceased to babble; for she was very talkative; more talkative than the magpies and the grasshoppers.

One day, one of the nymphs, while carrying to Mistral the scents she had gathered, met Echo on the way. "Good evening, Echo, my little sister," she said.

"Good evening," replied Echo, and commenced her babbling, which lasted so long that Mistral passed the summit before the nymph could reach it.

So great was Mistral's anger that evening, that he blew four times harder than usual, and the trees bent, the sand among the rocks flew, and all over the earth, one heard nothing but sighs. All the mountain nymphs had already hidden in crevices of the rocks, but the poor nymph whom Echo had delayed ran madly, carrying balms to the summit. Mistral, who saw her from afar, blew sand in her eyes, to punish her. Poor little nymph, she sat down and cried, until the sun disappeared and she fell asleep under the pines.

But the next day, meeting Echo, the anger rose in her throat. "Echo, wretched Echo!" she cried, "it's you who held me back by your interminable chattering. The earth has not received its evening scents, and Mistral has punished me severely. Do you think I can forget all the harm you have caused? No, from now on, you can only repeat the last words of what anyone has said, so that you can never again delay anyone."

So, the unhappy Echo lost the power of speech. She sat down beneath the pines on the side of the path, and wept bitterly. "Everything speaks, except me, the spring which falls from above on to the rocks, the pines whose branches never cease to move. What do they tell? The interminable stories of nymphs, of Mistral, of the great sun..."

While she thought of the happiness she would not have, a soft footstep approached. It was Narcissus, the young shepherd. "A man of earth, and yet so beautiful!" thought Echo. "He must be the son of some nymph, for he is as beautiful as the sunrise."

Hardly had he passed through the pines than she followed him, quietly.

"Who is behind me?" cried Narcissus.

"Me," replied Echo, hiding behind a pine.

"Why are you running away?" asked Narcissus.

"Why are you running away?" asked Echo.

"Wait until I find you... I am coming," said Narcissus.

"I am coming," replied Echo.

And with these words, she burst through the thick foliage, and appeared before Narcissus. Her tears had dried, and her eyes were shining, like periwinkles. But Narcissus, seeing her, turned in his tracks, and fled.

She remained alone beneath the pines, and wept so long that she turned into a rock. There remained of Echo only her voice.

And this voice is still heard in the mountains and the woods. When one calls, she replies, and her voice is always very sad, for she thinks of Narcissus, who left her alone, one day, beneath the pines).

What is interesting about this innocent adaptation of a rather more sophisticated classical Greek tale, is that its author was an unusually silent girl, whose voice, when she spoke, was just as faint, sweet and plaintive as that which she gives her heroine.

Radiodiffusion Française accepted some of her stories, which were broadcast in the Children's Hour of Radio Paris. Her fiancé remembers also articles on the Indian woman singer, Mira Bai, Nadia Boulanger and Nevada. The last, he preserved: *Cinquante années de gloire.*

CINQUANTE ANNEES DE GLOIRE!

Comment donc est passée la période des grandes cantatrices? Il y a à peine vingt ans de cela et déjà c'est un conte d'autrefois! Où donc sont-elles allées, ces femmes dont les voix magnifiques ont étonné le monde entier? Comme des fées qui ont fait vibrer des cordes magiques, elles sont passées dans l'oubli, mais où sont-elles cachées dans ce monde?

Patti, Nevada, Emma Calvé, Melba, Tetrazzini!

Il en est une à qui mes années d'enfance ont été liées et c'est en hommage à elle, la grande Nevada que je vous conte sa vie merveilleuse.

Il n'est pas un pays en Europe, pas une capitale où sa voix n'ait vibrée, laissant des traces d'enchantement, de merveille, laissant même de quelquechose dans les coeurs qui bien des fois n'y était pas, une petite lueur, d'amour qui ne s'y trouvait pas avant.

Car, parmi toutes ces glorieuses figures, elle était la plus humaine, la plus femme.

Enfant d'Amérique, des montagnes de la Nevada, elle fut aussi un peu enfant de la France car Gounod était son parrain. Et, comme dans un rêve nous voyons s'écouler les grands événements de sa jeunesse.

Liszt accompagnant la jeune cantatrice, Massenet, St. Saëns, Rubinstein, Delibes, Gounod, son parrain, Verdi et Mugnoni dirigeant l'orchestre.

Elle parut et reparut dans toutes les Cours d'Europe.

Paris l'aima si ardemment qu'on exigea constamment sa présence sur la scène. Londres la réclamait, Berlin, Vienne... mais ce fut dans le coeur de Paris, à la Rue de la Pompe qu-elle établit son foyer.

La Scala de Milan était alors en grand danger. L'Italie entière frémissait car la faillite menaçait et la grande Scala allait sombrer.

La Nevada fut appelée.

Elle vint aussitôt. Après quelques représentations la Scala fut sauvée. Miracle magique d'une voix féminine! L'Italie unanime lui en rendit hommage. Elle l'immortalisa comme les déesses de leur antique pays en élevant à Naples sa statue sur le monument Bellini, où tant de chanteurs passent et passeront, où tant de colombes et de pigeons se poseront sur ses blanches épaules.

Les grandes villes de Russie ont donné son nom à plusieurs de leurs avenues et boulevards, pour que sa voix ne puisse jamais s'éffacer.

Mais Nevada n'est pas seulement la grande cantatrice, elle est aussi la grande âme, la douce mère non seulement de son enfant chérie, mais de tous ces enfants qui sont venus comblés de dons et de richesses et que ce monde ingrat et égoïste abandonne à l'obscurité des grandes villes, lutter contre leur propre faim et leurs propres peines. A ceux-là elle a ouvert ses grands bras maternels et combien de ces jeunes qui ont lutté en vain dans cette foire d'argent qui ont passé des nuits à faire vibrer vainement leurs pauvres instruments dans quelque grenier de Paris, elle a doucement guidés et quelques recommandations de sa part leur ont ouvert les portes à la gloire que le monde entier leur attribue de nos jours.

Le jeune Casals, génie inconnu dans sa propre patrie, fut présenté par elle à la Cour d'Espagne, dans ce pays où elle était étrangère.

Sarrasate, Granados, tous lui doivent le jour. Mais hélas! il n'y avait qu'une Nevada.

Idole du public, comblée de succès, elle a su lier sa glorieuse carrière à sa douce vie de famille, ce qui est rare et presque introuvable dans la vie des femmes célèbres.

D'une touchant franchise, elle dit un jour ces paroles à un journaliste venant l'intervuer, paroles qui contredisent tous les principes concernant les conditions de succès des femmes célèbres:

"Ma carrière et ma vie ont commencées le jour de mon mariage."

Mignon, son enfant, qu'elle nomma ainsi d'après l'Opéra qu'elle interpréta peu avant la naissance de l'enfant, vint au monde douée par miracle de la voix de sa mère.

Mignon grandit et jeune encore, sa voix transporta les foules.

Je vois encore le public anglais, au naturel si sobre, l'acclamer frénétiquement et lancer des fleurs de tous les balcons.

A Paris elle fut à l'Opera National une Marguérite incomparable, d'une beauté innaccessible comme celle de ces princesses aux longues tresses d'or qui ne vivent que dans les contes de fées.

La Scala de Milan l'acclamait, New-York la célébrait, mais Mignon, à l'apogée de son succès et à la fleur de son âge, alla se cacher loin du monde car la douleur était venue sous son toit.

Son père souffrait durement, et un destin insurmontable et cruel était venu éteindre la voix de son illustre mère.

Auprès de leurs chevets elle passa ses jours et ses nuits.

Pour eux elle sacrifia sa grande carrière et même son plus tendre amour.

A quelle époque lointaine appartient-elle? Dans quel pays voit-on un si grand amour filial?

En ce moment où je vous parle, elle est encore auprès de sa mère, souffrant avec elle. Et ces deux femmes sont cachées dans les brouillards londoniens.

Et comme si la nature ne voulut point qu'elle voie le monde sans la gloire qu'elle lui donna jadis, elle a perdu la vue pour toujours.

Mais Mignon est auprès d'elle, conduisant ses pas tremblants, écoutant vibrer encore dans la faible voix cinquante années de gloires passées.

Noor Inayat.

Fazal Manzil
from across the grounds,
the foundation stone in the foreground

The four children
left to right Vilayat, Claire, Noor, Hidayat

A concert in Fazal Manzil
left to right, Hidayat, Claire, Noor, Vilayat

*Noor on horseback
on a beach in Holland*

Noor's brother, Vilayat

Noor playing the vina

Noor sitting among the sand-dunes near a beach in Holland

Noor playing the harp

By the Van Tuylls' lily-pond

Noor with dog whose broken leg she had set in splints

Detail of Sufi group picture, taken at Suresnes in front of the Sufi ball
From left to right in the front row Madame Egeling, Noor, Vilayat, Mrs. Maheboob Khan-van Goens, Claire

Noor

(How time has passed since the period of the great singers. Hardly twenty years have gone by, and yet it seems like an era. Where have they gone, those women whose magnificent voices astonished the whole world? As fairies caused magic cords to vibrate, they have passed into oblivion, but where are they, in this world? Patti, Nevada, Emma Calvé, Melba, Tetrazzini?

There is one with whom my childhood was connected, and it is in homage to her, the great Nevada, that I relate her marvellous life.

Yes, there is not a country in Europe, not a capital where her voice has not vibrated, leaving traces of enchantment, of wonder, leaving something in the hearts which often was not there before, a ray of love. For amid so many glorious figures, she was the most human, the most womanly.

Child of America, of the mountains of Nevada, she was also partly a child of France, for Gounod was her godfather, And as in a dream we see the great events of her youth pass by. Liszt accompanied the young singer; Massenet, St. Saëns, Rubinstein, Delibes, Gounod, her godfather, Verdi and Mugnoni directed the orchestra.

She appeared everywhere, in all the courts of Europe. Paris loved her so ardently as to insist constantly on her presence. London proclaimed her, Berlin, Vienna... but it was in the heart of Paris, in the rue de la Pompe, that she established her home.

The Scala was then in great danger. The whole of Italy trembled with the fear the great Scala should fail. An appeal was made to Nevada. She came at once. After a few performances, the Scala was saved. Magic miracle of a feminine voice! The whole of Italy rendered her homage. Italy immortalised her as one of the goddesses of antiquity, erecting her statue on the monument to Bellini at Naples, where so many singers pass and still will pass, where the doves and the pigeons rest on her white shoulders.

The great towns of Russia gave her name to several of their avenues and boulevards, that her voice should never be forgotten.

But Nevada is not only a great singer, she is also a great soul, the gentle mother not only of a dear child, but of all the children who laden with gifts and riches are relegated by an ungrateful and egoistic world to the obscurity of the great towns, there to struggle against hunger and trouble. To them, she opened her great arms, and many who had struggled in vain in this market of silver, who had passed nights playing their poor instruments in some Parisian attic, were guided by her, and her recommendations opened to them the doors of the glory which today the whole world accords them.

The young Casals, a genius unknown in his own country, was presented by her at the Spanish court, in a country where she was the foreigner. Sarrasate, Granados, all owed their luck to her. But alas, there was only one Nevada.

Idol of the public, laden with successes, she was able to unite with her glorious career a happy family life, which is rare and almost impossible to find amongst celebrated women. Touchingly frank, she uttered once, to a journalist who had come to interview her, words which contradict all the principles concerning the conditions of success for celebrated women: "My career and my life began on the day of my marriage."

Mignon, her child, whom she named after the part she had sung shortly before her birth, by a miracle was born endowed with the voice of her mother. Mignon grew, and was only young when her voice transported crowds. I still see an English audience, naturally sober, frantically acclaim her and throw flowers from every balcony. In Paris, she was at the Opéra Nationale an incomparable Marguerite, with an inaccessible beauty like that of those princesses with long golden hair who exist only in fairy tales. In Milan, the Scala acclaimed her; New York celebrated her; but Mignon, at the apogee of her success, and in the flower of her prime, withdrew to hide from the world, for sorrow had come to stay beneath her roof.

Her father fell gravely ill and an insurmountable and cruel destiny had silenced the voice of her illustrious mother. By their bedsides, she passed her days and nights. For them she sacrificed a great career, and even a more tender love.

To what bygone epoch did she belong? In what land does one see so great a daughterly devotion? At the moment at which I write, she is still by her mother, suffering with her. The two women are hidden behind the fogs of London. As though nature had not wished she should see the world without the glory in which she used to shine, the elder has lost her sight forever. But Mignon is beside her, guiding her trembling steps, still hearing in her feebled voice the resonance of fifty years past glories.)

Miss L. Hayat Bouman, a Dutch disciple, and at that time Vilayat's secretary, who spent this summer, 1938, in "Fazal Manzil," remembers some amusing incidents. Noor kept a number of rabbits in the garden, which were extremely tame, and used to follow her about. During three weeks when the maid was away, she and Miss Bouman did the cooking. The door into the garden was generally open, and the rabbits, perceiving Noor at work, would hop boldly into the kitchen and sit up on their hind legs round the table where she was working, to beg their mistress for scraps. In theory they were forbidden the rest of the house,

82

but on one or two occasions Miss Bouman caught a rabbit climbing up the stairs.

On July 5th, the anniversary of Pir-o-Murshid's birthday, a celebration was always held in "Fazal Manzil". The evening before, Noor proposed to Miss Bouman that they should get up at five o'clock the next morning, go down to the flower-market in Paris, and buy at wholesale enough blooms to fill all the public rooms and passages of the house. They could bring them back in a taxi, and have most of the arranging done before the rest of the family was up.

Vilayat, who had been apparently reading, interrupted this conversation, and - perhaps a little appalled by the prospect of such floral saturation - said it would be damp at such an hour and they would catch colds, and anyway the house did not need to be filled with flowers.

"Babuly," says Miss Bouman, "flared up - a thing that was extremely rare - and declared she was not a child! It was an extraordinary spectacle because a girl like that just couldn't be angry. She hadn't got the voice! It was a thin, childish little lisp."

Yet it seemed to her that in her demure way "Babuly" ruled the house. The Begum and Claire were spending the summer in Nice. Noor used to write to them every day, but Vilayat and Hidayat needed reminding. Sometimes when they came in for lunch they would find a pencil and pad laid in each of their places at table between the knives and forks. "Babuly" would explain sweetly, "That is so that you can write to Mother while you're waiting for the soup."

The winter of that year she spent with the van Tuylls. The Baroness remembers that during these months she was reading the Koran and the Holy Bible side by side, and making cross-references in a note-book. She went with the Baroness to Leiden, where they took Hindustani lessons from a Professor. He taught with the Devanagri script, whereas Noor had learned previously with the Persian; but she took philosophically this momentary setback, saying that the Devanagri would help her later with Sanskrit.

The Baroness now taught her to play the vina, an Indian stringed musical instrument bearing some resemblance to a guitar, which she had learned from Inayat Khan—though she was doubtful of the wisdom of Noor's taking another instrument, and thought she dissipated her energies in too many directions. "Nevertheless," she says, "she understood her father's teaching."

83

Twenty Jataka Tales was accepted by the firm of Harrap in England, and appeared in 1939, when the shadow of war was already falling across Europe. To Inayat Khan's children the National Socialist Party in Germany could not but be repulsive; its policy of racial discrimination and suppression of liberty was the antithesis of the affirmation of the innate goodness of human nature in which they had been brought up. Noor became furiously upset when she read of the persecution of the Jews or heard of the bullying of helpless people by the SS. Yet she asked herself what she could do in a social sense. She did not want to take part in a propaganda of hate against the German people—her own principles prevented it—and it seemed to her that as she had a gift for interesting children, and could supply them through the medium to her stories with moral spiritual food, her part might be to work for those who were growing up.

She decided to enlarge her scope. She had for some time had the idea of founding a children's newspaper, in which liberal use would be made of the children's own contributions.

The title was to be *Bel Age*. She invited a Monsieur Pinchon, an artist living in the rue de l'Hippodrome at the side of 'Fazal Manzil', to do some of the illustrations, and in the summer of 1939 took both illustrations and texts to show Monsieur Alexis Danan, a well-known journalist and editor, whom she hoped would publish it. He was charmed with the material she had put together, but feared that the cost of production of anything so beautiful as she had in mind would make it impractical to market. When he explained this to her, she replied naively that in that case it should be sold very expensively to rich children, so that it could be distributed free to poor ones. He never felt that it was a very practical proposition, but such was the effect on him of her soft persistence that the first number was in proof when the war started and the publication had to be postponed.

Her ideas founded on the 1914-18 war, Noor imagined that nurses would be required to serve behind the lines, and she and Claire began a course of training in Nursing and First Aid with the French Red Cross.

It was during the months of the 'phoney war' that the un-official engagement which had lasted so long was terminated by Noor herself. This was after a long internal struggle and great unhappiness. To Madame Prénat she said that the break had come in the end because she wished to remain free for action, either to go to the front as a nurse or to England with Vilayat if the Germans should break through. But naturally there is a great deal more to the story of what underlay this relationship, which had even affected her health, and of how she was able to find the resolution to break it, than can be told here.

Her first fiancé never ceased to hold her in high regard. In 1950 he wrote to me (in English, which is not his language): "She brought a new light and life. She had the best heart one could ever meet. Her presence was a great relief for those who were suffering. One glance of her was like a thousand suns. In her presence everything became clear; she showed the way to rise above difficulties. With her sweet voice she would speak to those she met, and her power was great. She never feared in accomplishing things. She loved nature. She loved the trees, the leaves, the snow, the flowers, the birds ... "

VII

It was on an afternoon in June 1940 that Noor and Vilayat, side by side on a sofa in the sitting-room at 'Fazal Manzil', were trying to decide what they should do. The sound of guns in the East lent urgency to their discussion.

The question where their duty lay could not be simple for them. By birth the natural guardians of a tradition supposed to be above nation, race, and creed, it might be argued — and indeed it *was* argued by many of their father's disciples — that their first responsibility was to the Movement, and to the preservation in times of trouble of values threatened with extinction. Should their care not be to resist the great gusts of hatred tearing the peoples of the world apart, and to shelter through the storm that flame which represented the common humanity of all men? Their connection with Britain was so slender it seemed likely that they would be exempted from internment, and so long as they were careful to preserve a strict neutrality they might be allowed to carry on. They went backwards and forwards examining their motives; they did not want to use their 'consecrated' position as an excuse to remain out of the fighting — nor yet to enter it solely to avoid being considered to take an easy way out.

Suddenly it appeared to them both that in their hearts they were not above the conflict. They wanted the Nazis to lose. This made a mockery of their pretension to a priest-like standpoint and left them no alternative but to join the ranks of those who were fighting to bring about their check.

They went upstairs to find the rest of the family, and told them they were going to England. Their mother and Claire they persuaded to come with them, but Hidayat, who was married, said he would take his wife and children to the South of France. He would give them a lift, if they liked, in his car as far as Tours. As Vilayat's car was undergoing repairs, they accepted.

"But we shall have to leave *at once*", he said. "The roads will be thronged."

Noor ran round to the houses of several friends living in the neighbourhood to say good-bye and—since they would have simply to abandon 'Fazal Manzil'—to ask them to invade it and take out any things of value and keep for them until after the war.

The party for England went first in Hidayat's car, Hidayat and his family and the uncle following in the latter's car. They had to keep very close so as not to get separated.

To say that the roads were crowded would be an understatement. They were entirely filled, from kerb to kerb, with traffic all going one way—out of Paris. Every conceivable kind of vehicle was moving in the slow procession, lorries, cars, vans, even poor little push-bicycles. Whole families were travelling, children crying, and the most pathetic household and personal treasures sticking up in the air. Tears were trickling down some of the old people's faces.

Soon after they had got out of the precincts of the city, the dive-bombing began. Planes roared over their heads and swooped with a sickening shriek to drop their loads from a height of only a few feet. From other low-flying craft, machine-gunners strafed the helpless cortège. In front of them, and behind, they saw frightful casualties. Noor put her arm round her mother and drew her close. Vilayat, at the wheel, swore he would join the RAF.

It was night when they reached Tours. They found there were no further trains until the next day, but were able to get their cars in under an outbuilding of the station. Like a lot of other people, they had thought the roof would afford protection; but it was made of glass and kept falling in on them. Some people were injured.

In the early hours of the morning they extricated themselves from the 'shelter'. The Begum, Noor, Claire, and Vilayat said good-bye to Hidayat and his family and the uncle—the Begum anguished at parting from her son, not knowing if she would ever see him again—and then made their way into the station to look at the indicator. They found there was a train coming through to Bordeaux shortly, and hoped that from there they might be able to get a boat to England.

As it drew into the station the crowd seethed round it terrifyingly; nevertheless, carried forward by the mass of people, they managed to get aboard.

Sandwiched in the corridor, Noor and Claire began to worry about their Nursing and First Aid Certificates. They had passed their examinations, but had been informed that the French Red Cross no longer had the authority to issue certificates to British subjects—the fall of the country seeming so imminent—and had been referred to the British Red Cross. When they arrived at the address for the latter, they found it had left, lock, stock and barrel, for England, and the premises were closed. Now they wondered how difficult it would be to trace the certificates when they got to London, and whether they would have any proof that they had passed the examinations.

When, towards the middle of the day, the train drew into Bordeaux St. Jean officials on the platform told them that nobody would be allowed out. The town was full, and they had orders not to allow any more 'refugees' to enter. (Noor and Vilayat did not like this word.) Some of the passengers tried to get down by main force, but they were pushed back and the doors shut upon them by the desperate station staff. "You will be taken on somewhere else!" they assured them through the windows.

The train began to move on again. Looking anxiously out, they perceived that they were following the course of the river. At Le Verdon, a small port about fifty miles down the estuary from Bordeaux, they stopped and were allowed to get out. The crowd poured through the barrier into a street already surging with people. At the Town Hall they learned that all the British residents in France were being evacuated, by arrangement with His Majesty's Government. This partly explained the enormous press in the town, which had absorbed in three days more than four times its own population.

Vilayat, who was a British subject, having been born in London, asked whether they might be given a paper authorizing them to pass through the town of Bordeaux to the docks. The official with whom they spoke was—after a little difficulty—successful in contacting the harbour authorities, and was able to inform them they would be allowed a passage but would have to wait several days for a boat as there was a considerable waiting-list.

There was nothing now to do but search for lodgings, and eventually they found a room where they accommodated themselves as best they could—the Begum and the two girls sleeping in the bed and Vilayat on the floor.

In the morning Noor and Claire began talking again about their certificates. They had learned that the British Red Cross was being embarked from St. Nazaire, and it occurred to them they might be able to intercept it. Their mother and brother were horrified. The Begum pleaded that if they did not keep together now, they might never see each other again. Vilayat pointed out that St. Nazaire was over two hundred miles up the coast, without counting the detour round Bordeaux. All normal communications would be disorganized, and to propose hitch-hiking under such conditions was lunacy.

But the girls were too headstrong to be deterred, and set out, assuring them they would be there and back in a couple of days. They found the roads north thronged. The long, slow-moving ribbons of traffic were occasionally dive-bombed and strafed, but at least they had no difficulty in obtaining hitches. They did not dare stop for meals, but were able to buy from time to time a roll or a sandwich. Sometimes they had to make wide detours because the roads ahead were blocked by bomb damage. They travelled all through the night and all through the next day, and it was already turning dark a second time when they reached the outskirts of St. Nazaire.

They found their way to the docks, but did not know from which basin the boat carrying the Red Cross would leave. Several times they asked directions from men on the quay, and hurried along, groping and staggering over the cobbles and trying to read the names of ships and wharves in the gathering gloom.

Suddenly they were stopped by a *gendarme* who wanted to know what they were doing snooping around the boats and to see their papers. They showed him their passports, and when he saw that Noor had been born in Moscow he did not like it.

She tried to explain, but he said their story was not satisfactory and took them to a prison, where they were locked in a cell for the night.

The next morning they were allowed to see the governor. He was a nice man and realized quickly that they were telling the truth. He apologized for their apprehension, but said, "You understand that the officer was only doing his duty. In an hour so grave for our country he could not risk allowing spies to stay at large."

He telephoned on their behalf to the enquiry office of the dock —only to be informed that the ship carrying the British Red Cross had sailed during the night. Anxious to make up, he had the captain of the ship contacted by wireless. The captain replied that he would take the girls on board and they could be incorporated in the British Red Cross if the harbour authorities would have them sent out. Triumphant, he returned to tell them what he had been able to arrange, but they explained that their mother and brother were waiting for them near Bordeaux and they must go back to them.

Meanwhile, in Le Verdon, the Begum and Vilayat were becoming quite desperate at their prolonged absence. Realizing that when they arrived it might be necessary to make a dash for the docks, and the bus service was not adequate, Vilayat bought a motor bicycle.

During these days, in every house and in all the shops where there was a wireless, it was kept constantly on, so that if there was an announcement everybody would hear it. On the morning of June 17th Vilayat was in a baker's when the announcer cut in, and then the aged Marshal Pétain told the people he had asked Hitler for an armistice.

Vilayat took the bread mechanically and went out. In the street the people were standing with bowed heads.

Saturday, June 19th, his birthday, looked in the beginning like being a very black birthday indeed. The girls had not returned, and the first thing he learned when he went out was that the British Government was evacuating that morning and the last boat taking British subjects was leaving from the port of Le Verdon in half an hour.

To go without Noor and Claire was unthinkable. He told their mother that when his sisters got back they would all have to make for the Spanish border and find a way through the Pyrenees.

Just then they came in, with passionate apologies, having been away five days in all.

Vilayat raced on his motor cycle to the basin. The boat, a small Belgian vessel, the *Kasongo,* was still there. He was able to speak to the captain, who said he would not leave a family stranded if they could be fetched quickly. No luggage would be accepted.

He went back and told Noor to get on the pillion. As they went, he heard her call to the people who were standing to watch them go, "We shall come back!"

He took her to the dock and went back for his mother, and then for Claire.

The ship slipped her cable immediately and moved out into the Gironde. On the receding quayside the motor cycle that had served its turn lay amidst a wilderness of other passengers' abandoned luggage.

THE ESCAPE FROM BORDEAUX

"Conditions on the cargo-boat were far from being either safe or comfortable, but because of the pluck and optimism of people like Noor they were bearable."[1] The weather was beautiful and summery, and at night the moon shone far too brightly for the boat's safety. "In his little room the radio operator was going slowly out of his mind, receiving SOS messages and submarine and enemy-plane warnings"[2] (He had to be put in a mental home when they reached England.) All the passengers stayed on deck because the ship was transporting Congolese wood and the cabins were infested with Congolese beetles.

Among those on board were Mr. Julius Hoste, proprietor of the Belgian newspaper *Het Laatste Nieuws,* his wife, and his daughter Magda, who became a close friend of Noor's. The two

1 Magda Hoste, letter to author.
2 Ibid.

girls began talking to one another while they were helping to peel the potatoes, and Magda was instantly attracted by the sweetness, gaiety, and courage of Noor, who was so different from anybody else she had known well. She was struck by Noor's curious voice, highpitched but soft, and by her bird-like quality.

The *Kasongo* docked at Falmouth. After the fantastic disorganization of life in France, it seemed strange as they came in at the quayside to see everything in the streets of this small Cornish fishing-town so quiet and orderly. And then quite suddenly a feeling overtook Noor and Vilayat—although they had never thought of England as their country—that they had come 'home'.[1]

The Mitchell family had always asked them to call if they should come to England; they decided to presume on this invitation, and took tickets straight to Southampton. Travelling all night, they arrived in the early hours of the morning, and since the Begum was exhausted, went immediately to 6 Northlands Gardens.

Basil, who came down in a dressing-gown to open the door, says, "I shall never forget the spectacle they presented on the step—all four incredibly dirty and tired, with red eyelids."

They stayed for a few days. The Mitchells were themselves considering leaving Southampton, which had become 'unhealthy', since the docks made a natural target for bombing. Finally it was decided that Mrs. Mitchell and the Begum, with their daughters, should go to Oxford, where Basil had some acquaintance amongst the dons' families.

Basil, who was expecting papers from the Navy, went to London with Vilayat. Noor, having seen her mother and Claire settled in lodgings in the Cowley Road, came down to London to join Vilayat for a couple of days and to try to trace the Red Cross certificates.

On July 10th [2] a large party met for tea in the Tottenham Court Road Corner House: Vilayat, Noor, and Magda from the ship; Basil and two friends, Theo Cadoux and Harold Herzmark, who had like himself, just come down from Queen's College, Oxford, and myself. Conversation was more personal than is usual amongst so many people, as there were already considerable links between us.

We on the English side were very depressed by the fall of France, a catastrophe still hard to assimilate. It was as though the very fountain of the gaiety and intellectual nerve which had irradiated Europe had suddenly been put out.

Vilayat related the full story of their adventures since they left 'Fazal Manzil', including his sisters' 'mad' dash to St. Nazaire.

[1] Vilayat.
[2] Diary of T. J. Cadoux.

Noor was still pursuing their certificates, and had that morning been to the Headquarters of the Red Cross in St. James's Palace and some other offices, but had not been able to get hold of them yet.

I recall being, at the time, amazed at the importance attached to the Red Cross certificates. It would have been simpler to sit for the examination again. Even if that had meant taking the whole course again, it was not a very long course, and would surely have been wiser than risking life to recover the originals. I can only think that in the fevered tempo of the crisis, Noor and Claire saw themselves as needing to be ready, without a moment's delay, to assist in nursing great numbers of the wounded. Also, though retrospectively, I see in this episode an illustration of Madame Bouvard's observation that Noor's heroism came always with an extremity of nervous tension.

That afternoon, she did not speak very much, but whilst Vilayat was talking I observed her. Hers was not a personality which obtruded; she had rather to be sought. She was very small, with indefinite brown hair, but tiny gold flecks in hazel brown eyes. These were very eloquent; both timorous and trusting, they made me think of a deer. But the most singular thing was her voice, which had struck Magda, too, so forcibly. It was exceedingly gentle, high and faint; it trailed in a curious way and might change pitch several times upon a syllable, quavering as though it were about to die out—and indeed sometimes it could scarcely be heard. It was the thinnest little pipe—aerial as a bat's squeak—such a voice as creatures out of fairyland might be expected to use, for it had no 'body' at all. It made me think of the woodlands. She had something of the stillness of a bird-watcher amongst the birds, that quality which enables him to remain so little felt as a presence that they will hop upon him. There was something elfin about her; it was as though the vibrations of her personality were so graduated as to pass almost unhindered through those around her.

She obviously felt no need of making conversation, and had very nearly the manners of a 'little girl'. She was quite friendly, but had none of the conventional smiles or phrases which people usually present on such occasions.

When Vilayat spoke of the bombing of the roads, her eyes flickered. She said, as though it were something incredible she were confirming, "The planes came down so low we could see the men in them, and they must have been able to see everything they were doing."

She said she had felt it wrong to be leaving, and wished she could have worked with the patriotic forces which she was sure would be organized in France when the country recovered from the shock. She even said she thought she would be a good person to send back from here as a liaison agent, because she did not look English, and if she were caught nobody would know what she was. I never forgot this remark.

She said, "Vilayat is joining the RAF, and if he becomes a fighter pilot he will be risking his life every day. Nursing seems so little in comparison."

The news that General de Gaulle had escaped from France and was rallying Frenchmen under the Croix de Lorraine had fired her spirit. She was wearing the newly-elected emblem of the Free French, a little double-barred cross in silver, pinned to her frock.

Vilayat left the party early, as he was going that evening to Oxford. Noor was staying another day, as her mother had asked her to buy a coat, and most of us arranged to meet again the next day.

The following afternoon the same party reassembled, minus Vilayat and Magda.[1] Noor's search for a coat had so far proved unavailing. The Begum had said she would like one fastening with a single button in the front. This style had been very much in vogue the year before, but had quickly gone out. With Basil she had worked her way through all the dress shops from Marble Arch to Oxford Circus, and thence down to Piccadilly Circus, but could only find coats that buttoned straight down the middle.

I suggested that her mother had probably not realized the kind she had in mind was no longer in fashion, and might be just as pleased to have one in the newest style.

She considered this, and would have liked to be able to ask her mother, but there was no telephone in their lodgings in Oxford, and she felt she should come back with what she had asked for.

After this there was no help but to continue the search. She did not know her way about, and Basil, though willing, was no use as a guide to women's shops, so I went with them. We worked our way up Regent Street on the other side, explaining in every house our strange errand. She would not be persuaded to try on any coat that did not fit the picture in her mind's eye, but would just run her glance over them, and say in her soft voice, "No, it isn't here."

Basil said to me aside, "She will persevere until she gets what she wants. She is so quiet, yet so persistent. I always think she is like the little stream that wears a valley through the mountains."

I found myself considering Noor during this expedition. She was twenty-six, but seemed much less. I was a year younger, and

[1] Diary of T. J. Cadoux.

92

yet felt older in point of ordinary sophistication. I wondered if this was because she had always lived at home with her mother, or whether the reason was more radical. She was guileless, but if she did not discuss, it was because she knew her mind. Hers was the kind of simplicity which profound people often have and which is not necessarily related to inexperience.

It was nearly five o'clock when I happened upon the coat we were looking for, and then we had just time to escort her to the coach station at Victoria, from which she was going back.

A few days later I received from Oxford a postcard reading:

> Dear Jean,
>
> I don't know how I shall be able to thank you for all the trouble you took. It was so sweet of you. The coat is a little large, but it is easy to have it fitted.
>
> I do hope I shall see you soon again!
>
> Cheerio! Kindest greetings,
> **Noor (or Babuly)**

For the next few weeks she lived in Oxford with her mother and Claire. They were in very straitened circumstances, having only the little money they had brought from France. Vilayat had volunteered immediately for the RAF, but in August he developed paratyphoid, and was incarcerated at Headington Isolation Hospital. Noor and Claire were very anxious and went every day to enquire about him and on visiting days to look at him through glass.

The life at Oxford was in itself in a process of uneasy transformation. From being a university town it had become suddenly a centre for evacuees, and the streets, instead of being crowded with throngs of undergraduates with their distinctive college scarves, were filled with mothers pushing prams or leading young children.

Some vestiges of the old life remained, however. One or two of Basil's friends, who were still there for one reason and another, took Noor and Claire out a little, especially on the Isis and the Cherwell in the Queen's College punt.

Noor could now have settled to a pleasant life, but she had been in the war already, and in the strange tranquillity of Oxford she remembered what she had promised the people in Le Verdon.

At the end of August the Battle of Britain began. There was not much to see at Oxford, but when she came to London for the day, she realized the force of the Blitz.

In the early autumn, having at last run the certificates to earth, she obtained a post at Fulmer Chase Maternity Home for Officers'

Wives, near Slough. One of the girls with her [1] says, "Our work there consisted in doing all the domestic chores, driving and helping with the babies—hardly any nursing, as there was a trained nursing staff." Noor became increasingly restless, for she felt that anybody could do the sort of work she was given at Fulmer Chase. She wondered if she should join the Services. She was not a girl to whom a uniform and the prospect of communal life 'somewhere in England' presented any attraction; and she knew that such a course would cause pain to her mother, who found it shocking that girls should go away and live in camps like soldiers.

Yet the conviction grew that her present work was too trivial. She balanced her loyalties—to the mother whom she loved and to the countries she loved—and in the end she broke to her mother that she was going to volunteer for the WAAF. This choice was dictated by sentiment. Because Vilayat was in the RAF she wanted also to be in Air Force blue.

To her immense shock, her application was refused.

The recruiting sergeant said she was not eligible for service in His Majesty's Forces because she was not a British subject.[2] (Her brother's case was different, since he had been born in England.) She was so hurt and angry at what she felt to be a rebuff that she wrote to the officer in charge of the recruiting, saying she had always understood that as the holder of a 'British Protected Person' passport she participated, if not in all the privileges of citizenship, at least in the right to serve under the Crown. She received, almost by return, a reply regretting that an unfortunate mistake had been made. Certainly there was no ruling which could prevent her from joining the Air Force. 'On the contrary,' the letter said, 'we are honoured you should wish to serve with us.'

WAAF

Noor enlisted in the Women's Auxiliary Air Force on November 19th, 1940, giving her name, after some reflection, as Nora Inayat Khan, and her religion as Church of England. She then became 424598 Aircraftwoman 2nd Class, and was posted on the same day to Harrogate for training in wireless operation.

Recently she had come to have the feeling that she had grown up in something the nature of an 'ivory tower', isolated from the swift main currents of the life of the world. She wanted to enter these, and on the 'ground level'. The child of a man of extraordinary personality and connections, she had spent her childhood

---

[1] Wendela Wheatling.

[2] Mr. Gordon Walker informed me that since he did not find any record that Noor Inayat Khan ever took out British naturalization papers, it must be supposed that her status remained always that of a British Protected Person.

under the branches of the ancestral tree, overshadowed, yet invested with an aureole. Now, in joining HM Forces, she entered upon a new life, and the people she would meet would know nothing of her background unless she told them. This she decided not to do. That she was half Indian they must know, but she eliminated from her personality anything that could appear exotic or 'interesting'. She wanted to find what she was in herself, and could do by herself.

She consulted with Vilayat how she should fill in her form, and he told her his experience when he volunteered. The sergeant taking his particulars surveyed them in some perplexity, or perhaps disapproval, and then asked, "But which is your *first* name?"

"Vilayat."

The sergeant considered this, and then asked, perhaps trying to be helpful, "But what do your *pals* call you?"

"Vilayat."

There was another pause. "The boys'll never be able to pronouce that. Couldn't you think of an English one?"

A pause on Vilayat's side. "Victor?"

"Make it Vic. That'll be better."

When they came to the place on the form where it said 'Religion', the sergeant suddenly exploded: "For Pete's sake don't tell me what your religion is! I don't want to know! Just write down C. of E. on this line, and it'll make everything much simpler."

Noor decided to be guided by this history. For a Christian name, 'Nora' was an obvious choice for her. Although etymologically different, it sounded much the same, was short and preserved her initial.

At Harrogate she found herself one of about forty girls. They were the first WAAF's to be trained for wireless operation.

She had her troubles, of course. The lack of privacy caused her some suffering, the constant noise and bustle and 'Music for the Forces' fatigued her, the heavy meals disagreed with her, and the shoes hurt her feet. The tide was rough, nevertheless she kept swimming. During the first weeks some of her possessions were stolen. Opening her kitbag to take out her hairbrush, she discovered that it and some other articles were missing. Her little exclamation of dismay attracted the attention of the other girls. They pointed out that it could only be one of the WAAF's who had rifled her bag, and wanted her to report it. She winced and shook her head, and said, "I expect she needed it."

After just a month they were all given a few days' leave. Noor spent them in Oxford with her mother. Fortune brought Vilayat back at the same time, and on December 15th they came in together to a tea-party at the Mitchells', both in Air Force blue.[1]

[1] Diary of T. J. Cadoux.

On December 23rd she was posted to Edinburgh with the same group of girls as before. Here they were trained by officers of the GPO as wireless telegraphists. One of the girls, Mrs. Dorothy Ryman, who was on the same course, remembers that during the six rather tedious months which they spent in Edinburgh she never once saw Noor without a smile or a pleasant word. One thing in particular has stayed in her memory as showing a rare good humour and sportsmanship. To their great enjoyment, the girls were allowed to learn Scottish folk dances instead of the inevitable PT. Although Noor suffered from dreadful chilblains all through her stay in Scotland, with swollen and terribly painful feet she danced throughout each session, though her 'dancing' looked as if she were hopping about on redhot coals. The other girls teased her mercilessy, but instead of asking permission to drop out, or growing angry at their joking and shrieks of laughter —which, however unintentionally, must have been rather cruel — Noor took it all with smiling good humour. The girls grew to respect her for it, and although she was too quiet to be popular in the usual sense of the word, everyone on the course liked her immensely.

On June 10th, 1941, Noor and a girl who had been her friend from the beginning, Joan Clifton, were posted together to RAF Bomber Command at Abingdon. This was an advanced training school for bombers, and consisted of a Group HQ and six or seven dependent stations. The Group HQ was in radio communication with the dependent stations and the latter with the planes which were up.

To one of these stations Noor and Joan were posted. They were always put on watch together, and for a long time remained the only WAAF to be working side by side with the men at the transmitting and receiving sets. They worked to a scheme of shifts of unequal length, so arranged that they had to acquire the knack of going to sleep at whatever time they came off duty.

Neither Joan nor Noor liked being tied by Service life and a lot of its irksome details, but they got infinite pleasure from the things they did together and the sense of using every free moment fully. They were fortunate in being billeted for a long while off camp in a big old house outside Oxford at Boar's Hill, which was taken over for WAAF personnel, and in getting a top room small enough for just the two of them. Here they tried to make themselves as self-contained as possible, decorated the walls with gay travel-posters, had vases of flowers everywhere, and did all they could to make it look homelike. They rented a radio from Oxford, and had a never-failing source of pleasure in listening to music which they both loved. They also used to listen in to Morse broadcasts from abroad, until they came to the conclusion that they were rather overdoing it, as they found themselves muttering Morse in their sleep!

The 'spit-and-polish' aspect of the station dismayed Noor, and five minutes before any parade she was sure to discover something wrong with her uniform: that the buttons wanted cleaning or one had come off.

She was desperately bad at drill, with surprisingly enough no sense of time. Nor did she have any sense of coordinating her movements with a given beat, and nearly always marched out of step. The badness of her drill may have been partly caused by her feet, which because they were bound when she was a baby, had not grown properly, and were swollen and malformed. Probably she never in her life walked without some degree of pain. All shoes hurt her, the Service ones very much indeed. Often her feet were covered with lacerated blisters.

As the newness of the work wore off Noor became bored and impatient. There was none of the sense of urgency which she would have had if it had been a question of working to bombers out over enemy territory rather than trainees on practice flights. Noor felt she had got stuck in a groove and was very anxious to get a commission.

Yet Joan remembers her as a happy person, with her lips always parted in a smile. A little thing would happen and one would see the corners of her mouth going up, and sometimes she would burst into a peal of laughter.

It seemed to Joan that Noor and her brother and sister had no country, and no feeling of belonging anywhere. Noor felt a stranger in England, but when she went to India she realized she did not belong there either. There was only one place where she felt completely at home, and that was France. There everybody accepted her quite naturally, and she didn't feel a stranger.

Each of the girls had an old bicycle which was very precious, and they used to cycle to and fro between camp and duty. At times it was tiring, but it gave them air and exercise, and memories of the little shared joys of those rides which they took together—the barking of a fox nearby, and the unearthly shadows from the moon when they were pushing their bikes up the steep hill after coming off midnight watch; above all, one May night when they stopped and listened to a nightingale visible in the moonlight, singing in a may tree just above their heads.

They used to cycle miles when they were off duty, going into Oxford, where Noor's mother was then working in a hospital, to visit her and other friends. Nature, with all its many beauties, meant much to Noor, and they would cycle happily exploring new parts, perhaps singing together Schubert's 'Röselein Rot' or some other song, or enjoying the early spring scent of the larches. One

97

day in Youlbury's beautiful garden they picked in March what they thought was a kind of palm, and their joy was immense when after a day or two it opened out into the gloriously and delicately scented Stellata Magnolia.

On thirty-hour passes they would skip sleep and hitch-hike up to London, or wherever they felt like, taking great risks on picking up a suitable hitch back to be on duty in time. Somehow they generally made it and with time to spare.

They read a great deal, and discussed everything together; and Joan remembers that Noor's one desire after Service life was over was a quiet married life with lots of children, to whom she was devoted.

Noor had a deep sense of family responsibility, and was always worrying what would be best for her mother or Victor or Claire, and how best to help them in any way at all. She had a particular kind of unselfishness which rarely allowed her to think of herself. But although she was one of the most unassuming creatures possible, she would fight for those things she held to be right morally, or for some small personal right, showing great strength of character under her quiet demeanour.

The days that Joan and Noor spent together at Abingdon were happy ones, with the joy that comes from a harmonious sharing of duties, pleasures, and thoughts.[1]

Joan is, in parenthesis, pretty sure Noor went down in the Air Force, as C(hurch) of E(ngland); at any rate, she attended all church services with the other girls.

It must have been during the time she was at Abingdon, that Noor at last received news of Hidayat, whose fate, since they said good-bye to him at Tours, had been an anxiety to her, to Vilayat, to Claire and to their mother. She wrote, in a letter (bearing neither address nor date).

Brother dear,

Just received a wire from Bhaiyajan [2] saying: ADDRESS LES TILLEULS DIEULEFIT DROME ALL WELL HIDAYAT.

Some French people in Edinburgh had told me that all the British of the coast had been sent inland in the Doubs. Now is the Drôme anywhere near the Doubs? I believe it is, in which case he is probably with the lot. Did I tell you that every Britisher is receiving so many pounds a week... I forget how many exactly. So at last we know where he is. I really don't know if it is advisable to reply.

Brother dear, I met Basil and Myrtle yesterday...

[1] Joan Wynne née Clifton (from "On June 10th", p. 96 close paraphrase of a long letter from her to myself).
[2] "Little brother".

98

The reference to the Mitchells permits the dating. It was probably in a street in Oxford — so close to Abingdon — that Noor ran into Basil Mitchell with his younger sister. The letter goes on to give news of Basil's two sisters from which I can work out that it must have been written in early September, 1941. Theo Cadoux's diary confirms the presence of Noor in Oxford on September 13th (at the wedding of the elder of Basil's sisters) and 15th (with her mother in Fuller's [tearooms]).

The Drôme was in what was, at that date, still Unoccupied France.

Towards the end of 1941 both Noor and Joan Clifton put in for commissions, Joan being recommended for Code and Cypher and Noor for Intelligence. Joan came up for her Board the earlier, passed it, and was sent on a Commission Course about April 1942. Noor's file at the Air Ministry shows that on May 11th she was posted 'for duties as a wireless operator' to a different Group, and for the next few weeks she wrote to her brother from a station in Compton Basset, Wiltshire. Here she was one of a group selected for a specialized and rather secret course of instruction in signals and some technical aspects of wireless which ordinary operators did not need to know. She was one of the first wireless telegraphists in the WAAF to be picked out for this extra training, which involved a great deal of bookwork and lasted about seven weeks.

Vilayat had trained for some months in the RAF when it was discovered in a test that his eyes were not good enough for a fighter pilot. This was a great shock to him, as he had loved flying passionately. He might have remained in the Air Force in another capacity, but had so entirely set his heart on this one role that he preferred to change his service.

He decided now for the Navy, but was granted a postponement of his call-up papers so that he might study first privately for an examination in navigation, which would open to him interesting possibilities. Whilst studying for this he was living—in more or less constant relations with the pawnbroker—in a strange room in Bloomsbury, near the top of Premier House in Southampton Row. He received it in part return for his services as superintendent of the fire watchers guarding the premises by night. As the raids during this summer were infrequent he was able, more often than not, to sleep during his hours of duty and to study in the day-time.

It was a small cubicle, bare as a prison cell, with splintering floor-boards, and was mainly remarkable for a vast sink, set right in the very middle and occupying most of the space. He balanced some boards on it, and these served on different occasions as draining-boards, kitchen table, dining table and writing table, not to mention bookshelf. He did all his navigational work, drew his charts, etc., on them. They accommodated also some brackets of test-tubes, which, abandoned by the last occupant, were left undisturbed by the new. They contained substances, some turquoise blue, some green, some golden yellow. He did not know what they were, but said they added 'a flash of colour' to the room. Normally they were kept corked, but one day his elbow sent some through the window, and a few minutes afterwards a policeman came upstairs to ask from which room a phial of evil-smelling gases had been launched.

An addict of heights, he loved to stand on the little balcony and watch the traffic crawling in a quiet stream below. When Noor came up with an overnight pass, he would sleep on this balcony, straight under the stars, and she would have the little iron bedstead inside.

She knew that her brother adored this room and would not have it prettified; at the same time, she used to perform a certain unobtrusive service to it in the interest of hygiene, and would tactfully deposit a packet of cereal on the corner of the floor where he kept his food.

His room lay on the way from my flat at 1 Taviton Street to the offices of the Postal Censorship, where I worked during most of the war. Sometimes I would call in on my way back and we would have tea off the boards on the sink. Noor was there as often as she had a pass long enough to come to London.

They were desperately poor. This was partly because they were both contributing to enable Claire to pursue a course of medical studies in Edinburgh. She wanted to take a degree and go in for bacteriological research. Although so feminine and shy, her mind had a scientific bent, and if she had it in her to become a doctor, Noor and Vilayat were anxious that the lack of means should not prevent her. Yet they had to help their mother too, and the situation threatened to become untenable. Sums as small as ten shillings and even five shillings were constantly pushed backwards and forwards between them as though they were precious as life blood. Of just sixty letters written by Noor to Vilayat at this time, there is hardly one which does not refer to such amounts, whilst nearly all mention the difficulties of her mother and Claire.

On Sunday, June 14th, *The Fairy and the Hare* was broadcast in the Children's Hour of the BBC. Noor did not, however, receive anything for it, as she had sold the copyright to Harrap outright.

On Vilayat's birthday, a few days later, she called whilst he was out and left the score of Bach's D Minor (the card that was attached, in her hand, does not state the composer) and a copy of Nehru's *Autobiography*, for which she had saved; but a note attached to the presents asked if he would mind taking to the pawnbroker's two Swiss sovereigns enclosed.

On one of her leaves, Vilayat took her to the cinema to see Walt Disney's *Fantasia*. She enjoyed it, of course, but had one point of criticism, which she explained to me. It concerned the treatment of Beethoven's *Pastoral Symphony*. This was a serious work, and she did not think it was right to have drawn lambs gambling about, and other creatures with funny faces. However pretty and charming the drawings, most people had their own feeling about what Beethoven's music meant, and did not want it reduced to the level of this fantasy. Gravely, she said, "I don't think one should make people laugh to Beethoven's music."

They used to go to the Zoo when they had a little money. He made friends there with a Phillippine eagle and she with an Indian deer. He took me once to look at a small creature with enormously large eyes, spindly legs, and white spots, and said, "This is what my sister loves. I'm going to write and enquire whether it ever has progeny. It would be so nice after the war to give her a fawn." He liked to see people in terms of an animal symbol, and said, "Tipu Sultan was a tiger, my father was a lion, I am a gargoyle, and Noor—Noor is a deer." Her flower, he remarked, was the rose, whereas his was the lotus.

By this time, Vilayat had met my mother. My father had been an officer of the (British) Indian Army, for which Vilayat had a kind of hate-love. When he came to my flat, he would stand in front of my father's sword, which I had hung on the wall, gazing at it. At last he found the courage to ask me to take it down. "I would so much like to know what it feels like in my hand." He and my mother liked each other, but their conversation highlighted the fact that they knew different Indias. Though he had not as yet been there, except for the brief visit as a child, he felt that he had by inheritance an occult insight; she that she had been in contact with the reality; and sometimes the opposition between their viewpoints was almost violent. On one occasion, when he had just left us, my mother almost burst out, "He thinks India's a land of saints and holy-men! They may exist, but what is on more immediate view is the poverty of the wretched people, the shocking barbarity. I wouldn't even like to tell Vilayat some of the things I've seen." The chasm dividing them was bridged at a different level. While Vilayat played his own compositions on her piano, she painted abstract forms inspired by his music. This rose from my mention that I heard the colours of sounds. We all three discussed the possibility of a real correspondence between colour and sound, as different octaves of a vibration. She said she did not see the colours of sounds, but would try to paint the soul of his music, if he would play it to her.

101

Vilayat told me he would like his sister to meet my mother. On July 29th, 1942, she gave a small party; my uncle and aunt came, and Noor and Vilayat. My mother showed her latest pictures, including the series of abstracts, which interested Vilayat the most, and of course the lotus and swan-like forms she had painted to his music. Later, I remember her sitting side by side with Noor, turning for her the pages of an album of photographs taken by my father and herself in India. One showed an enormous elephant, kneeling, herself in the howdah on its back. "Do you know who that elephant belongs to? The Nizam of Hyderabad. I understand your father admired his elephants." And she told Noor the story of how she came to be riding through Hyderabad on one of the Nizam's elephants.

The portrait of Noor which forms the frontispiece (and which was exhibited at the National Society, in London) was, of course done from a photograph for she only met Noor once; but having met her, she was able to remember her colouring, and the impression made by her personality.

As the date of her Board approached Noor thought of everything that might affect her chance of making a good impression. Her appearance, she felt, was as important as her knowledge. She wrote to Vilayat:

> Signals,
> RAF
> Abingdon,
> 24th/Aug

Brother dear,

I wonder if it would be possible for you to send me a pound for a permanent wave. I just loathe to have to ask you now whilst Mams [1] is in London which must involve extra expenses and I want you, Bhai[2] to let me know straight away if it is difficult. You see, I realise that it is of primary importance as I shall be interviewed by several officers next week. And I really do want a lady-like hair style, which is the first condition for looking well-kept and well-bred. There's no use my having a setting that just lasts for the day. I must have one ready for every minute. I would go to the hair-dresser's next to Queen's [presumably Queen's College, Oxford] which looks rather aristocratic. I would be so grateful to you, Bhai, but if it is not possible this week because of extra expenses, I shall ask Mother to get a pound out next time she goes to the bank...

Matron has given Mother an easier job and put two nurses

1 Affectionate for Mamely, Mamaly or Mamuly (spelling doubtful) — I have never seen this pet-name written in full, though I have many times heard it spoken: Mother's Daughter; that is, Claire.
2 Brother.

to replace her as Mother had an awful physical break-down
the other day. She was literally over-worked . . . I consider it
very blameworthy for putting a frail person like Mother on
a job where two are required...

We are now on a very intensive course which we follow
en dehors of duty hours and every subject is presented to us
mathematically — if you saw little Bib . . . just rushing through
pages of trigonometry and spheres etc. just struggling with
time to keep up with it. But the amazing part is that maths
seem so clear to me now. Besides, I have absorbed so much
recently from reading technical wireless books that the
matter is much fresher in my mind than in the men's whose
training is further back. Consequently, I always manage to
have quick, appropriate answers to problems brought up...
It's too funny...

So cheerio Bhai! Love to Mams. Love galore.

Bibel [3]

In fact, Vilayat confided the burden of this letter to me.
As he was unable to produce a pound, and did not wish to have
to ask his mother to draw one from the bank, or to deny Noor,
would I, he asked me, lend him a pound which he could send
to Noor as from himself. Naturally, I did. Vilayat transmitted
the sum by wire, so that it was utilised in time for the great
occasion.

Noor wrote:

Brother dear,
    Really I don't know how to thank you! It is so sweet of
you and by wire too and 10/- extra! That is very extravagant
on your part. And as you show the example, I'm going to
be extravagant too and have a real "Eugene perm" for 25/-.

Babs

On the afternoon of Noor's Board, August 28th, I called in at
Vilayat's room on my way back from the office. I thought she
might have returned, but he was still waiting for her, and we
made some tea. It was perhaps half-past six when she arrived (and
I saw for the first time the new hair style) and we asked her
eagerly, "How did you get on?"

"I don't know—not very well, I'm afraid."

We saw at once that she was tired and dispirited. She sat down

---

[3] Babuly, Father's Daughter, was like her younger sister's pet-name,
subject within the family to various distortions and abridgements,
Dabs, Dib, Dibel.

103

and pulled off her cap. Her forehead was damp with perspiration, and she ran her hand through her hair as though she needed to let the air to her head.

"I'm afraid I've been ploughed," she said. "It was a very long interview. They asked me my attitude to Indian Independence."

Since they had come to England and met in London politically-minded Indians, brother and sister had become more conscious of Indian affairs. They had followed anxiously the development of Sir Stafford Cripps's mission to India, and shared in the disappointment of the Indian leaders concerning the proposals he brought. The particular bone of contention at that juncture was the control and organization of defence. Noor thought the Indians should be allowed to organize, in every town and village of the Indian sub-continent, a Home Guard, similar to that in these islands, but answerable to an Indian Minister of Defence, and equipped with all the arms available, ready to repel a Japanese invasion. "At present we have to depend on the British to protect us, and that is humiliating—apart from causing delay." India had a vast coastline, and if the Japanese landed on an out-of-the-way part of it there would be a loss of time whilst British-commanded forces were rushed up. But a Home Guard, organized on the village system, could meet them immediately, and perhaps prevent them from even establishing a bridge-head.

She had talked earnestly, trying to get the officers composing the Board (Joan thinks there were about fourteen of them) to enter in their imagination into the feelings of the people in the villages living under the threat of a Japanese invasion as we were of a German one. Mr. Churchill had said that if the Germans came we would fight them on the beaches and in the streets of the towns. The Indians were not less eager to defend their land, but it was difficult if they had nothing but sticks.

She saw from their faces that her insistence on arms was making a bad impression, and struggled to keep from her voice a mounting antagonism. She understood the British were refusing to allow the Indians control of arms for fear they would use them against the Government. But she thought it was a mistake. Such a gesture of confidence would inspire—as could nothing else—a loyal allegiance, until a total transfer of power was made, later, in a reasonable spirit. If they were not allowed to participate in their own defence the effect would be deplorable. The people would fall into a sullen apathy, and in such a mood many of them might drift into collaboration with the Japanese if they came.

One of the officers put a crucial question: if the Indian leaders should take measures embarrassing to Britain, would she support them?

She replied that she would feel it her duty to support those whom she recognized as responsible Indian leaders in any measures they might consider necessary. She realized that with this answer she demolished her chance of a commission.

The officer asked her whether the position she had just stated did not seem to her inconsistent with her oath of allegiance to the Crown.

She said that so long as the war with Germany lasted she pledged her loyal service to the Crown and the British Government. After the defeat of the Axis powers and the re-establishment of peace she would reconsider her attitude in the light of the way that Anglo-Indian relations had developed, and if the position of India had not improved she might feel it her duty to support India against Britain.

She was still hot and shaking as she told us all this, and exasperated by the thought that now she would have to remain in Abingdon for the whole of the war.

Vilayat thought the firmness and integrity she had shown might, all the same, have made a good impression, and that she might get the commission.

But she shook her head. "I should like to have appeared deliberate and cool and well-balanced. But I got angry and I could feel my face flushing. I gave the impression of being emotional, and that's no good."

Vilayat was always very concerned about the unworldliness of his sister. A few evenings after this, I watched with him from his balcony while the sun went down behind the roofs of Victoria House and the British Museum. "Noor-un-nisa is a saint," he said, "but she is still a negative saint. There is an innocence which is literally ignorance, and there is the innocence of knowledge. Noor's is still the first. In the terms of the allegory, she has not 'fallen'. Noor does not see evil. It is a kind of blindness in her." After a silence he continued, "We were brought up in such a way that we could not be like other children. The whole atmosphere was so rarefied. In 'Fazal Manzil' it was as though we looked at life through stained-glass windows. It was like growing up in a church—or in a conservatory, where plants are forced. We needed to come out into a more normal climate. When Noor went into the WAAF I thought she was going to sustain a very painful shock—and I still feel that it has to come."

The part of the sky where the sun had gone down changed from rose to indigo and purple. When he spoke again it was almost prophetically. "I have a presentiment that my sister will have to meet in this life the most utter blackness of the world. There is a valley down which she will have to walk alone. I know if I were to try to prevent her it would be wrong, because it would be interfering with something that is necessary to her evolution. And yet I shudder."

Vilayat passed his examination, and on September 2nd received papers requiring him to report to HMS *Collingwood* on Monday the 14th. The Saturday before, Noor came down and devoted the whole day to helping him pack up such possessions as he had accumulated. In the evening she staggered away with a big parcel which she was going to take to her mother's place in Oxford. There still remained some stuff, but, she said, she would return and deal with it after he had gone—which meant that she would devote her next thirty-six-hour pass to clearing up.

At about eleven o'clock in the evening, on the 21st, I answered a ring at my bell, and found Noor-un-nisa on the step, a small, shadowy figure. A thin little voice said, "Jean, I'm so sorry to trouble you, but I wondered if you could possibly put me up for the night. I tried first at the YWCA and then thought I'd just slip along and see if there was a light in any of your windows. I could just see the crack under the black-out."

She had been dealing with Vilayat's things from the afternoon until this time. As I brought her up the stairs she said she did not want to be a nuisance, and did not need a bed. "All I want is a wee bit of floor. I didn't want to sleep at Vilayat's now that the bed's gone because there is such a terrible draught under the door. I thought if you could give me a corner somewhere it would be warmer... I remembered you have a carpet..."

I had a spare bedroom, into which I brought her.

Blinking in the light, she seemed quite enchanted. "Oh, what a darling little room! It will seem funny sleeping in a bedroom!"

With her quick appreciation she noticed at once a red lacquered Chinese table, and whilst she was examining it I went into the kitchen and put on something to make her a hot supper.

She was obviously cold and tired, and I wondered what more I could do to make her comfortable. I remembered her feet, and got a pair of soft red moccasin slippers, and put them in front of the fire in the sitting-room to warm for her when she came in.

She was delighted with the little attention, and exclaimed, "It's nice to be made a fuss of! I only begin to feel like myself when I get out of my Service shoes!"

I was grateful to the occasion that had brought her, and even more that she was happy to be here. We talked until late, and I remember that when we said good night I did not doubt she would sleep.

In the morning I went to the office and Noor went back to Vilayat's, where she was going to wash the floor, as she wanted to leave it nice for the landlord.

A few days later I received a letter of thanks from her.

Jean my dear,

I have been dealing with Vilayat's experimental devices which we were obliged to get rid of. One tube is being considered at a laboratory next to Premier House and they asked me where they could return the apparatus in the case they could not make use of it. The only address I could think of was yours, Jean, I do hope I am not intruding. But if they do burden you with it I shall collect it at the beginning of next week and bring it down to Oxford with other things.

I did enjoy my stay with you, Jean. I think it was the best evening I had spent for a long time.

I do hope to see you again soon!

Yours,
Babuly

When I received this, I wondered if there had been a misunderstanding. Vilayat had told me the bracket full of test-tubes was not his but had been abandoned by the previous tenant of the room.

I thought a good deal about this. It seemed to me she had a bleak life, and I wrote saying she should not hesitate to come and stay with me whenever she was in London.

Not long afterwards, returning one day from the office, I found a hand-delivered note:

Jean dear,

Thanks a thousand times for your sweet card. It is lovely to know I may come to your darling flat. I do enjoy it. Unfortunately this time I shall have to be leaving London at 5 o'clock. I have just slipped into your guest-room. I hope you don't mind. Jean. I just wanted to collect something. I am not taking anything more as there is a possibility of Mother's being transferred to London. Do you mind therefore my burdening you a wee while longer?

Do excuse this awful handwriting. I am sitting on the staircase.

Yours
with love,
Babuly

I have been awfully interested reading the book, Jean. Longing to tell you how. Cheerio.

Pleased, I was for a moment puzzled. Then I realised that someone must have let her in at the front door. My guest-room, being outside the locked, self-contained part of my flat, she had been able to let herself into. She had deposited in it a certain number of the personal things Vilayat had abandoned when he left the room in Premier House. I remember that they included huge long rolls of navigational maps. I think it was my own mother and I who in the end disposed of them. The book I had lent her was probably one of Geoffrey Hodson's.

Noor had joined the Air Force primarily because Vilayat had done so. Her simple desire, as she had always said, was to be in the service he served in. Now that he had changed the light blue for the dark, the former no longer held the same attraction for her. She felt stranded in something he had quitted, and wrote to him:

> I'd love to go into the Fleet Air Arm now that you are in the Navy. I might be able to manage after being commissioned...   Bibel.

Joan had for some time been engaged to be married and at the beginning of October went to Ireland, and settled with her husband in Co. Wicklow.

Noor was sincerely glad of her friend's happiness. At the same time, her own sense of loneliness was perhaps increased. Joan was married and Vilayat was in Fareham, with the interest of starting in the Navy a new career. She had the feeling that other people were moving forward in their lives, while only her own stood still. Abingdon was unspeakably dull, and she seemed to have no prospect of another posting.

Then she received, out of the blue, a communication requesting her to attend an interview at the War Office with a Captain Selwyn Jepson.

INTERVIEW AT THE WAR OFFICE

It is now generally known that there existed during the last war an organization called 'SOE', the initials standing for 'Special Operations Executive', but in those days it was mentioned only in 'top-secret' circles; it had other titles indicating less potent activities, but its real function remained a close secret until some time after the end of hostilities. Even so, its name did not fully describe its activities, which in fact were the organizing and carrying out of sabotage of the German war machine in Occupied Territories. [1]

For this work it was necessary to recruit and train secret agents for infiltration into enemy-controlled countries. The 'French Section' of this organization was the largest single section in it, for obvious reasons.

It was Captain Selwyn Jepson's[2] job to find people, either in the armed Services or in civilian life, who might be employed for this highly important and very dangerous work. Having found suitable volunteers—they could be nothing else—he would arrange for their training and introduction to his colleagues, led by Major Maurice Buckmaster. [3]

Selwyn Jepson had a number of contacts in the Services who, without knowing anything of his work except that it came under the generic heading of 'Intelligence', would from time to time pass on to him the names and whereabouts of men and women whose qualifications were known to include bi-lingual ability in French. Having received such a name he would then ask them, out of the blue as it were, to come and see him at the War Office, where SOE had the use of a room (an ex-bedroom in Hotel Victoria, Northumberland Avenue) which was the limit of War Office responsibility so far as the Organization was concerned.

Naturally, these people had no idea when they arrived what the interview was about, and as often as not went away after-

---

[1] The opening paragraphs of this chapter were composed by Mr. Jepson himself, but since they are written from the standpoint of a member of SOE ('F'), I think I should make it plain that there existed not one but two SOE sections operating in France; one called the 'French Section' ('F') of which Lt.-Colonel Buckmaster was the head, and the other called 'Republique Française' ('RF'), of which the head was Lt.-Colonel Devavrin, better known under his code name of 'Passy' (for he visited his agents in the field). SOE as a whole was a British-directed organization under the command of Major-General Sir Colin Gubbins and responsible through the Minister of Economic Warfare (first Dalton and later Lord Selbourne) to the Cabinet. In principle the difference between the two sections was that 'French Section' (despite its name) was purely British-directed, whereas 'RF' was of semi-independent French direction within the SOE framework. In practice it was much more complicated; there were innumerable Frenchmen serving in French Section (even two on Lt.-Colonel Buckmaster's staff in London), and a sprinkling of Englishmen (notably Yeo-Thomas, Dismore, Whitehead, and Thackthwaite) serving in 'RF'. Perhaps the real distinction was one of flavour: in the French Section all instructions and orders were issued in English, and in 'RF' they were in French. The two sections duplicated each other in almost every area of France, overlapping territorially but utterly separate in structure and organization.

One other point needs to be made. Contrary to popular belief, SOE was not an organization for espionage. Its activities were twofold: sabotage and the long-term building up of arms and organization among local Resistance movements against the day when they would be called upon to rise in support of the invading Allied armies.

[2] Later Major, now reverted to civilian life.

[3] Later Lieutenant-Colonel, now reverted to civilian life.

wards no wiser than they came. But in those instances in which Selwyn Jepson judged the man or woman to have the particularly rare qualifications of personality and capacity, in addition to perfect French, which would enable him or her to become an agent, he would lead gradually to the real purpose of the meeting, very often seeing them two or three times before deciding to broach the subject.

But he remembers that in the case of Nora Inayat Khan he was able to come to the point more swiftly than usual, and at this first interview. He found her singularly direct thinking, "in spite of a great gentleness of manner", and she "seemed to have an intuitive sense of what might be in my mind for her to do. Also, I realized it would be safe to be frank with her, that her 'security', as we called it, would be good, that if she felt herself unable to take it on, she would not talk about the reason she had been called to the War Office—which, as a WAAF, was in itself rather odd.

"Having drawn a picture for her of the state of affairs in France, and the opportunities the German occupation gave us for interfering with their war effort, I explained what the work would entail, that if she came to us she might ultimately find herself as a wireless operator working in the underground with other British officers engaged in sabotage operations. To my mind she stood out as almost perfect for this aspect of the work; she was obviously careful, tidy, painstaking by nature, and would have all the patience in the world. A W/T operator, at his or her best, must have infinite patience and great coolness. As usual, I stressed immediately the extreme danger, that in the event of capture she would be interrogated by the Gestapo—a thing no human being could face with anything but terror—that since she would not be in uniform she would have no protection under the international laws of warfare—in short that she might not return.

"There was no monetary reward for the mission. She would receive her ordinary Service pay, without increment or bonus of any kind, and it would be held for her over here during the time she was in France. If she came back alive, it would be paid to her on her return, otherwise to her next of kin. Her only personal satisfaction would be the knowledge of the service she gave.

"But she listened to me quietly, and with complete understanding, and I had scarcely finished when she said, with the same simplicity of manner which had characterized her from the outset of our talk, that she would like to undertake it.

"Normally I would be uneasy and reluctant when anybody accepted the idea at once like that. It could, and usually did, mean that it was being accepted without proper thought, or for some motive other than the pure sense of patriotic duty or 'call' to a personal effort in the war much beyond that generally experienced

110

or undertaken. But in her case I had no misgivings on this score. She had thought about it as deeply and finally as a less direct-minded person might have spent days in doing. As a writer myself, I had a natural feeling of kinship with her—she had told me, of course, about her work as a children's writer and broadcaster—and I could not help saying, even if it was in the face of my duty in my job, that she might be justified in feeling she *might* be more valuable in the service of humanity as someone in contact after the war with the minds of the children who would have to live in the partially destroyed world which must follow it—the men and women to be, who would have to rebuild. That this might be rather an academic point of view in the light of our desperate situation, but since we were undoubtedly going to win in the end, it could be excused perhaps.

"She shook her head. She was sure and confident. She would like to try to become an agent for us, if I thought she could make it. I had not the slightest doubt that she could, and said so, and with rather more of the bleak distress which I never failed to feel at this point in these interviews, I agreed to take her on.

"I saw her again, of course, during her training, and had several conversations with her about this and that, and sometimes about the job she was going to do, but I see her very clearly as she was that first afternoon, sitting in front of me in that dingy little room, in a hard kitchen chair on the other side of a bare wooden table. Indeed, of them all—and they were many—who did not return, I find myself constantly remembering her with a curious and very personal vividness which outshines the rest . . . the small, still features, the dark, quiet eyes, the soft voice, and the fine spirit glowing in her."

Maurice Buckmaster, like Selwyn Jepson, was impressed by the readiness and confidence she showed. He says: "She never for one moment doubted she could do the job. She made me even some positive suggestions, proposing what she thought she might do. She had some ideas of her own. It was by her own wish she was sent to work in the Paris area, the most dangerous in France. In her case there was an additional danger, because she had been brought up there, and risked being given away if she should be recognized. I pointed this out to her, and had meant to draw her attention to one or two other points there were to consider, but found she had thought of them already—so there was not a lot I had to say to her. She went into this business with her eyes open. She appreciated the military importance of the mission and understood the risks, which she faced with a cool courage. In the field, later, she acted sometimes with great audacity, which was however justified by the military situation. Her motives were of the highest."

At this time, also, Noor was introduced to Miss Vera May Atkins,[1] who was to brief her for her mission. She did not, however, come really to know Miss Atkins until some time later.

She was told now that she would be discharged from the WAAF and enrolled in the women's Transport Service (FANY).[2] She could expect to be called in a few weeks. Until then she would return to Abingdon.

II

To Vilayat, Noor wrote a letter almost more concerned with the recent German occupation on November 11th, 1942, of the hitherto Unoccupied zone of France where Hidayat was, and with her family generally than with her own terrible impending adventure:

Brother dear,

The recent events are so overwhelming. I wonder what is happening to poor little Bhaiyanjan! Do you think we ought to wire—to get in touch with him?

My visit at Air Ministry was just a previous coming into touch with the branch I shall be working for: combined Navy, Army, Air Force Intelligence Service in the capacity of an Air Force Officer. I shall be called for it in about three weeks time. I saw Mother, too, she is just waiting for a vacancy. Actually, I was asked yesterday if I wished an officer's

[1] Later Squadron Officer, WAAF, now returned to civilian life.

[2] A problem which had for some time exercised the French Section, and Selwyn Jepson in particular, had been how to put their women agents—some of whom had been drawn from civilian life—into uniform during the period of their training in England. They could not, obviously, train in plain clothes, since this would be bound to excite curiosity; they had to have a uniform which would provide them with a 'cover story' they could tell to their friends and relatives, and at the same time provide them with a sense of being in the Services.

The ATS could not provide a cover, on account of a clause in their constitution forbidding members to take part in active military operations.

Jepson made contact with the Commandant of the Women's Transport Service (First Aid Nursing Yeomanry), a civil organization which had in its constitution no such limiting clause. The Commandant readily gave permission for women members of the French Section to be enrolled in the FANY corps, to wear its uniform during their training, and to remain members while in the field.

It was still considered desirable, however, to obtain for these women officer's rank in one of the Armed Services before they were sent out into the field, since in the event of their capture the Germans might (it was hoped) hesitate to sentence them to death—even although they had been operating in plain clothes—if they could say they were officers of His Majesty's Forces. If nothing else, such status might procure them better conditions of detention.

In the end, the WAAF agreed to give honorary commissions to women agents of the French Section, and this is how Noor came to hold later an honorary commission in her original Service.

allowance for any member of my family after which the officer agreed that on the grounds of our having lost property and money in occupied territory Mother is entitled to a superior income (damage income). She will be receiving this as soon as I start on the job, so that we might be able to manage a little flat in London in some time. Wouldn't it be grand!

I wish I had news about you, Bhai. Actually Mother was so anxious that I believe she had wired you. By the way, if you have not been able to send anything to Mams don't worry because I shall be able to, tomorrow, and if you need some, do let me know...

I don't know when I shall see you again, I have such a lot to talk to you about. Actually, I am afraid I must reserve every available day to see to Mother and her affairs until she is settled.

Do, do let's hear from you soon, Brother dear—and tell me if you advise us to do anything about Bhaiyan. I wonder whether he has procured himself a French naturalisation. I do hope so.

Cheerio,
All the love in the world,
Babuly

There followed a period of waiting in Abingdon, much longer than she had been given to expect, which tried her sorely. 'The waiting in the Services is enough to kill a person before action,' she wrote to her brother.

Since he had been forced to abandon, some months ago, his dream of becoming a fighter-pilot, Vilayat's mind had turned on little else but the idea of going back to France to work with the 'Maquis'. He had talked about it to me, he had talked about it with Noor, but did not know how to get himself recommended for such a mission. When he received Noor's news, veiled as it was, he leaped like an arrow to the conclusion that his sister had found a way to go back. And he was furiously envious and exasperated, because he thought she might go while he was stuck at Fareham.

It was during this waiting period that an episode in Noor's personal life reached its dénouement. One of the airmen training on the station had for a long time admired Noor and asked her to marry him. She liked him, without being deeply in love. She craved the warmth and affection of a home life, and said she would think about it after the war if they were both still alive. He was not satisfied, and tried to persuade her to marry him there and then.

She was uncertain, and hung back. She wanted Vilayat to meet him; so he came up specially, and they dined all three in a restaurant in Oxford.

Vilayat's impression was on the whole favourable: the young man was refined, sensitive, and devoted to Noor. But she demurred, saying he had only known her on the station, and therefore only knew one side of her, and that for an Englishman it would feel very peculiar to be married into their family.

Shortly after this he mentioned that she reminded him of a girl to whom he had been engaged previously. Noor insisted at once upon his telling her how he had come to be estranged from this girl, and where she lived.

On her next leave she took the train and called upon the girl in her home. She told her how she had come to know her former fiancé, and felt that the quarrel could be made up. "If you go and see him now I believe he will realize he still loves you."

The girl accepted Noor's advice, and shortly afterwards the reunited pair were married.

Another small but significant glimpse from this period comes from an aircraftman[1] who had just been posted to Abingdon as a wireless operator. He, two other men, a corporal, and Noor were for some time sharing a section of the Aircraft Watch, and their job was to maintain contact with the planes from the station, which were on training flights. The hours were pretty arduous: 4.30 p.m. to midnight; on again at 8 the next morning to 4.30 p.m.; then from the succeeding midnight to 8 a.m. After that they would go off duty until 4.30 the next afternoon, when they started all over again. In other words, they spent twenty-five hours in thirty-six on duty.

Noor was already an accomplished operator, with a speed of twenty or twenty-two words a minute, and she was always ready to help her less experienced colleagues, when conditions were fairly quiet, they used to put down three 'biscuits' (small square mattresses) and take it in turns to get a little sleep, two of them rolling up in a couple of blankets while the other two kept watch. Often Noor would forgo her sleep for the sake of the others, if she thought they were tired, even if she needed some badly herself. That, it struck him was the outstanding thing about her: that she always thought of others before herself—indeed, he doubts whether she ever thought of herself at all. He was struck by the inner poise which never seemed to leave her but gave her, he felt, an understanding of the meaning of life. Although she did not, so far as he remembers, ever speak of her religious beliefs, she seemed to him to have a serenity and a tranquillity which could only come from spiritual harmony within herself.

[1] Mr. F. R. Archer.

114

From another man on the station [1] comes a recollection which has an irresistible appeal in view of her future record. Her nickname with the RAF, he says, was 'the mouse'. This was not meant to be derogatory, but referred to her mouse-brown hair, her tiny voice, her shy ways, and her timidity.

III

Noor used to come and stay with me now when she had a night to spend in London. She told me simply that she had been transferred to the Intelligence, and I did not ask questions.

She took an amazing joy in the small guest-room, and said she felt it was 'hers' because she could come in and go out when she liked, and that after so much communal living she felt that she rested more deeply for being able to sleep in the personal atmosphere of a home. "Sometimes after I have gone to bed I lie awake with the light on, looking round the walls of your little room, and just enjoy feeling myself in it!"

The moccasins she completely adopted; she kept them in 'her' room and used to change into them as soon as she arrived.

I used to keep a box of incense sticks on a small table between the armchair and the fire. Sometimes she would lean forward to light one, and play with it, watching it burn. Beside them was a small bronze Buddha, to which she took immediately, as a familiar figure. She said it made her remember things she had had to shut away largely from her mind: "I feel sometimes I am developing a thickened skin in becoming used to the life of the station."

She told me of a museum in Leiden where there was a Buddha in the gardens. One approached it through an alley of almond trees, and when she was there they had been all in flower against a blue sky. She would like to go back and see it again one day.

As she spoke I felt her nostalgic longing for loveliness, as though she felt herself an exile from another world. She apologized for 'prowling' round my flat as though it were a museum, discovering at different moments, with a little cry, some Egyptian figurines, a Persian incense burner, and an early Italian Christ. As she liked Egyptian things I gave her a scarab, a whitish-grey one, and she said she would wear it.

But she attached herself most to a Tibetan prayerwheel I used sometimes for meditation, which had been presented to my parents by Kusho Horkang Dzasa, the Prime Minister of Tibet, after being received by them at Fort William, Calcutta, where my father had held a staff appointment. She liked to take it in her hands, and would say, "There is such peace in it. It seems to

1 Mr. Charles Dcakin.

115

bring blessings." In spite of her strong Indian patriotism she had no feeling against the British Indian Army, and appreciated its tradition.

In the course of these evenings I came to know her quite well. She was a good person, in the truest sense, and very serious. She admired easily, and had a human respect which extended even to the leading personalities of the states against which we were fighting. She did not like vulgar jokes about Hitler, Mussolini, and Goering. She said once, "I don't think we ought to represent these people so as to make them appear ridiculous. After all, they are persons of a certain importance, and we shouldn't seek to cheapen them." We made the discovery we had both seen Mussolini at performances of *Rigoletto* and remembering how carefree and good humoured he had appeared then, permitted ourselves a regret he had joined up with Hitler.

She was always the most assiduous little ministrant. I would have liked to treat her to the small luxury of breakfast in bed, but she always forestalled me. I would wake up shortly before eight to find her sitting quietly at my side, balancing a tray on her knee and pouring out. The first time this happened I could not imagine how she had managed to come in and so establish herself without waking me sooner.

After she had gone I discovered when I went into the kitchen that not only had all the dishes and pots left over from the previous evening's meal been washed up, but even the floor shone with a damp gleam. When next she came I said I did not want her to wash my floors. She explained that she had been used to getting up at six in Suresnes, and on the station to sleeping in very short periods. "So I was just looking around your flat for a way to occupy myself for a couple of hours!"

After that, I always saw that she had a book. The first she chose from the shelf was Leadbeater's *Man Visible and Invisible.*

As I had read several of her father's books, *The Unity of Religious Ideals, The Inner Life, Metaphysics, Moral Culture, Rassa Shastra, Gayan, Diwan* etc., which either had been given me by Vilayat or acquired by me on his recommendation, I would have been interested to talk about his teaching with her; but on this subject she resisted my attempts to draw her out. The resistance was so marked, that eventually she explained it.

Choosing her words with some difficulty, she said that having been brought up against a particular background, people who knew her against that background expected her to be a particular kind of person. "I don't know if I am like that. I don't know what I am." Perhaps at a later time she would go back to it, but at the present time, she had taken the opportunity offered by the war, to find her own feet, among people who did not know her against a Sufi setting. She said she told the girls she met in the WAAF nothing about her family. "They must know I am Indian, from my name, Inayat Khan, but I don't tell them anything else." She modified this by saying she avoided telling them anything which could feed the imagination. She wanted to be accepted for what she was, on her own; to discover herself. "I want to find out what I am!" She could only do that amongst people who did not know her background.

I did not doubt that the teachings in which she had been brought up underlay her deeper thinking (even perhaps to an extent greater than she realised) but at this time, she clearly felt that she had been living in a world of images of her father and his family in the minds of the disciples, and felt it as absolutely necessary to herself to make a naked contact with the ordinary world.

She told me now that she was trying to procure for her mother some lands in the United States she believed should have come to her as her share of the Baker family estate, and had been to a lawyer. She wanted to provide for her mother and Claire in case she should not come back from the war. Vilayat might want to go to India, and she did not wish to leave a charge on him. "Our house in Suresnes would be too full of memories for them to be happy to go back. But Claire has always had a fancy to go to America, and it is Mother's country. If they had a nice little property in the New World, it would be just the thing to give them a fresh interest in life."

So she calmly provided for her decease. It was perhaps true, as Basil once said, that Noor-un-nisa was "as nearly wholly selfless as it is possible for a human being to be." Vilayat was always troubled about this. On leave from Fareham, he remarked, "She thinks all the time about other people. She doesn't ever consider there is such a person as herself. That idea doesn't occur to her." Much later he wrote to me: 'Noor-un-nisa was born for sacrifice, like the Iphigenia of our school books. As a child I used to struggle hard at times to repress an obsessive thought that she would not live long. Indeed, she had something of the ethereal fragrance of those angelic adolescents who rarely outlive a score of years. I don't suppose she was ever conscious of herself. This gave her a forthright transparence that would attract friends like a magnet. If, however, a matter of principle were at stake she would defend it so fiercely that the less discerning would despair of seeing her revert to the same meek and carefree person.'

Yet I would have said that Noor was too interested in human development not to watch her own. She tended towards the doctrine of reincarnation, and regarded the soul as immortal and pursuing an endless evolution. For example, she did not like the discipline of the Service, but thought she might have had compressed into these three years an experience which it would otherwise have taken her a lifetime to acquire, and which she needed to pass through at this stage—having been previously an anarchic personality—before she could go on to the next step.

"When it is all over I may find myself equipped for something quite new which I could not have tackled before."

The idea of self-culture underlay many of the things she did. I remember her taking from her knapsack Milton's *Poetical Works*. She had read the whole of *Paradise Lost,* and though she found it very difficult and was only enjoying it moderately, was beginning *Paradise Regained*.

She was toying then with the idea of taking an Honours Degree in English after the war, because she thought this would give the literary background she needed if she were to write seriously.

She always had the idea that one day she would write something important; but in this connection she felt acutely the limitation of her human experience. One day, after reading something I had written, she spoke frankly about this, saying that she hoped eventually to be able to write realistically, about adults against a background of modern life; but at present she could not, because she had not lived sufficiently. She had, in fact, never had a love affair going beyond a certain point, and perhaps because she had always been so much with her mother and with children, was in truth rather childlike (in some respects) for her age; but the interesting thing to me was that she could take the measure of her condition. "So long as I only write children's stories it doesn't show that I know so little," she said; but she wanted to go right into life.

We used to talk sometimes about Indian affairs. The imprisonment of Gandhi, Nehru, and other Indian leaders in August had made a deep impression on her, and she began to feel the shadow of imprisonment falling across her own future if she should go out there after the war. Yet though she believed in Independence, and was prepared if need be one day to fight for it, she was not wholly at one with the action Gandhi had taken. She did not think the Indians should use pressure to force the British out at a time when they were embarrassed by the need to fight an external war.

She had a point of view which was in keeping with her way of thought concerning the value of renunciation. If India were willing to sink her claims whilst Britain was herself at a disadvantage, and support her without stint, it would create such confidence that after the war Independence would automatically be given. Although impatient at Abingdon, she thought that her being in Air Force blue might have some value if people saw that an Indian was serving with them.

I can see her now, standing before the mantelpiece, as she said,

"I wish some Indians would win high military distinctions in this war. If one or two could do something in the Allied service which was very brave and which everybody admired it would help to make a bridge between English people and the Indians."

Noor thought it should be possible to the spiritual man to take up the sword, provided he was not moved by hate. "If I did not believe that," she said, "I could not engage in the war against Germany."

I can remember her reading from the Bhagavad Gita:

Perform thou action, for action is superior to inaction.
Renunciation and yoga by action both lead to the highest bliss; of the two yoga by action is verily better than renunciation of action.
What is action, what inaction? Even the wise are herein perplexed. He who seeth inaction in action, and action in inaction, he is wise among men, he is harmonious, even while performing all action. Hoping for naught, his mind and self controlled, having abandoned all greed, performing action by the body alone, he doth not commit sin.

These teachings, given in the frame of Krishna's advice to the vacillating warrior, were particularly apt for Noor's case.

We talked of the end of the war. Noor saw dramatically the four armies, British, French, American, and Russian, converging upon Berlin, and wondered where she would be at this time. She wanted to get a job there, or wherever the Western Allies met the Russians, because she thought that being a half-Oriental she would be able to understand them better than our officers would, and could create good will as a liaison officer.

She said she felt it distracting to have a foot in so many countries—England, India, America, France, and Russia—and yet not to have one she could call her own, and that she envied people for whom the question of loyalty was a straightforward one. I said it was in some ways a position of strength; she could consider herself a citizen of the world. She said, "Yes, but they all pull different ways and sometimes I feel I'm coming to pieces in the middle. If I could bring all the ends together in myself then I might be able to make something of it."

Early in December her mother, who had joined the Red Cross, took rooms at 4 Taviton Street, only a few doors from me. At the same time Noor's duty brought her to London. Her file shows that on December 1st she was 'Reclassified Leading Aircraft-woman', and I remember she told me obscurely she had been attached to "Headquarters". She now stayed with her mother, but came in to ask me to write her a recommendation as a fit person

119

to use the Reading Room of the British Museum. She wanted to read some books on Polish folk-lore.

I was surprised she had time, but she explained that her interviews, though important, did not occupy long·in the day. She would like to publish a book of Polish tales to follow the Jataka. "I shan't be able to do very much towards it now, as I am only in London for a couple of weeks. But if I begin collecting the material I shall have some notes to start from after the war."

TRAINING FOR A MISSION

There was still a certain delay before Noor could be called to the FANY. Just before Christmas she was returned to Abingdon. I sent her for her birthday *Fairies at Work and at Play*, by Geoffrey Hodson. Her thoughts were at this time more than usually with Claire, who had ended by being called up in the ATS.

On January 30th, 1943 Noor came down to London for the day and met her friend Joan, who had returned from Ireland on a short visit. "She told me," says Joan, "as nearly as she could, what she was doing. She said she expected to be sent to Scotland on a parachute course, and I understood enough to know what this meant. But she was still in blue." She told Noor she expected a baby in June. Noor was convinced it was going to be a girl, and chose for her the name of Carol Ann. If she had not been posted overseas by June, she would apply for a week's leave so that she could come to Co. Wicklow and welcome Carol Ann into the world. Yet in case they should not meet again, Noor asked her to try to comfort her mother if she did not return from 'Foreign Service.'

According to her file, Noor was posted to 'The Air Ministry, Directorate of Air Intelligence', on February 8th, 1943. On February 10th she sent Vilayat, now at Rosyth, a telegram:

COMMISSIONED BUT IMPATIENT. LOVE NORA.

It must have been immediately after this that she was finally released from Abingdon, being seconded to the FANY, and was sent to Wanborough Manor, near the Hogsback in Surrey, for training under an ex-Guards officer, Major de Wesselow.

With her trained Mrs. Yvonne Beekman—whom she was to meet again only on the journey to Dachau—and Mrs. Cecily Lefort, also doomed to die.

The Escorting Officer to these three women was Mrs. Joan Sanderson. The physical training on this course was not very severe. The girls did a ten-minute run before breakfast, but no

PT. They were taught to shoot, throw a hand-grenade, and handle explosives, and did a great many observation tests. Mrs. Sanderson was particularly struck by Noor's exceptional reliability and unselfishness.

It must have been during this period that Noor wrote Vilayat a letter which refers to all four of Inayat Khan's children; to Vilayat's being at sea, to news of Hidayat, to Claire's having now joined the ATS, and to her own new and exciting training:

4 Taviton Street
London W. 1 [sic]

Brother dearest,

I am in London for a short while and wonder where in the big, big world you are. I do hope you will soon be coming back.

We have good news for you. Little brother is well. Erica heard from him some time around New Year and Lucy past [sic] the news over to us.

I guess you have been through such a lot of adventures and many hardships too. I hope to see Claire soon and am endeavouring to do all I can about helping her to get fixed up. It's rather hard going through all the breaking in when first joining up. We know something about it, don't we!!

Well, the biggest thing we are longing for now is to see you back again. So come quickly. I am a busy little girl now, and life is just full of activity and interest. I feel I am making up for all the time lost at Abingdon. I hope I will be here when you come back.

Cheerio brother dear! All the love in the world,

Babs.

I recall her saying to me she thought Claire hated the ATS, but that life in the services was good discipline. Certainly, Vilayat was hating the Navy.

He took very ill to the life of the lower deck, and suffered from a feeling of frustration. In the middle of February Noor received a fretful letter from PJX/383550 V. Inayat Khan, H.M.S. *Quantock*. He had been carrying sacks of potatoes about the ship for three days, and had now been transferred to picking cigarette ends from the deck. 'If I don't get a commission,' he wrote 'I shall join the Maquis.'

Noor was very alarmed. She knew her brother's proud and not altogether wise temper, and had a terrible vision that he might leave the ship to make his own way to France and be classified here as a deserter.

In the middle of March she came to London again, for consultation with her chiefs in the French Section. I was sitting in Gordon Square, trying to study in the timid sun, when, happening to look up, I saw a girl coming through the cherry trees. Her step and figure made me think of Babuly. But she was in khaki instead of blue. And then she saw me, and turned towards me smiling.

"I've been seconded to the FANY," she said, explaining her uniform.

"What does that stand for?"

"First Aid Nursing Yeomanry."

I was perplexed. She had done nursing at the beginning of the war, but since then every step she had taken had involved her more closely in military operations. Then she gave me in one phrase, "That covers many things", the clue that it might be a cover — though it was a phrase which, at the same time, could have meant nothing. I was aware of a subtle change in the atmosphere surrounding her. It was as though the strings of an instrument had suddenly become tuned more tightly, and I had the sense of an impending dénouement.

Perhaps because I felt I should make a total change of subject, but also because Vilayat had told me she saw fairies as a child and still half believed in them, and I wanted to hear it from herself, I took the occasion of our being in a garden to say something about its having a fairylike quality.

She responded at once. Her father used to like this garden and was accustomed to sit under the cherry tree beneath which she had found me. "It was his tree, too. Perhaps he felt the atmosphere".

This took me by surprise, for although I knew the Inayat Khans had lived in a house on Gordon Square, I had not reflected the place must hold childhood memories for Babuly. She told me now that she could remember playing here as a very small child, her father sitting beneath that tree. I told her Christina Rossetti had lived in a house off the other corner of Gordon Square, and probably sat in it, too, and we talked of cumulative influences.

As we walked up Taviton Street, she asked me, "Can you actually see fairies?"

I had to confess that I could not, though I did feel in Gordon Square, particularly in that spot, a kind of heightened life.

She did not have to go in to her mother's immediately, and I asked her into my place, for coffee. Over this she said, "I wish we could see them. I suppose we are not sensitive enough."

I ventured to say, "But I thought you could see them."

She said she used to think she could. When she was very small, she used to see diminutive human figures within the cups of flowers. As she went down a garden, every flower had such an inhabitant. She used to enjoy looking at the little people as much

122

as at the petals surrounding them. She talked to them as she went along. One day she heard some grown-ups speaking, and realised with horror that they thought the little people did not exist and that she only imagined she saw them. This was a great shock to her, for she had never doubted the little people in the flowers were as real as the flowers that held them. If really the flowers were empty, then she had been talking to companions who were not there.

Very upset, she asked her father, hoping he would assure her he could see the little people in the flowers, too. But he said if something was real to the imagination, there was a plane on which it had reality (Vilayat had told me of this answer, too, but regarding Father Christmas). This had left her doubtful, for she felt that though he spoke very gently, it was not to hurt her feelings. He might have said the same if he did not see the little people, or believe them really real. Now that her seeing them had been brought into question, she herself could see them no longer.

As she walked round the garden, she could see only empty flowers, and felt miserable. It had been like losing a faith.

She felt she understood the desolation of those who had lost the religious faith in which they had been brought up; they felt as she did over the loss of the fairies. The difference was that with loss of religious faith, it usually happened to people when they were grown up, through intellectual analysis; for her, the crisis had come when she was very young; over fairies.

It might seem strange that fairies should be so important. She did not doubt the reality of the One Life in which we all had our being; did not doubt our immortality. It should not matter so heavily whether there were fairies in the flowers or not. In the WAAF, she told me, now, there was a girl who was tremendously sensitive to colours. She loved them, they affected her moods; they seemed to her alive; when during a particular course of instruction they were undergoing, it was explained to the girl colours were merely the effects of light waves reflected back from surfaces at different speeds, she felt they were no longer real things, and became miserable. Her world had gone grey, and the shock was so great she could hardly go on with her work. Noor felt she knew absolutely the dejection of this girl; she had tried to tell her the colours were real, no matter what the scientific explanation of what caused them, and that it was possible to enjoy them as before; but she knew the girl was suffering as she had suffered over the loss of fairies.

She said it was so terribly easy to destroy what another person lived by. The damage could be done in a minute, and to repair it could be so very difficult. She said, "I felt if somebody wise had been there, he would have helped her." I replied that she herself

123

was wise and her words must have helped. She shook her head, and repeated that if someone really wise had been there, he would have found the way to explain in terms that would give the girl back her joy. At that moment, I had not the slightest doubt she was thinking of her father.

I told her that my grandfather, who was an army man, and not given to vapours, always maintained that when he was a very small child, in Lincolnshire, diminutive men came in from the outside and perched in a row on the rail at the foot of his bed; frequently. But he never allowed this to be mentioned outside the family.

"People are afraid of being mocked!" she said.

I thought, also, of Shakespeare: "In a cowslip's bell I lie."

"What do you think fairies are?" she asked.

I referred to the Theosophical and Rosicrucian doctrine concerning a stream of evolution sister to our own, but having bodies composed of much finer matter.

"Yes," she said, "that's what I think they are." In the tenderest voice, she added, "I would never speak badly of a flower, for fear of hurting the feelings of the fairy in it, that was doing its best to make it beautiful." She was sure they knew what one said about them, even if one only said it in silence.

Suddenly I thought of something that would be meaningful to her. I took from my shelf a book which reproduced a drawing from an Egyptian tomb, showing a slight feminine figure rising from a shrub. She gave a soft, "O-o-oh!" and took it in her hands.

Then I found, in the same book, the head of a goddess emerging from a lotus.

She said that sometimes, at Suresnes, she had practised meditation in the hope of recapturing the clairvoyance which had enabled her, as a child, to see fairies. In her present life, she had no time to herself, but if she should ever have a period of solitude, she would use it for the purpose of meditation.

During the week she came in to ask if I possessed any modern German novels I could lend her. I had only Goethe's lyrics, and Heine's *Buch der Lieder*. She shook her head. She had read Goethe's *Faust* in the country, and did not think she should absorb any more verse. "I thought if I could get hold of a rather better modern German novel it would give me the kind of language I could use suitably."

"But if it's in connection with your work you need German, surely you can apply for instruction."

She replied that 'they' did not consider it was relevant to her work. It was only her idea.

On an Airgraph form, stamped March 18th, 1943, she wrote to Vilayat:

Inayat 4 Taviton St. London W.C. 1

Brother dear,

It's grand hearing from you... Good news for you, little brother is well. Erica heard from him some time in January. Mother is so much happier at her new address and Claire is overcoming her first trials courageously. I shall see what I can do for her. I am at the War Office at present and life is full of activity and interest. I'm just so impatient to see you... I do hope you will be sent to Cadet school soon...

On another Airgraph form, stamped 25th March, 1943, she wrote:

Inayat, 4 Taviton St. W.C. 1

Brother dearest,

Wherever you are, I hope this word will reach you... Little Claire is on an army secretarial course, and is enjoying it. Apparently she is in the right line for a commission. Mother is expecting a post as Red Cross Deputy Superintendant at the end of this summer...

Soon after this, Vilayat was informed he would proceed to Lancing College. For some reason I have now forgotten, I received his news earlier than Noor. Amongst her letters to her brother, now confided to me, I find this:

I have been invading Jean with questions about you. I was so excited to hear you are classed in a group training for a commission. I knew it wouldn't be long before you would. I am anxious to see you!

I sent your woollen underwear to you... Bhai, my pen is broken and leaking.

Cheerio. Good luck;

All the love in the world,

Babs.

Although her mother had been my neighbour now for some time, the reticence of her disposition had been so strongly impressed upon me that it was only when I needed to speak with Noor one Sunday afternoon that I knocked at Number 4.

I had met the Begum only twice before, each time accidentally. When I went in, Noor was preparing tea for her and was going out to buy her some aspirins. But she set a second cup, and asked me to stay with her mother.

After her daughter had gone the Begum talked to me about

her. "She spends so much of her time in doing things for me, and I'm afraid I have done wrong in allowing myself to depend on her. She has no life for herself."

"And yet I would say she is a happy person."

Her mother passed her hand over her forehead. "Yes. ...I don't know why it should have been given me to have such a daughter..." She said she had not wanted her to go into the Forces. "I thought she would meet a rough type of girl, and she has always been so carefully brought up." She was glad Noor had left the WAAF. She could not make out what the FANY was, but she hoped it was something less rough.

Noor's next move was to Aylesbury, in Buckinghamshire, where agents selected to serve as wireless operators were trained for this special work. That she should serve in the field in this capacity, in which she was already qualified, was an obvious decision; and yet it set a precedent, for she was the first woman to be sent as a wireless operator. Teams consisted normally of three persons— organiser, wireless operator, and courier. Of these, the wireless operator was always the most likely to be arrested, the nature of his work being the hardest to conceal. Previously, women had only been sent as couriers.

An operator, to serve in the field, had to have a speed of twenty-four words a minute (only twelve being required of a GPO-telegraphist); but Noor had attained to twenty-two whilst at Abingdon, and therefore had an enormous pull over those having to be trained from the beginning.

From Aylesbury she went to the school in the New Forest where agents underwent a course of training in Field Security. Here they were taught how to avoid detection and capture in enemy territory, to notice if they were being followed, and to disembarrass themselves of a sleuth.

After a certain amount of preliminary instruction they were sent out on 'scheme', that is to say, briefed with a 'mission' to accomplish in a distant town, usually Bristol or Edinburgh. Wireless operators would have to find an unused building from which to transmit back to the school. All the time they would have to be on the lookout in case they were being shadowed by a 'Gestapo man' (an officer with whose face they were unfamiliar, and who would have been briefed to spot them). If, in the streets of the town, they should become aware he was following them they would have to try to lose him by making twists and turns through the shops and other places where it was difficult for him to follow.

It must have been in the course of one of these 'schemes', when she was cycling, as she told me, in the neighbourhood of Great Malvern, in a tremendous hurry, that she came to a cross-roads with traffic-lights showing STOP. She could see nothing on the roads but herself, so she put her head down over the bars and pedalled as hard as she could.

She was already across when a man's voice behind her thundered, "Stop!" Looking over her shoulder, she saw a policeman who had just emerged from a place where he had been unnoticable. She stopped, dismounted, and came back.

"Didn't you see the lights?" he demanded.

"Yes," she said, "but I didn't see *you*, or I wouldn't have done it."

He took this answer as impertinent—which it was not meant to be—and required her name and address. Later she received a summons. Unable to attend the court, she was fined in her absence ten shillings—for her quite a sum.

But she was certainly enjoying herself at this period. I remember she was looking very well whenever she came up. The khaki suited her better than the light blue, and the FANY uniform gave her a trimmer silhouette. But beyond that, she *gleamed*; her skin and eyes were bright and her hair seemed to have become more glossy. She said. "The women I'm working with are of a very superior type. We have the feeling of having been specially selected, and it's quite a different atmosphere."

Towards the end of the course trainees were given a mock Gestapo interrogation. Conditions were made as like as possible what it was supposed they would be, with very strong lights beating down on the 'prisoner', who had been briefed beforehand with a cover-story she must defend. In a corner an officer of the FANY would be seated, making notes.

"I found Nora's interrogations almost unbearable," says Mrs. Sanderson. "She seemed absolutely terrified. One saw that the lights hurt her, and the officer's voice when he shouted very loudly. Once he said, 'Stand on that chair!' It was just something to confuse her. She was so overwhelmed she nearly lost her voice. As it went on she became practically inaudible. Sometimes there was only a whisper. When she came out afterwards, she was trembling and quite blanched."

Though it is probable Noor did not know it, Colonel Frank Spooner (a retired officer of the Regular Army), who commanded a group of the SOE training schools in the home countries known as the Finishing Schools or Group C (because trainees came to them after having passed through A [Arisaig] and B [Beaulieu]) had recommended against her being sent into Enemy Occupied Territory. Speaking to me in his home in Guernsey, years afterwards, of the reasons which had led him to make an adverse report on her (which naturally he had not before him) he was at pains to explain that nothing he had said had been intended as a criticism of her as a human being. Frankly, he had not been too happy when he realised the agents he would have to train included women — he felt women should be protected from danger rather than sent into danger — but given the premise, he would have preferred women of considerable worldly sophistication and toughness. Noor appeared to him too emotional and too impulsive . . . too vulnerable. Also, though she was eager to face danger, she was too highly strung and too nervous. Once, when he trod behind her, she started. Walking up and down his country home, he explained to me that he would have preferred someone with "a more phlegmatic kind of courage"; and above all, "harder". That she had been awarded a posthumous George Cross did nothing to change his opinion.

That she had behaved with gallantry in a certain situation was to her own credit, but it was still his view she should not have been sent into that situation. He felt that he had been regarded in some quarters as a kind of grumpy bear who had tried to block the path of a wonderful girl, and been so imperceptive as to write a bad report on her. He emphasised that he had only his memory, since obviously it would have been improper to make notes or keep a copy of a report he had made in his official capacity. If he had written somewhat rudely, and it leaked out, what he would like it to be remembered, by those fond of her, was that he had not to judge — would have been incapable of judging — her understanding of philosophy or music but simply her suitability to be an agent. "To be an agent is not the highest flower of humanity." He spoke with not unfriendly gruffness. He had tried to stop her being sent to France, and had in his rough way written a report which he had thought would make certain she was not sent.

(What he had actually written, as it emerged when the Foreign Office opened the agents' personal files to a historian, appears to have been this: "Not overburdened with brains but has worked hard and shown keenness, apart from some dislike of the security side of the course. She has an unstable and temperamental personality and it is very doubtful whether she is really suited to work in the field."[1])

Colonel Buckmaster, however, preferred Miss Atkins' assessment of Noor to his. Colonel Spooner then "really stuck his neck out" by appealing to the higher authority of Robin Brooke against the decision to send Noor into the field; but in vain. "If I had had my way," he said, "your little friend would be alive today."[2]

[1] SOE in Franche, M. R. D. Foot (H. M. Stationery Office, 1966), p. 337.
[2] During the time that I was writing Madeleine, nobody told me of Colonel Spooner, or that a senior officer had recommended against Noor's being sent. I learned of his existence only after the publication of my book, and as a consequence of publication. It was when he heard

128

On May 8th, 1943, Noor came to see me and to tell me she had ten days' leave, which she was going to spend with Joan at her home. She would have to go in civilian dress, as members of HM Forces were not allowed to enter Eire in uniform. As she had put her civilian clothes in store she asked me if I could lend her a dress and a coat. She was smaller than me (her file at the FANY shows: Height, 5 ft. 3 in.; Weight 7 st. 10 lb.) but I found something to fit her.

We spent much of that evening looking at my latest acquisition, the enormous British Museum facsimile of *The Papyrus of Ani*. I spread it out on my divan for her. She sat on the divan with it, and turned every plate. She was most interested in the tableau of *The Weighing of the Heart,* but was rather taken, I recall, with the green, kneeling "Millions of Years" and liked Ra in his boat. I was working through Gardiner's *Egyptian Grammar,* and with its aid, and that of Budge's *Hieroglyphic Dictionary* was trying to read the papyrus.

Babuly asked, "Do you find it's harder than Latin, or easier? Do you have declensions and conjugations of caterpillars and little black storks and men doing things?"

I explained to her the structure of the language, to the extent that I had been able to understand it — the ideograms and phonograms — and, turning back to the *Hymn to Ra,* near the beginning, which I had already puzzled out, took her through it, at snail's pace, explaining each of the picture symbols, and how they linked together to form words and sentences.

She pointed to the small crouching hare with long ears, and asked, "What does he mean?" Why the author of *The Fairy and the Hare* was struck by him, was obvious. I had to confess, "By himself, so far as I know, he doesn't mean anything, but with a wavy line underneath him, representing water, he is the infinitive of the verb 'to be'."

She said, "This must all mean something. A hare on water must mean, to these people, something to do with the mystery of being."

She felt that she could easily become engrossed; but that it must not happen at this moment. If she went into that, she would never come out. Now she must be practical. After the war, she had already in mind to learn Sanskrit, and to read the *Vedas* in the original.

She suddenly sat up with a gesture in which all her coiled energy seemed to pulsate, as she exclaimed, "But there are so

I was coming to the Channel Islands, in 1954, just after the appearance of my second book, **The Starr Affair**, that Colonel Spooner took the initiative of inviting me to stay with his wife and himself at their home, so that he could tell me of the role he had played in the story of Noor Inayat Khan,

many things I want to do! I want to take up my music again! I have been leading such a one-sided existence during these last three years, and I don't want to get to think there's nothing else in the world but wireless and the war!"

I did not see her again for about ten days, and when I did it was briefly. She rang, apologized for not being able to stay, and said she had just rushed in to return my clothes. I did not doubt she had been to Ireland and come back; in fact, she had not been away.

Though I did not know it, either then or even when the first edition of this book was published, a first attempt to infiltrate Noor into Enemy Occupied France was made by the light of the full moon in May. She was flown from Tangmere to Compiègne, but it was found there was no one on the field to meet her, and she was brought back again.[1] As the full moon fell on the 18th, I suppose now that it was just before this she dashed in to return the dress and coat I had lent her.

Her chiefs in the French Section had found themselves in an embarrassment. The wireless operator of their team in Paris had asked for another to share his duties, which were becoming beyond his capacity to handle. There was not another operator fully trained whom they could send. They had, however, Nora on the way to the completion of her training, and radioed back asking if he could hold out for a few weeks longer. But his reply sounded so desperate that they contacted her as she was going on leave and asked her if she would be willing to go right away. Jepson sent her measurements to the Parachute School, but they said they had no harness small enough to fit her, so he arranged to have her taken by a plane that would land.[2]

She agreed to go, and Miss Atkins briefed her at once.

Her cover-story was that she was a children's nurse—they thought of this for her because it fitted her personality—and her name was 'Jeanne-Marie Regnier'. A false identity card and ration book were made out to her in this name.

Her code-name, for the French Section, was to be 'Madeleine'.

Thus, she would be referred to by her associates, in everything which concerned the work of the Section, as 'Madeleine', but in social situations as 'Mademoiselle Regnier'. Persons she met in France who were not members of the French Section would hear only the name 'Jeanne-Marie Regnier'. Only members of the French Section would know the name 'Madeleine', which had to be most carefully guarded. Her radio post would be the 'Poste-Madeleine'.

With her equipment were issued four boxes of pills. One con-

[1] **SOE in France,** by M. R. D. Foot (H. M. Stationery Office) p. 292.
[2] Selwyn Jepson to the author.

tained a kind that would induce a total sleep of about six hours, and were intended for administration to 'the enemy' in his tea or coffee, if occasion should render this convenient and desirable. One contained stimulants, for herself, if dog-tired and faced with the necessity of making an all-out effort. Another contained capsules to produce stomach disorders, for herself, if she should need to 'sham' an indisposition. And the last contained one pill only; it was lethal, for herself, if she should be captured and prefer not to face a Gestapo interrogation. (These were issued, but Miss Atkins does not think she took them with her.)

Miss Atkins had felt some difficulty in coming to know Nora. She liked her, but was conscious of a deep reserve. "She seemed to me the most quiet, retiring, reticent, and self-contained person it was possible to meet. At first I thought she was extremely shy; later I realized it was not shyness but something else." She had so arranged it that each of the women agents had been at some time alone with her, and had the opportunity to speak of any personal problems she wished. But Noor did not avail herself of these occasions. "I was there to be helpful if Nora wanted help, but I had the feeling that anything I might say by way of personal counsel or encouragement would probably be irrelevant to what she was thinking, and would just run off her."

But just at the end she opened up, and Miss Atkins was amazed by the soul she displayed. "She had a purity of motive that was hardly of this world. She had such high ideals. Her mind was so far removed from all ordinary worldly and earthly consideration that it was almost incomprehensible to me how she could do this job."

She had one request to make: Miss Atkins was to send her mother periodical bulletins to the effect that her daughter was well. In the normal way these would cease when she was captured, and she would be informed instead that she was missing. It would not be known in London until the end of the war whether she had been executed or was being kept in a camp, and all this time her mother would live in suspense. She wanted Miss Atkins, therefore, to keep up the bulletins unless they had definite intelligence she was dead.

To Miss Atkins this seemed a heavy charge. She asked, "Will it really make you happier if I agree to do this?"

She said it would.

Since she would not be finishing the course, she went privately to Mrs. Sanderson to say good-bye, and gave her as a memento a pair of cuff-links she had been wearing.

At Taviton Street she was 'furiously busy' trying to arrange her mother's affairs so that her sister could pick up the threads. Claire was at this moment home on leave. She noticed that Noor received telephone calls several times a day from a man-friend, and realized it was the same one who had rung her on the last occasion when they were both home with their mother. Her sister called him by his Christian name (which slips Claire's memory). "It was a nice name. English, but a little unusual."

On almost the last day Noor broke it to them that she was engaged. She had met him at the War Office two or three months ago, and they had fallen in love immediately. He was a British officer, and his father was English. Claire thinks Noor said that his mother was Norwegian, though it might have been only that he had been brought up in Norway. She gathered he had lived most of his life in that country. They had meant to be married before they left England. They expected to be sent overseas about the same time, and Claire had the impression they were engaged in the same Service (though she did not know what this was). But Noor's sudden order to stand by had taken them by surprise, and they found it impossible to get the ceremony performed in time. The engagement was nevertheless formal, and they would marry after the war. But she would not give her mother and sister his family name, or any address by which they could get in touch with him or his people.

Noor told her mother and sister that she was going to be away for a long time, and would not be able to write very often. They were mystified, without for a moment suspecting the truth. "I thought she must be going to an island," says Claire. "I never dreamed it was to France."

"If ever they ask you to do anything called liaison work," Noor told her, "you must say no."

Claire did not understand. "What would be meant by that?"

Noor did not explain. She just said, "Because you have been brought up in France they might think of you for something that would be called liaison work. But you mustn't do it, little sister. You promise me?"

Claire still did not understand—did not understand that women were being sent to France and her sister was one of them. But Noor looked so serious as she took her hands that she said, "I promise I won't do it."

Then Noor gave her a sealed envelope. Vilayat was now at Lancing College, following a course for a commission. She said, "If he fails the examination, and if you think he is going to do anything lunatic, give him this, and tell him to try what's written inside first."

Claire was worried by this trust, and gave it to her brother, in fact, immediately after he obtained his commission. It contained the address of an officer of the French Section.

Noor had evidently meant to say good-bye to her mother and

sister on the step, where she kissed them both. But Claire, clinging to a few more minutes with her, insisted on walking along at her side. She thought she could not mind being seen to the station, and yet felt a mounting premonition that Noor was going to tell her not to come any further.

They took the tube from Euston Square to Baker Street, and got out. Then, in the underground circus, Noor came to a decision, stopped, and said firmly, but very tenderly, "This is where we say good-bye."

"The last thing she said to me was, 'Be good'. They were very childish words..."

THE LAST STAGE

Noor had now gone to Chorleywood [1], in Hertfordshire, where agents standing by for infiltration stayed together in a large country house. Inevitably the atmosphere was a little nervous; each one, engrossed in her own cover-story, would begin to see weak points in it and ask the opinion of the others. Miss Atkins received a letter signed by two other women saying they did not think Noor was the type to be sent.

She felt she must see Nora again, and wrote asking her to come up and meet her for luncheon at Manetta's in Clarges Street. They went down to the bar, where a red leather sofa ran round the wall, and Miss Atkins chose a table on the extreme left, at which they could talk without being disturbed. When they were settled she asked her if she was quite happy about her work.

Noor looked very startled and said, "Yes, of course!"

Miss Atkins told her frankly of the letter she had received. She realised that Noor was very shocked and hurt that the idea could even have occurred to anybody that she was not suitable.

All the same, she said, "You know that if you have any doubts, it is still not too late to turn back. People have come as near to it as you are now and still changed their minds. If you don't feel you're the type—if for any reason whatever you don't want to go—you have only to tell me now. I'll arrange everything so that you have no embarrassment. You will be transferred to another branch of the Service with no adverse mark on your file. We have every respect for the man or women who admits frankly not feeling up to it. For us there is only one crime: to go out there and let your comrades down."

Noor thanked her for what she had said, but insisted that she felt she was a proper person for the mission, and had no doubt about her ability to carry it out. She had wanted to do this from the

[1] So known from its nearest railway station, this was one of Colonel Spooner's schools. The actual location was Chalfont St. Giles, Buckinghamshire.

beginning. Then she told Miss Atkins that during the time she had been in London she had been staying with her mother and sister and had had to say good-bye to them, and she had found this the most difficult and painful thing she had ever had to do in her life. Her mother thought she must be going to Africa, and had given her all sorts of advice about living in a hot climate. She had felt as though she were perpetrating a deliberate deception and being very cruel. She said, too, how much she wished she could have known before she went the result of Vilayat's examination. Miss Atkins said she would make it her business to find out how he got on and have Noor informed by radio. This seemed to make her feel happier.

By the time they parted Miss Atkins felt quiet in her mind that it was only these considerations concerning her family which had recently clouded her spirits temporarily.

I I

About a week after she had left London Noor came to see me again, unexpectedly. It was a little past eleven in the evening, and I was just going to bed when my bell rang. I put on my dressing-gown and went down. On the stairs I wondered if it could be Babuly.

It was she! A shadowy little figure stood on the steps with an attaché case, and a small voice said, "Jean, I'm so sorry to disturb you, but I wonder if I could come and stay with you again tonight, as I used to." It was like the first evening.

"I guessed it was you," I said affectionately. "There is nobody else who comes to see me at this hour." As we came up the stairs in the darkness it struck me as odd that she had come to me instead of going to her mother. But I did not ask the reason.

It was not until we were in the lighted sitting-room that I saw how her eyes were shining. "I'm going on Foreign Service," she said. "The waiting has been so long I have thought sometimes I would never go. But I do think now I am to go at last!—in three or four days."

If she was really going to German-Occupied France, would she tell me as openly as this? My mind cast a map of the world. The Continent, except for the neutral countries, was all German-Occupied. And yet to where else could there be any interest to send her?

I asked, "Will you be able to give me an address, where you are going?"

I was almost surprised when she answered, as though she had thought of it before, "Yes. If you will give me your address-book, I will write it in now."

134

I gave her my address-book, and she printed into it a cypher, 'c/o The War Office, Whitehall, S.W.1'.

"I have given this address," she said, "to my mother and Vilayat, and no one else. If you write to me your letter will be put in a bag, with those that come from my family, and then the bags will be forwarded at certain intervals with whatever has been collected." She said it had been difficult to ask her mother not to write too often, as, of course, she did not understand the reason. "They haven't put any limit on the number of letters I receive, but I think they must expect me to use my discretion. I feel that if too many letters came for me it would not be fair on the people who have to bring them."

I said I would not write at all.

"Write if something happens which you feel I would wish to know. Anything about Vilayat... I would feel it a comfort to know you would do that."

I promised.

"Jean," she said after a moment, "it may be I am exaggerating the difficulties of communication. In spite of everything I've been told I still can't form a picture—and won't be able till I get there—of what conditions will really be like. If things run quite smoothly I should be able to send back letters once a month. If I find that, I'll write to you. I shan't be able to say much, so they won't be very interesting. It'll only be to say I'm alive and well, but in the circumstances you might like to know even that."

She had stooped to change into the moccasins. I was about to go into the kitchen to put on some tea, but as she straightened again, I stopped, transfixed by the realization of how beautiful she had become. Her eyes had diamonds in them; there was a brilliance all about her as though she carried the stars in her hair. The thought went through my mind that she had spent the earlier part of the evening with a man with whom she had found a real love. (She had not told me of her engagement.)

"You are looking very beautiful," I said, gazing at her with involuntary enquiry. "Something has happened to you."

She was confused. "I expect it's because I'm happy. Everything I've ever wanted has come at once."

Whilst we had our midnight supper I looked at her. Certainly there was a change. She had acquired, as though overnight, a maturity which had previously been lacking.

She asked me if I could tell her something about her horoscope. She had been born with the Sun in Capricorn, and complained because she thought it was a 'material' sign. I said I would rather call it 'practical'.

She said she saw herself in the symbol of the sign as a goat

135

ascending a mountain. "The goat is a very obstinate creature, and so am I. And I like goats. I bring them into most of my stories. In Switzerland I used to watch them. They can climb in places where you would think no creature could find a hold, and they always go to the top, and they will stand for hours with all four feet bunched together on a tiny pinnacle of rock where no other animal could balance."

"Capricorn is a sign of ambition. Yet you're not ambitious . . ."

"Oh, but I *am*!" she exclaimed, squeezing up her little fists. "For the *highest*!"

She said somebody had once read her handwriting, and had told her that if she had to learn how to do something, she would let someone show her the way, and then she would do it that way just once and no more; after that, her own way. This was true.

She asked me to read her palm. She had a hand remarkably firm in its consistency, with the short fingers that often go with an impulsive nature. When I tried to bend them back I found they would not go at all. This worried me, on account of the usual correspondence between the flexibility of hand and mind.

When I spoke of it, she said, "I think the hand shows truly. There is something hard and rigid in me."

I warned her not to confuse hardness with strength, pointing out that a green twig, because of its suppleness, was stronger than a dry one.

She seemed to take this in deeply, but was troubled. "I believe this is something which I have to learn... but I can't see how to apply it. It seems to me in the path I've chosen I almost have to be hard and unpliable."

I observed the development of her thumbs, which showed the Will as the dominant principle.

"The difficulty," she said, "is to know the difference between will and wilfulness. I have a great deal of the latter, but I have always considered it a fault. I don't take people's advice."

I remarked that it was curious how people always had the impression of her as a very gentle person—perhaps on account of her stories.

She said, "I *like* gentle creatures, but I don't think I *am* gentle."

She thought she had a tendency to become a tyrant.

"A tyrant?"

"Yes, a domestic tyrant." Because she was the eldest she had had to manage the rest of the family when they were small, in place of her mother, but it had gone on too long. "I tend to supervise them. I used to think I was 'looking after' them, but I have come to see that I'm domineering under this cover, and

136

organize them in my own way." She thought she was actually hindering their development. "Claire would find herself more quickly if I were not accessible. It's time I should go. For me it will be better to be out of the home atmosphere, and it will be good for them not always to have me around."

She had a great space between the lines of Head and Heart, a deep Line of Mars, and a Life Line only half the normal length, starting from high under the first finger—all indications of a generous but reckless character. She spoke herself of the shortness of her Life Line, saying it had often stared her in the face when she had been making plans for the future. "When I was a child I used to hope it would grow, but now I see it isn't going to."

I said I did not believe in absolute predestination. Certain tendencies in the character could generate probabilities, that was all.

"Then if I have a short life, it is because I am reckless," she said. "That seems fair enough."

She asked me to go on with the examination. "If you don't mind telling me every little bit you can get out of it, I shall be very grateful. It might be useful to me in my work." She wanted to know what were the traits in her character through which she was most likely to come to grief.

I was touched by the confidence with which she put her hand into mine, and we talked into the small hours. At last she thanked me, and said, almost gravely, that she would keep in mind what I had told her. "I'm sorry to have wanted to talk about myself all the time, but I thought in the circumstances you would understand. I'm glad I plucked up the courage to come this evening."

Still later she told me about what she considered to be her most important story, the manuscript of which she had deposited with a publisher in Paris just before they had to leave.

Although she had given it the character and atmosphere of a fairy-tale, she had tried so to select the incidents that they could all have a natural explanation. At the same time, it was an allegory, and there was to be nothing in it that was not symbolical. "So it was very difficult to write." She had wanted to create something which children could remember, and understand in a different way when they grew up.

She had set it in Switzerland, where two children used to look up at the peaks where the goats climbed, and noticed that in the evenings they turned to gold. They made up their minds to fetch some of it down and give it to the poor people in the village. On the lower slopes they met a herdsman who told them a secret they must keep if they would reach their goal. Afterwards they were stopped by robbers who tried to make them give it up and tortured them.

She broke off her narrative and said she had always been afraid of being tortured. As a child she used to read stories of martyrs, and had sometimes lain awake at night imagining that one day she might be tortured for a secret. She had supposed then such things belonged to the Middle Ages, but since what had happened in Germany that kind of question had become real again for some people. She wondered how brave she would be in a Nazi concentration camp, or if she were really tortured for a secret. "I don't see how one can know . . ." She looked down slightly, then suddenly drew her nails into her fist with a little jerk, and said in a very low voice, "I don't think I would ever speak."

She took up the story again. Her children did not reveal the secret, and because they were brave a fairy guide appeared and led them on to the right path. They reached the peak of gold at last, and in the same moment they found that they had become gold themselves. Exalted, they gathered up as much of the golden earth and nuggets as they could, and started down. But as soon as they got out of the golden circle they found they were carrying in their arms nothing but earth and stones. They understood then that the gold belonged to the place and could not be brought down. At first it seemed they had climbed for nothing. Then it dawned on them that they could still show the poor people the way to climb up. But that would be much more difficult. "And I left it there," she said, "with my children just realizing this problem." She said she had tried to put into this tale the thing she had found it most difficult to learn.

We had talked so far into the morning that there was no longer any question of going to bed. We put out the light and drew the black-out, and saw that the stars had grown faint in a grey sky.

After we had had breakfast I came down with her to the front door. On the step she looked at me with eyes which became suddenly very eloquent, then said simply, "I shan't be seeing you again for a long time, so I will say good-bye. It's the end of a phase. Thank you for *everything*." And she kissed me, which she had never done before.

III

On June 15th Noor was released from the Air Force under the provisions of the Defence Regulations, 1941, and on the following day she was given an honorary commission as Assistant Section Officer in the same Service terminated on appointment to an emergency commission on July 5th, 1944—when she was in prison.

On the afternoon of the 16th Miss Atkins called for her in an open car, to take her to the field from which she would leave for France. In three years less three days she was keeping the promise she made when she left. It was a lovely June day; the air was fresh, the sun shining, and the English country at its sweetest. As they drove through the Surrey lanes the hedges were filled with dog-roses and honeysuckle, and when they passed into the more open country of East Sussex marguerites bobbed their heads in the fields of green corn, and here and there a lark rose singing. Noor hardly talked at all, but to Miss Atkins, glancing at her, she seemed serene. There was a smile on her face during nearly the whole of the journey. She followed with her eye the clumps and clusters of flowers as they passed, and occasionally exclaimed upon their beauty.

It was nearly evening when they arrived at a little white-washed cottage with green shutters, hidden amongst the trees. When they stopped the car the silence was profound. The doors and windows were all closed—for a reason. Miss Atkins let them in. The hall was full of smoke, and from a room on one side came the noise of men's voices. This was the mess of the pilots operating a Lysander wing engaged on 'Special Operations'. Different parties arriving or departing were not supposed to come into contact. Miss Atkins and Noor hurried upstairs, talking loudly, so that any others would avoid them. They went into a room reserved for them. On one of the chairs lay a novel called *Strange Women*. Noor said, "I suppose the boys like to read about strange women!"

Miss Atkins remarked, "Perhaps some day someone will write a book about the strangest women of all!"

She helped Noor get herself ready. She had in her handbag her French identity card and ration book, and a pistol—in case there should be an incident immediately she landed. But her transmitters, and a case containing her personal effects, were to be parachuted out to her afterwards so that she could land unencumbered.

Noor made a simple toilet, and as she finished she noticed a silver bird Miss Atkins was wearing on her dark tailor-made suit. She exclaimed, "You always manage to have something pretty and attractive on your suit! I never have anything, and I feel so plain."

Miss Atkins took off the bird to give her, but she protested, "Oh, no, I didn't mean it like that. I wasn't asking for it."

Miss Atkins insisted. "I should like you to have it. It's a little bird, so perhaps it will bring you luck." And she pinned it on her lapel.

One of the boys knocked to say he would take her to the field.

It was quite dark outside now, and a nearly full moon had risen. Only on nights when the moon was large were aerial operations possible.

BOOK II

MADELEINE

Only the actions of the just.
Smell sweet and blossom in their dust.

J. SHIRLEY

INTO THE DARK

On the night of June 16/17th, 1943, two Lysanders left together. Between them, they carried Noor, C. Skepper, Cecily
Lefort and Diana Rowden. The small, two-passenger aircraft were
known affectionately, as Lizzies and sometimes as hedge-
hoppers, so low did they fly. They were used because they could
land within a smaller space than any other type, and could be
employed where the approach was dangerously enclosed. The
landing was on a sloping field at Le Vieux Briollay.

The man who was waiting for them in the grass was, though
none of them could have suspected it, one of the most
controversial double agents of all time. "Gilbert", or, to give him
his right name, and rank, Flight Lieutenant Henri Eugène Alfred
Déricourt, RAF. The Air Movements Officer of the Section,
responsible for receiving and despatching aircraft which landed,
he had by this time been for at least six weeks in contact with
German Intelligence. In its files he had a number, BOE 48,
meaning forty-eighth agent of SS Sturmbahnführer Boemelburg,
the Chief of the Gestapo in Paris. That the Germans knew
Déricourt's function is certain; that he made it his custom to tell
them the actual times and locations of Lysander landings, less so.
After the war, he was tried and acquitted on a charge of
intelligence with the enemy; and I have a particular reason, which
I shall expose later, for believing that the Germans never knew
Noor had been landed by Lysander.

Déricourt may have been strong enough, in his position with
the Germans, to choose what he would and would not deliver to
them; but that it should have been he, the most interesting and
sensational of all the "doubles", who gave Noor a hand-down, sets
in dreadful relief her inexperience.

He led the new arrivals across to the gate of the field, where

141

he had waiting a bicycle for each of them, and told them the way to the nearest railway station, Angers.[1] Remy Clement, 'Marc', told me he sat with Noor in the train from Angers to Paris. "She was very afraid". It affected him.

THE GREAT CATASTROPHE

On the evening of Thurday, June 17th, Noor arrived at the apartment of a Frenchman, Lieutenant Emile Henri Garry. This was at 40 rue Erlanger, a street in Auteuil, one of the more elegant quarters of Paris. She had been given this address in London, and told that it must be her first point of call. She had been told also a certain phrase, acting as a password, which she must use in order to make her identity known; but owing to some mistake, she had understood it was an elderly lady whom she was to meet here, and had bought on her way a posy of carnations to give her.

Garry, for his part, had been informed that during the week an agent from England would be arriving, and would make himself or herself known with the aid of a certain password; he had also been told the phrase by which he must reply; but he had expected to receive further instructions informing him of the day, and approximately the time, when this person would arrive.

When Noor rang he opened the door, and for a moment they both stood looking at each other in some surprise.

Noor had understood that the old lady lived alone, and was therefore taken aback when the door was opened by a man. She did not know how to introduce herself, but realizing that she must account for having pushed his bell, stammered at last, "I think I am expected."

Garry said, "Oh yes. Will you please come in?"

He brought her into the sitting-room, and she saw, seated on the couch, a young woman.

He said, "Allow me to introduce my fiancée, Mademoiselle Nadaud." [2]

Noor, who was still more surprised to see the young woman, said, "How do you do," and extended her hand; but she did not make known her own identity.

Garry and Mademoiselle Nadaud were, on their side, puzzled. It had flashed upon them both that the visitor might be the agent whom they were expecting from London. She would not,

---

[1] The above account is as Dericourt gave it to me. For a full consideration of his case, see my **Double Webs** (Putnam, 1958); or, better, the expanded and revised edition published by Pan Books in 1961 under the title **Double Agent?**

[2] This account is as given me by Madame Garry, nee Nadaud.

otherwise, have said she was expected. Yet if it was she who had arrived in advance of any further notification, they did not understand why she did not make herself known by the proper password. Garry's password was the reply to hers, so he could not use it unless she gave hers first.

He invited her to sit down, as though it were quite normal for him to be entertaining somebody of whose identity he was ignorant. He offered her a cigarette, which she took, and made some remarks which were meant to put her at her ease, if she was his 'contact' from London. To these she replied, with some others which were designed obviously to test whether he knew who she was.

Noor, as she explained afterwards, was wondering whether they were perhaps relatives or connections in the Resistance of the old lady whom she had understood was her proper 'contact'. She could not believe them to be outside the network, or they would not have received a visitor who presented herself so strangely. Nevertheless, she felt she ought to await the appearance of the old lady before declaring herself.

Mademoiselle Nadaud, who had also been wondering what the explanation could be of this strange scene, decided that their visitor probably was the agent from London, and that it was her own unexpected presence which was causing her embarrassment. She had doubtless expected to find Lieutenant Garry alone.

She said, therefore, that she would make some coffee, and went out into the kitchen to do so.

Suddenly she heard a peal of laughter, and realized that bona fides must have been established.

When she returned with the coffee on a tray Garry and Noor were already chatting with confidence.

"She expected me to be an old lady!" he exclaimed. "And she brought these carnations to give to me!"

They both persuaded Mademoiselle Nadaud to accept the carnations.

Noor, it transpired, had been all the time studying Garry; he was a tall man, with curly brown hair, a strongly cut face, and a somewhat serious expression—indeed his eyes were almost stern. She had felt a confidence in him and had suddenly taken the plunge and spoken her password, to which she had received, of course, the proper reply.

Neither Garry nor his fiancée could understand how she came to have been told about an old lady. "There is no old lady who lives here!" they said. Besides themselves, there was Garry's sister Renée, who lived in the flat, and also a "South African" Major, an officer of the French Section—code-name 'Antoine', real name Antelme,[1] and cover-name 'Rattier'—who generally stayed with them, though on this night he was away.

Noor told them her story since she had arrived in France the previous night. She had been landed by plane in the country near Le Mans. (Note that Noor had the prudence to veil the secret of the exact landing-place of the Lysander. She would have passed in the train through Le Mans on the way from Angers to Paris.) She had not, so far, had any meals, She had in her bag the faked French ration book with which she had been issued in London, but was not sure of the way in which to use the coupons, and had not thought it prudent to offer them, either in a restaurant or across the counter, before seeking advice. The only thing she had dared to buy was the posy of carnations.

"Then you haven't had anything to eat for twenty-four hours!" exclaimed Mademoiselle Nadaud in dismay.

"I haven't had anything to eat since I left England, yesterday afternoon."

"But you must be weak with hunger after travelling for so many hours on an empty stomach. Have you had nothing to eat at all?"

"I had a glass of Vichy water in a café."

"That didn't sustain you much!"

"No. But I thought they couldn't ask coupons for it!" She said this with a little smile.

"Then it is much more than coffee that you need," exclaimed Mademoiselle Nadaud, and went back to the kitchen to see what she could find. It was unfortunate that they had just finished their evening meal when Noor arrived; she whipped round the shelves, however, in search of such things as would cook quickly, and after a few minutes was able to bring in some steaming plates.

Noor, who must have been famished, ate prodigiously. Whilst she was consuming the burden of the first plates Mademoiselle Nadaud, perceiving the rate these were going down, went back into the kitchen and made some more, and so kept her supplied.

Whilst she was eating they told her a little concerning themselves and their sector. Garry had been working for the French Section for a little over a year. He worked under a British officer, 'Prosper', and was the chief of the sector covering the Department of Sarthe; he had therefore headquarters in the capital of Sarthe, Le Mans. He retained a residential address in Paris, and travelled between Paris and Le Mans according to need. To cover his activities he had a false *carte de travail*, declaring him to be an engineer of the Société Electro Chimie of Paris. (He was, in

---

1 Full name Joseph Antoine France Antelme. Information from his young nephew, Daniel Antelme, when he came to see me in 1959 on a visit from Mauritius, where in fact his family lived.

fact, an engineer.) His code-name was 'Cinema'. [1] He did not need a cover-name, as he could still live under his own. This was often the case with the French members of the Resistance networks. British officers infiltrated needed, for obvious reasons, to have cover-names (identity card names) as well as code-names.

They knew already Noor's code-name, 'Madeleine'. She told them now her cover-name, 'Jeanne-Marie Regnier', and they said they would call her from the beginning 'Jeanne-Marie', as it was wiser to forget her real names.

She told them she had just parted from her mother, who, of course, did not know where she was, and that to make the decision to leave her had cost her a great struggle. They both felt she was very young to have been sent on such a mission; they had the impression she was not more than twenty or twenty-one.

They asked her if she had arranged where she would spend the night. When she replied no, Mademoiselle Nadaud said at once that she must stay with them.

She accepted very willingly. Actually, she was already looking very sleepy. The food and warmth were beginning to have their effect, as well as the sense of having come to rest at last amongst friends, after a day and a night spent in lonely and terrifying adventures. They saw that her eyelids were beginning to close, and Mademoiselle Nadaud went at once to make her up a bed.

II

The British team which Noor had been sent out to supplement consisted of 'Prosper', the organizer (really Lieut.-Colonel Francis Suttil, in private life a barrister); 'Archambault', the wireless operator (really Major Gilbert Norman)—he who had been appealing for assistance; and the courier 'Denise' (really Miss Andrée Borrel, a young French girl). These three lodged mainly in Paris, but their working headquarters were in the Ecole Nationale d'Agriculture at Grignon—a small place to the north-west of Versailles, chiefly distinguished for its School of Agriculture. The school worked under the direction of a Monsieur Vanderwynckt, and served as the cover for a plexus of networks, of which the overall chief was 'Prosper'. The area covered by the 'Prosper' organization was divided into a number of sectors. Professor Alfred Serge Balachowsky, of the Institut Pasteur, was the Chief of the Sector of Grignon, as Lieutenant Garry was Chief of the Sector of Le Mans.

Very soon after her arrival in Paris—probably next day—Noor was taken out to Grignon by 'Archambault', after Balachowsky

[1] Later changed to 'Thône'.

145

had obtained the permission of the Director, Monsieur Vander-wynckt. She came in the afternoon, and was introduced to Madame Vanderwynckt and the two daughters, Madame Balachowsky, and two young women belonging to the network. After the introductions had been made she exclaimed, "I know Archambault! He was brought up in Saint Cloud,[1] and is two years younger than I am."

'Jeanne-Marie' made herself quite at home, and later went with the young women into the kitchen to help them get some tea, and came back carrying a tray. She poured out for everybody and began to toast before the fire some slices of bread which she had brought in.[2]

One of the young women, noticing this, and that she had poured the milk into the cups before the tea, pointed these things out to Madame Balachowsky, with the comment, "You can tell that she's English!"

Madame Balachowsky thought it good to pass this remark on to Jeanne-Marie. In France, she reminded her, people did not cut up a loaf to make toast, and in pouring out tea they always put in the milk last. To put the milk in the cup before the tea was, to the French mind, a distinctively English custom. Such a thing would be sufficient to betray her. Jeanne-Marie thanked her for the warning.

A little later Professor Balachowsky came in. He entered the dining-room carrying a portfolio belonging to Noor which he had found where she had left it, in the entrance hall. He asked her if it contained anything important, and she replied that it contained her code, which she had brought from London.

He remonstrated with her, explaining that she should never leave unguarded a case containing important papers. "I picked this up; somebody else could have done so too!" So far as he and his colleagues knew, the staff of the school was trustworthy; but she had no right to assume such a thing. Now that she had come to German-Occupied France she must learn to bear constantly in mind that agents of the Gestapo were everywhere, even sometimes in the places one believed to be strongholds of the Resistance, and conduct herself constantly as though she were surrounded by spies. He gave her some practical advice concerning the precautions she should take for her safety in her daily life. Madame Balachowsky, who had noticed by this time one or two other typically English things which Noor had done, added some further remarks.

Later in the afternoon, perhaps about five o'clock, Archambault took her out to show her the greenhouse from which with his

---

[1] Where Noor attended her second school.
[2] This account is as given me by Professor and Madame Balachowsky.

transmitter, since her own had not yet arrived, she made her first transmission to London from Occupied France. [1]

After she had been taken out by Archambault, one of the young women said to Madame Balachowsky: "Haven't you been discouraging Jeanne-Marie? You have perhaps told her rather a lot of things for the first day, and it is enough to frighten her and to make her think that she does everything wrong."

Madame Balachowsky said that she had not meant to discourage Jeanne-Marie, but it was in her own interest as well as theirs that she should learn as quickly as possible those things which might lead to her being arrested. She did not have the impression that Jeanne-Marie, who seemed an intelligent girl, had taken her comments badly.

The school was a magnificent building, situated in the midst of extensive grounds, surrounded by a wall nearly fifteen feet high. Within these precincts there was also a building known as the 'Château', where Monsieur Vanderwynckt lived with his wife and two daughters and his son-in-law, Monsieur Douillet. Here they gave Jeanne-Marie a room.

At meal-times there was often a large party in the dining-room, the entire Vanderwynckt family and its connections, Professor and Madame Balachowsky, and the British team, now swelled by the addition of Jeanne-Marie, all gathered round the table. Under these conditions there was rather the atmosphere of one large family, living a communal life and having its own jokes. Despite the state of tension in which they all lived, the meetings round the great dining-table were often very merry.

'Prosper', the big Chief, was specially liked. The Balachowskys had a high regard for him. "He was," says Madame Balachowsky, "exactly one's idea of an English gentleman, refined, responsible, and always considerate."

The Balachowskys did not actually live on the premises, since they had a flat in a big modern block in the suburb of Viroflay, one of the dormitory suburbs of Paris, on the other side of Versailles. Nevertheless, they spent much time in Grignon.

Jeanne-Marie told them a little about herself, saying that she had a brother in the Navy, and that she herself had served in the Air Force before volunteering for this mission. She gave her own 'true' name, rather strangely, as 'Nora Baker', [2] and said that she had just parted from her mother, who did not know she was

[1] Miss Atkins says that the first message from 'Nora', that she had arrived safely and made all her contacts, was received within forty-eight hours of her departure from England, an exceptionally short time.
[2] The Begum was known as Mrs. Baker in the Red Cross and at 4 Taviton Street. Noor probably did not wish to give the name of Inayat Khan in case, if she were captured, Germans connect her with either of her brothers, and be able to use the relationship as a way of putting pressure on one or another.

147

doing this work and believed her to have been sent to North Africa. They had the impression that her thoughts were very much with her mother, and the fact that she had had to steal away from her, without giving her true information where she was going, seemed to weigh upon her.

The Balachowskys found her charming and extremely courageous, very conscientious in her work but often extremely imprudent during the first days. They were both rather concerned about what they felt to be her 'Semitic type'. Not knowing that she was partly Indian, they were sure that she was Jewish. "It was," says the Professor, "something in the cast of her face—in the formation of the bones—which was typically Semitic." The Sicherheitsdienst, or Counter Espionage Service of the German Police—the organization occupied with the French Section—was not, in fact, concerned with Jewish questions. They believed that at the Headquarters of the Sicherheitsdienst, on the Avenue Foch, Jewish prisoners were treated the same as any others—race here was irrelevant; but the danger was that if her appearance should attract the attention of the arm of the Gestapo which applied itself to Jewish questions, her cover-story might break down under close examination.

For those who were not a part of the network, Jeanne-Marie passed herself off as one of the students attending the school.

Whilst awaiting the arrival of her own transmitters she worked every day with Archambault, sometimes side by side with him at his set, and sometimes in his stead, to let him go off. They used to work from the greenhouse under the supervision of the gardener, Marius Maillard, [1] a Frenchman, who used also to help with the reception of parachutings.

Sometimes they all went up to Paris. On the Sunday after her arrival in Grignon she formed part of a large luncheon-party in Paris, the others being Professor and Madame Balachowsky, Prosper (who had been away when Madeleine arrived), Archambault, Denise, Vanderwynckt, Douillet, and Maxime Roberte-Gaspard, the son-in-law of the Belgian Minister. Noor managed also to spend an occasional evening in Paris with her first friends, Lieutenant Garry and Marguerite Nadaud. On, perhaps, two occasions she shared a room with Garry's sister, Renée, who was living with them.

Major Antoine had now returned, and met Noor at the Garrys'. He was tall, broad-shouldered, deeply suntanned, and had about him a breath of the outdoors. He was perhaps about forty-five, and talked to Noor in a paternal fashion, almost as though she were a little child, whilst producing photographs of his own children for her to look at and telling her about their life on the ranch.

[1] Died at Dora, April 1944.

148

Between Garry and his fiancée, Antoine, and Noor there was always a warm friendliness and confidence, Noor's obvious youth, her natural trust and earnest enthusiasm endearing her immediately to the other three. Garry and his fiancée were intending to be married on the last day of the month, and it was arranged that Noor and Antoine should come to the wedding.

It was during these first days that Garry introduced Noor to two other Frenchmen, X [1] an important business magnate whom Garry had drawn into the French Section, and a Monsieur Vaudevire, Director of the Societé Française Radio Electrique, a firm nominally working for the Germans, but actually covering on its staff a number of persons serving in various Resistance networks.

It was on a bench by the Tuileries, in front of the Hotel Continentale, that all four met for the first time, Garry, Noor, X, and Vaudevire.

Shortly after this, X introduced Noor to a friend of his, Maître Y, [2] a lawyer. X, Y, and Vaudevire formed a trio which worked together, and with which Noor was to become closely associated.

On the night of Monday, June 21st, Professor Balachowsky went with some of his men to a farm near the village of Roncey aux Alluets to receive seven parachutes bearing a cargo which included either two or three transmitters for Jeanne-Marie, as well as a case of her personal effects. The parachute bearing this came down on top of a tree, over which it spread itself out in a complete cap, like a mushroom. When the Professor reached the spot with his men they found that the case itself had burst right open, scattering her lingerie over the lower branches. They worked until the dawn—not in the best of humour—to collect it. Parachutings were inevitably dangerous, since although a country spot was chosen, there was always the possibility that somebody might have seen the parachutes coming down. It was in the committee's interest to collect the cargoes as quickly as possible and to get away. They dared not, however, leave a tell-tale trail of things festooned upon the tree.

In the small hours, having packed Jeanne-Marie's lingerie back into the case, they deposited the cargoes temporarily in a place where they would be safe, and then bundled the parachutes into the Balachowskys' car, which Douillet drove back to Grignon.

On the following Thursday Noor had a rendez-vous in the afternoon with Professor and Madame Balachowsky, by the fountain in the Jardin du Luxembourg. As soon as she met them she put straight into Madame Balachowsky's hand a piece of paper on which was drawn a plan. This showed a road running below

[1] Who remains anonymous for reasons which will appear later.
[2] Who remains anonymous by reason of his close relation with X.

149

the farm at Roncey, with a place marked with a ×. There, on the following afternoon, two men would come with a wagon to receive from her husband and Roberte-Gaspard, after exchange of the proper passwords, the parachute cargoes dropped on Monday.

Madame Balachowsky was shocked that Jeanne-Marie should give her such a paper in a public place. She felt that she did not sufficiently realize the condition of France, and explained to her, "Things have come to such a pass here that it is unsafe for one person to give a letter to another in the street, if he does not want it to be intercepted. Secret police are everywhere, and they watch everything and ask what is the reason of it. You must regard every person whom you meet as a possible agent of the Gestapo—in the street, in the underground, in the restaurant. They don't wear it written on them, you know! They look like anybody else. Suppose somebody had asked to see that paper as you gave it to me?"

Jeanne-Marie was obviously rather shaken by this. Afterwards Madame Balachowsky talked with her for about an hour, giving her advice on the precautions she should take for her own security and that of others. "If you ever again have to give something to a person whom you have to meet out-of-doors tell him simply that you have something to give him, and then arrange with him to go together into the house of somebody who belongs to us, and give it privately."

As soon as the cargoes had been brought to Grignon the Professor gave to Noor her transmitters and also her lingerie. Despite its condition, she was very glad to get it!

That week-end there began a series of arrests which constituted collectively the biggest coup ever made by the Gestapo in France. Since the German Police struck practically simultaneously at widely scattered points, it is likely that they had an overall knowledge of the field before they moved.

On Thursday, June 24th, Prosper, [1] Archambault, [2] and Denise [3] were arrested in Paris. Monsieur and Madame Touret,[4] who kept the restaurant where they ate, and which they used as a letter-box, were also made prisoners.

Professor Balachowsky advised Noor that she should leave Grignon at once, since the school was likely to be the next place to be searched. Neither he nor his wife would return there. Only the Director, Monsieur Vanderwynckt, was obliged to remain.

[1] Executed in Germany (details still unknown).
[2] Shot at Mauthausen Extermination Camp, September 6th, 1944.
[3] Executed by lethal injection at Natzweiler Concentration Camp, July 6th, 1944.
[4] Deported to the Concentration Camps of Buchenwald and Ravensbrück respectively; returned after the Liberation in 1945.

He told her she should try to find a room in Paris and look after her own security. After so great a catastrophe it would be impossible to work for some time. It remained to be seen how far the wave of arrests would spread, and on what basis it would be possible to re-organize now that the big Chief had been taken.

Garry considered that in the circumstances of more than usual danger which had arisen, it was unwise for agents to congregate under one roof, and therefore did not invite Noor to stay with them. Instead, he appealed to another member of the network, Madame Aigrain, Directress of the Toile D'Avion, a big woman's shop on the Champs Elysées, and she agreed to take Jeanne-Marie. Her flat in the Square Malesherbes was particularly convenient in that it was very near to the rue Erlanger, so that Noor could run backwards and forwards between the two apartments in a matter of minutes.

Despite the disaster, Lieutenant Garry and Marguerite Nadaud were married, as they had intended, on Tuesday, June 29th. Antoine had meant to be one of the witnesses, and on the evening before they had smiled at the thought that he would sign the register in his cover-name of Rattier. The next morning, however, he was taken with some malady, and they had to leave him behind in bed. Noor, of course, was at the wedding.

The newly married couple returned that night and slept at the flat. Antoine appeared to be better.

In the morning the Garrys had to go to the Gare St. Lazare. When they returned the concierge stopped them in the vestibule to say that men of the Gestapo had come, asking for Monsieur Rattier, and had gone upstairs to their flat.[1] Monsieur Rattier had gone out just before they called. They thanked her for her loyal warning and made their escape as quickly as they could.

Their first duty was to intercept Antoine and Jeanne-Marie before either of them could return to the flat, to warn them that it was now occupied by the Gestapo. Noor, as it happened, had gone out early. Then they had to get out of Paris. They had, in any case, intended travelling during the week to Le Mans, for work there, but the raid on their premises made it desirable to depart immediately. All the possessions which they had in the flat, clothes and personal effects, were naturally lost to them, since it was impossible to retrieve anything.

Madame Balachowsky remembers that it was on this Wednesday morning that Jeanne-Marie arrived suddenly at their apartments

---

[1] Ernest, the interpreter at the Avenue Foch, confirms that the Garry's flat was raided by his Service at the end of June. To the best of his knowledge, they were searching for Garry and Antoine only, and knew nothing at this time of the existence of Madeleine. He did not take part in the raid on the first morning, but visited the premises after it had been occupied by his Service for some days.

at Viroflay, having cycled out from Paris. She had come to tell them that she would be going with the Garrys to Le Mans, and that on the next day Antoine would be coming to see them and to work in her stead. The Balachowskys had not met Antoine. He was in fact an officer of far greater importance than was generally realized even by those who were working with him. Noor described him to them as "very big, broad-shouldered, and very sunburnt", and added. "He does not speak very good French." She had, she said, cycled round by the Pont de Sèvres, not wanting to pass through the Ville D'Avray (which would have been the shorter route) since she had been brought up near St. Cloud, and knew too many people in the district.

She was extremely fatigued and had a bad cold, or perhaps influenza. She made them laugh with the account of all the cures she had taken, the cachets and the inhalants. Although she retained her sense of humour about this, they both realized that, as was natural, she had been badly shaken by the arrest of the British team the previous Saturday.

Having delivered her message, she said she would be going back to the Garrys.

"To their flat?" asked Madame Balachowsky. "You had better telephone first, to make sure that it is all right to go."

"Everything was all right there yesterday," said Noor. "I was at their wedding."

"That does not mean that everything is all right today," retorted Madame Balachowsky. "The situation changes very quickly now and there are arrests every day. Better telephone, in case the Gestapo have come during the night or this morning."

Noor thanked her for the warning, and said that she would do so. She went to the phone in their sitting-room, but Madame Balachowsky prevented her, exclaiming, "Not from here! The call would be traced, and they would come here next. Go back to Paris, phone from a public call-box, and if, instead of the Garrys or Antoine, you are answered by a man whose voice you don't know, who says he is a 'friend' of Garry, take it that the flat is occupied already by the Gestapo, and *don't go!*"

It must be supposed that Noor followed this advice; she did not go to the flat. Thus, the foresight of Madame Balachowsky saved her from arrest on this occasion. [1]

Meanwhile Garry had succeeded in intercepting Antoine, who, since he was now homeless, came to join Noor as the guest of Madame Aigrain. It was now a disadvantage that her flat was so near to the rue Erlanger. Since the Gestapo had asked for Rattier when they called, it was extremely inadvisable for Antoine to go

---

[1] Ernest confirms that had she come at any time during this day she would certainly have been arrested.

152

out. Like the Garrys, he had had, of course, to sacrifice everything except what he carried upon his person, and so was rather helpless. Madame Aigrain thus found herself playing mother to two British agents, one of whom was certainly wanted by the Gestapo already, and neither of whom was in good health.

The Garrys left on the same day for Le Mans—where, to conceal from their landlady and others their real activities, they presented themselves as a honeymoon couple, a cover-story which had the advantage of being true.

At two o'clock on the afternoon of the next day, Thursday, July 1st, the Gestapo came to Grignon.[1] Between eighty and eighty-five SS entered and occupied the school. They arrested Vanderwynckt[2] and Douillet[3] as well as a number of other persons.

On this day Noor, despite Professor Balachowsky's warning, came to Grignon. She wanted to transmit to London, and Madame Aigrain's flat was not convenient for this. She hoped, despite everything, that it might be possible to transmit from the greenhouse as usual.

She cycled to the school, left her bicycle against the wall, and approached the place stealthily. As soon as she was within the grounds she realized that the conditions were not normal. Then, perceiving that the building was occupied by the SS, she withdrew quietly, and, abandoning her bicycle, jumped on to a passing bus which took her to the station, where she got a train back to Paris.[4]

During the whole of this Thursday, the Balachowskys, who did not know what had happened, waited in vain for Antoine. At about midnight they gave up and went to bed.

The next morning, Friday, July 2nd, at about eight o'clock, whilst they were having breakfast, the bell of the flat rang. Through the glass door of the living-room they saw the maid admit a big, broad-shouldered man who asked in not very good French for Professor Balachowsky.

Madame Balachowsky exclaimed, "Ah, Antoine!"

The Professor got up and went straight out into the passage, and said, "Hullo! We have been waiting for you!" to the man from the Gestapo who had come to arrest him.[5]

[1] Ernest says that the information enabling his Service to raid the premises at Grignon was not obtained from the prisoners already taken.
[2] Executed in Germany.
[3] Executed in Germany.
[4] This is according to Noor's own account, later, to Raymonde. According to the French official citation for the Croix de Guerre, she shot and either wounded or killed some of the Germans who pursued her. See citation at the end of the book. The Balachowskys do not think that there was any shooting.
[5] Deported to Buchenwald; returned 1945.

Greatly to her surprise, Madame Balachowsky was not arrested with her husband.[1] The party of men who had come all went out again, taking the Professor with them and leaving her and the maid alone in the flat.

She had a responsibility now, which took precedence over everything else, to inform other members of the network of her husband's arrest, and to prevent them, if possible, from walking into a trap. She told the maid to remain by the phone and to tell anybody who called what had happened and prevent them from coming. Then she herself went downstairs, and after looking round very carefully to make sure her exit was not being watched, went out to warn members of the network living locally. To her own knowledge, she saved three persons from arrest by doing this.

At about eleven o'clock Jeanne-Marie telephoned to say that she was coming out to Viroflay. The maid told her the Professor had been arrested, and that she must not come. This was the last Madame Balachowsky heard of Jeanne-Marie.

On Sunday, July 4th, Madame Balachowsky went to Grignon and learned the extent of the raid there. The SS had moved out between four and five in the morning on the Friday. On the same afternoon that they arrived seven other persons living at different places in the neighbourhood had been arrested. In Paris, between twenty-five and thirty persons known to the Balachowskys had been taken.

It was only after a little time that the extent to which the networks in the provinces had been devastated became apparent. In the north and in the west, and even in the south, the arrests ran into appalling figures.

In Paris, Noor and Antoine, practically the only survivors of the holocaust, lay low in Madame Aigrain's flat. Antoine was virtually imprisoned for so long as the Germans, who had come to search for him, remained in occupation of 40 rue Erlanger, close by; but Noor must have gone out, for she transmitted (nobody knows from where) the news of the disaster, in so far as she was aware of its proportions.

Buckmaster replied that since all the members of the team she had been sent to join had been arrested she should return to England. He would have a plane sent to fetch her home.

To his amazement, she replied that she would rather remain. She perceived that her post had now become one of singular

[1] She had the explanation of this later when, at the suggestion of a friend, she called at the Avenue Foch to ask what reason they had for supposing her husband to have any connection with the Resistance. The member of the staff who received her replied, "Plenty!" but added, "It has been explained to us that you are a sick woman and had no idea of your husband's secret activities. That is why we have not molested you."

154

importance, and preferred not to leave it. Since she was now (as far as she knew) the only wireless operator working in the Paris area, [1] if she were to quit the War Office would be left without the means of knowing what was happening in the capital. In time, she suggested, she would be able to find, and to draw around herself, new persons to form networks gradually to replace those which had been broken up, and so rebuild the circuit.

Buckmaster [2] recognized an extraordinary situation. Overnight the 'Poste-Madeleine' had become the most important wireless post in France. If 'Nora' stayed she was very likely to be captured; yet so great was the military interest in her remaining that, since she was willing to make the sacrifice, he felt, as a soldier, he should accept it.

He replied giving his consent, and suggesting only that she should not, for the present, transmit; since hers was now one of the few transmitters working in the area, all the detecting apparatus at the disposition of the Gestapo would be trained upon it. She could always receive transmissions from London, since reception could not be detected.

"SETTLING DOWN"

Of the next period of Noor's life it is difficult to write a connected history. A number of witnesses exist to testify to having seen her at different times, but the chronology is often uncertain.

During the first part of July, at any rate, she continued to stay with Madame Aigrain. Throughout the days of the great crisis, and those immediately following, she was suffering from a violent cold, or more probably influenza, and under normal circumstances should have been in bed. Despite her condition, and despite the risk, she went out continually to search for a room from which she could transmit. Her first requirement was that it should have a window giving on to trees, into which she could fix an aerial. Until she could find such a place it would be impossible to settle down to regular work.

It must have been during one of these first days that she presented herself suddenly at the door of Mademoiselle Henriette Renié, her one-time teacher of the harp, whom she had not seen for nine years.

Mademoiselle Renié says that somebody rang the bell of her

[1] In fact there was another French Section operator, Lieut. Gaston Cohen, MC, who had, like herself, been sent out to supplement the Prosper network just prior to the disaster which overtook it. He too sent intelligence of the mass arrests to London and (for a time at least) carried on. However, he and Madeleine were not informed of each other's existence. It seems that there were also some non-French Section operators still carrying on in the Paris area.

[2] This account is as given me by Colonel Buckmaster.

155

flat. She went to the door. And there was her little Noor, whom she had not seen for so many years.

Noor could be sure of Mademoiselle Renié's trust and affection, and had come to ask her if she knew of a little room to let, or a hut. The Frenchwoman debated whether she could herself offer Noor refuge. She was surprised at seeing her, whom she had known as a very quiet and timid girl, with few indications of the reserves of energy and enthusiasm which had brought her alone to Paris.

Noor said it would be impossible for her to stay with Mademoiselle Renié herself. Suddenly the Frenchwoman realized why ——Noor was afraid of bringing reprisals upon her. But why? she wondered.

"I have come to Paris to establish a wireless post for transmission to England," said Noor.

"You—but you run the risk of death, if you are discovered."

"I know. The person whom I am replacing has been shot," Noor said, in her quiet and musical voice. "In London they were looking for a young woman who spoke good French and knew Paris well. I fulfilled the conditions; I suggested myself, and here I am. I know I risk my life, since that is how most people end who do this work." Then she added, speaking more quickly, "I have been so happy to see you and give you a kiss, but I must go away at once, for I am afraid in case I am already being followed. If anybody should have seen me coming in here, and anything should happen to you ... I would not for the world bring you into any trouble." [1]

And she slipped away, with a smile, leaving Mademoiselle Renié stupefied and filled with admiration for her courage and devotion, combined with such simplicity.

The next person to see Noor was probably Madame Salmon, the married daughter of the Grutars' family, whose house in Suresnes was only a few doors from 'Fazal Manzil'.

Madame Salmon was walking in the Champs Elysées when she saw Noor passing on a bicycle. She called out, "Noor!"

Noor, who must have been startled to hear her own name ring out so loudly, stopped and came back.

She smiled when she saw Madame Salmon, but said immediately, "Let's go into a side street." As soon as they had got to a place where they could talk she explained that she had returned to France as an agent of the War Office, and was known now under the cover-name of Jeanne-Marie. Nobody, she said, amongst the persons with whom she was working, knew the name of Noor.

Madame Salmon apologized very much for having shouted out

[1] Conversation according to the recollection of Mademoiselle Renié.

156

her name in the street, and was indeed annoyed with herself for her want of thought. "It seemed, in a way, so natural to see you cycling along," she said, "that I forgot for the moment you had ever gone away, and called before I realized what you must be here for. You haven't changed at all."

Noor gave a wry little smile. She was slightly disguised in the sense that she was wearing dark glasses, and had had her hair dyed red.

"I had this done to prevent people from recognizing me," she explained pathetically. [1]

She gave the appearance of having come straight out of a hairdresser's, the hair being set still in very small and tight curls. She was wearing a simple summer frock.

She said that she had only recently arrived, and was urgently looking for a room from which she could work. Madame Salmon did not know of a room, but said she would let her know at once if she heard of one. She herself belonged to a student organization for the clandestine publication of anti-German literature, the *Mouvement de Libération Nationale*. They decided to keep in touch, since they might be able to help each other, but for reasons of mutual security, thought it better not to exchange addresses. They would always meet in cafés, agreeing upon a rendez-vous each time. They parted, arranging their first at a café on the Rond Point du Champs Elysées, which afterwards became their most frequent meeting place.

Madame Salmon dates this first meeting with Noor as about July 18th, the time when she and her husband moved into a new flat in Paris.

When she saw her next her hair was entirely blonde, and set in large waves. Madame Salmon thought she looked more normal blonde, for she might have been one of those blondes who had became burned on the Riviera—whereas with red hair and her slightly olive skin she looked like no type which nature could have produced.

It does not seem that Noor can have heeded for more than a day or two the advice she had received from London not to transmit. From the first week in July onward she was working regularly with X / Y, and Vaudevire. In this group it was arranged that she should be known as 'Rolande'. The four met several times a week all through the summer at a bench in front of the Tuileries.

Maître Y used also to take her out in his car to transmit. His memory of her was obviously founded on their first meetings, for he describes her as "a little dark girl, always carrying her machine with her and always out of breath. I never had a rendez-vous with her which she didn't come to at the run."

[1] Conversation according to the recollection of Madame Salmon.

157

He would take her out into the suburbs of Montrouge, Levallois, and Noisy, and stop the car in a quiet lane where she could let out her aerial and transmit to England.

He was the chief of an important French Resistance organization. Until recently he had had two wireless operators of his own, but had lost them both when they were arrested during the week of the grand coup. Now he found himself without a means of communicating with his chiefs in England. He explained to Noor that he wanted to work for General de Gaulle [1], and asked her whether, in return for the facilities which he offered her from his car for transmitting to her chiefs in the French Section, she would operate for him to the Headquarters of General de Gaulle in England.

She replied that she would be glad to do so; thereafter, she became virtually his operator, replacing the two he had lost, in addition to continuing the regular work of the Poste-Madeleine.

The first thing which Maître Y asked her to arrange was for money to be sent from the funds of the Free French to pay his men. She made the arrangements, forthwith, for 1,000,000 francs (about £ 1,000) to be flown and delivered to him by hand

Maître Y used to take her out on Wednesdays and Fridays, and she would transmit from 5 to 5.30. He says that Vaudevire, who also had a car, used to take her out on the other days.

With X she was in continual contact, since he was acting for the French Section.

It was now that she was doing the work which earned her a posthumous mention in despatches.

One of the first messages which she received from London was a personal one from Miss Atkins, to say that her brother had obtained his commission. Noor sent back a message showing that she was enormously relieved.

Although Y and Vaudevire would always take her out in their cars, this was an imposition upon their time, and it remained from every point of view desirable for her to become independent. She continued all the time her search for a room with a window looking on to trees.

One day, probably about the middle of July, she visited the apartment in Paris of Dr. Jourdan, before the war the family physician of the Inayat Khans, to whom she had, as a little girl, presented a climbing rose-bush in a pot. Dr. and Madame Jourdan, as well as their daughter Françoise, now sixteen, were very much moved when Noor called to see them and explained her mission.

They were not able to tell her of a room with a window giving

[1] The Free French Services under General de Gaulle and the British 'French Section' worked independently of one another.

on to trees, but they agreed at once to her using occasionally the garden of their own property at Marly-le-Roi. Here there were plenty of trees amongst which she could put up her aerial.

At Marly, the 'Noor Inayat' had grown so as now to cover the whole front of the house with a mass of pink blossoms. Noor was delighted to see how her namesake prospered. She transmitted, thinks Madame Jourdan, four or five times from their garden here.

The Jourdans found her unchanged from the Noor they had known as a child, very gentle, very feminine, very sweet. The only difference was in her hair, which was blonde when first she came to see them, and which she dyed on several occasions afterwards.

Madame Jourdan was surprised to discover the weight of *Poste* which she always had to carry. She thought that having to carry it around all the time must have been one of the reasons why Noor always looked so tired.

It was, however, at the Paris flat of the Jourdans, rather than at Marly, that Noor allowed herself to relax. This was because, when she went to Marly, it was to work. When she came to their flat in Paris it was simply to call, like an ordinary person. She said once, "My only good moments are those I spend here. Everywhere else I feel that I am being watched, and must hold myself ready to escape if the Gestapo should knock on the door." Madame Jourdan noticed that she would sometimes sink down into a chair, as though utterly exhausted, when she arrived, and then take one or two larger breaths and begin to relax, as though she had come through peril to safety.

Nearly always she brought with her a little bunch of flowers to give them. The Jourdans always associated Noor with gifts of flowers. Most often it was a little posy of roses. Roses were her favourite flowers. But sometimes it was other kinds. Once she arrived at Marly with her transmitter in one hand and a huge bouquet of gladioli in the other. Madame Jourdan protested against her spending her money in this way, and exclaimed, "But our garden is full of flowers!"

Once she brought Madame Jourdan a little model aeroplane. She said, "It was made by a British agent. [1] The Gestapo are looking for him, and, so he can't go out. He is hiding in a house until a plane can be sent to fetch him back to England. He is very bored, and makes these little things for something to do. You see, it is nicely made." It was made of wood, carefully finished, painted with green paint, and then marked like a French plane.

[1] Probably Antoine. Madame Jourdan still has the little aeroplane, and had hoped that its maker might one day recognize it.

She did not ever tell them where she was staying, and they did not think it proper to ask her. They always knew that she was looking for a room. About the middle of July she told them she had found one.

Madame Jourdois, the concierge of 3 Boulevard Richard Wallace, Neuilly-sur-Seine, recalls that it was "a gentleman with an English accent who came in to arrange about the letting of an apartment to a Mademoiselle Jeanne Regnier".

No. 3 Boulevard Richard Wallace was one of several enormous blocks of modern flats, built in some white material, facing the Bois de Boulogne. These blocks were a prominent feature of the landscape, from many angles. Noor must have been very familiar with their appearance from the old days, because coming into Paris from Suresnes, through the Bois de Boulogne, they were visible most of the way as imposing white masses behind the trees.

The apartment which she had obtained here was a minute one, consisting of one small room on the ground floor of one of the sides of the block. It was only because it was so modest that it had been possible to let it to her. The rest of the house, like Ibis next door—and indeed practically the whole of these blocks—was occupied by SS officers. In No. 3 there remained, like isolated 'pockets of resistance', one or two normal tenants. These had come in a curious way. In 1940, when the Germans first arrived, they had commandeered the whole building. Subsequently a great part of them had gone out of Paris, and permission had been given for the apartments they had vacated to be let to ordinary persons. When, later, the Germans came back again, they did not in most cases require the tenant who had come in their absence to be uprooted, but found themselves accommodation elsewhere. If, however, any of the apartments became vacant again, the Germans generally came back to them. When Noor's predecessor left his little room the Germans looked at it but considered it was too small to be of use to them for any purpose, and allowed the concierge to let it to whom she would.

It was not perhaps an ideal situation for an agent of the War Office, but Noor did not seem to mind it, and often talked about the German officers in the building to Madame Aigrain and others.

She did not give her precise address to anyone. For security reasons she told her friends only that she had found a room 'at Neuilly'. To Dr. and Madame Jourdan she gave the telephone number of this room: Sablons 80.04. [1]

[1] It was by means of this number, which Madame Jourdan gave me, that I traced the address through the Telephone Exchange, in 1950, and made contact with Madame Jourdois.

160

It does not seem that Noor intended in the first place using this room as a base for wireless transmissions. There was, indeed, a tree in front of her window, but it was growing on the pavement and was very exposed. There were, however, other purposes for which she wanted a room of her own, and it seems that she used this one mainly as a 'letter-box' where she could leave and receive messages.

Madame Jourdois and her husband were quick to realize that they had in Jeanne Regnier a strange tenant. She never slept in her room, but only came into it at certain hours during the day. It was evident to them that despite her youth and sweetness she was leading a double life. They remarked how she was always leaving letters or packets, which men would come and collect.

At first Madame Jourdois and her husband could not make her out. She seemed to have no occupation, and no relatives, and yet was obviously 'a nice girl'. She could not, they thought, be more than twenty-two or twenty-three. When she came in, or went out, she was nearly always running. They hardly ever saw her walk. She was quite friendly, and was always confiding to Madame Jourdois letters and packets to be called for by strange gentlemen, but never responded to any invitation to talk about herself.

Madame Jourdois and her husband recognized that she had an English accent—and fancied the same was true of one of the men who came to collect her packets. Madame Jourdois commented on this once or twice to her husband, without voicing the question which was in her mind. One day her husband said to her, "These people are working for *us*. And the best thing we can do is see nothing, hear nothing, understand nothing—and let them get on with it."

Shortly after this Jeanne Regnier left with her one morning an envelope, saying, "A small, very thin man, with spectacles, will call to collect it."

Later in the day a person answering this description called, and said he understood that a Mademoiselle Regnier had left an envelope for him.

For no reason, the thought occurred to Madame Jourdois, "Some Germans look like that! Suppose the real person has been killed or captured and this German has substituted himself and will go off with secret papers." She replied, "I have no envelope. No Mademoiselle Regnier lives here."

The man looked surprised and rather taken aback, but went away.

An hour or two later another man came, bearing a note in what she recognized to be the handwriting of Jeanne Regnier: *Please give to bearer the envelope which I left.*

She did not think that Jeanne Regnier would write this if she had been captured, and so she handed the note over. Jeanne Regnier said nothing to her about this afterwards, and the understanding between them remained always tacit.

Déricourt told me that the address at the Boulevard Richard Wallace was known to him. It was an adderss at which he sent some missives to Madeleine. Moreover, Déricourt later told me, it was his courier 'Claire' (Julienne Aisner, née Simart, later Besnard) who found Madeleine this flat on the Boulevard Richard Wallace. It was, he said, the flat of 'Claire's' boy-friend, Brulé, who was going away and (so Déricourt understood) introduced Madeleine to his concierge before he left as being a relative who would occupy the place in his absence. This does not absolutely match the recollection of Madame Jourdois that it was a man with an English accent who introduced her, yet Déricourt could be a little wrong about what he only understood from Claire, without the whole of what he says being wrong. With Déricourt, it is always necessary to bear in mind that he was a "double" and that it was often in his interest to lie. "There are two kinds of lying: lying to be believed and lying not to be believed. When I lie to you, I try to do it in such a fashion I say to myself it is impossible you could believe me. And so I don't lie. If you believe it is your own fault." Even bearing in mind the disarming frankness with which he warned me I must learn to sift the truth from the fiction in what he told me—"Never believe me farther than you think you should"—I do not always find it easy. I can make some obvious discards, yet much of what he told me I have later found to be correct, and there are points at which I hesitate. Claire, he told me, later found Madeleine another flat, on the corner of the rue Berlioz and rue Pergolèse.

Noor never, however, lived at the Boulevard Richard Wallace. She was probably still living in the flat of Madam Aigrain, who had developed a protective, motherly feeling for her. 'Antoine' was there, too. In July, according to Miss Atkins, they were both sent out on a temporary mission to the country. This probably relates to their visit to Robert Benoist, at his parents' villa at Auffargis, near Rambouillet. He worked with a Captain Williams, who had lost his radio operators, and was therefore in need of contact with London. Williams' widow, the sole survivor, remembers Noor and 'Antoine' clearly.

Noor and 'Antoine' can only have stayed with the Benoists for a few days.

Immediately after they had left a raid was made on the villa of the Benoists by the Sicherheitsdienst from Paris, and Benoist, and Benoist's lame brother, Maurice.[1] and their parents and Williams,[2] were arrested, Robert narrowly evading capture.

It was as a result of this raid, in which many papers were captured, that Ernest of the Sicherheitsdienst learned for the first time of the existence of Madeleine, whom he was later to get to know so well.

Lise de Baissac and 'Denise' had been the first two women to be parachuted into the field, eleven months earlier and Lise de Baissac was now the longest surviving woman agent from London.[1] She had been working in the Poitiers area, but met Noor when she came up to Paris in connection with the arrangements for the massive evacuation; and she made a statement for me:

"I met Madeleine and 'Antoine' in front of a café on the Place des Ternes. Madeleine was wearing a light summer frock. She made on me the impression of a Madonna in an Italian painting— with her large, soft eyes and oval face."

Madeleine stayed only a few minutes, but after she had gone, 'Antoine' said to Miss de Baissac, as the latter remembers, "She is really wonderful. In the whole of Paris, she is the only operator working, and all the arrangements for this operation have gone through the Poste-Madeleine. Nobody here is able to understand how she keeps it up."

On 19 July, 'Antoine' was flown back to London.

II

Either at the end of July, or at the beginning of August, Noor took the very dangerous step of revisiting Suresnes.

The risk was enormous. In this suburb, where she had grown up, where she had lived from her childhood until 1940, everybody knew her—the more so, because the Inayat Khans were a conspicuous family. All the tradespeople knew them, as well as many of the families in the houses on the hill. Everybody knew that when the Inayat Khans had left in 1940 it had been to go to England; and nobody could fail to recognize Noor on her return. Many of the younger people had, as children, formed part

---

[1] Robert Benoist himself escaped for the moment and went to England. On his return he was met on the field by the waiting Germans who had replaced the French who were to receive him. Executed in Germany.

[2] Executed in Germany; his widow, who was arrested a month later, survives.

of the circle which used to gather around her when she told them stories from Indian scriptures or from her father's teachings.

To return here was to trust that there was not one single soul who would earn the money the Germans would pay for her betrayal.

She climbed the hill and walked straight up the rue de la Tuilerie, almost to the gate of 'Fazal Manzil'. Then she turned into the smaller road which flanked its garden, the rue de l'Hippodrome, and knocked on the door of the little white villa of the Pinchon family.

She was wearing dark glasses, her hair was dyed blonde, and waved, and she was brightly made-up. As usual, she was carrying her black case.

Madame Pinchon answered the door, and gasped, "Babuly!"

She explained her mission at once. "I have come as an agent of the War Office, to act as liaison between London and the Forces of Resistance in France, with a view to the Invasion."

Madame Pinchon gasped, "You!"

"I have come to establish a wireless post."

They were still standing on the step. Madame Pinchon brought her in hastily, in case anybody passing should hear. She went on explaining in the hall and the sitting-room: "What I am looking for is a house with a garden, where I can put up an aerial and establish a regular post. I thought that perhaps you would allow me to use yours. I have my transmitter with me now. You see, it is made up to look like a suitcase."

Madame Pinchon explained to her that the garden of their house was overlooked from two sides by premises commandeered by the Germans. "'Fazal Manzil' has been taken as a barracks." She saw Noor wince. "And the big house at the end of this road is also full of German soldiers."

Noor did not seem immediately to be impressed by the unsuitability of the situation. She said, a little plaintively, "There are trees in your garden. I could put up an aerial ever so inconspicuously."

Madame Pinchon refused. "It's impossible, Noor! This is not the place for your wireless post. You know yourself that from the side windows of 'Fazal Manzil' you can see right into our garden."

This reference to the view from the windows of her old home seemed to affect Noor. She exclaimed, "I must have a look at 'Fazal Manzil' from your back-window."

Madame Pinchon was not very anxious for her to look from the back-window. She said, "The soldiers might wonder why you were staring at the house, and perhaps they would come round and ask who you were."

Noor pleaded. "Oh, please! I only just want a peep."

She wheedled so much that eventually Madame Pinchon allowed her to go into the back sitting-room, where she crept to a position just behind the curtain. There she stood for a long time, gazing across the back gardens at the house where she had spent her childhood. Madame Pinchon felt that it was the house which had drawn her back.

When she could at last persuade Noor from the window she brought her again into the front sitting-room, and made her sit down whilst she went to the kitchen and made some tea.

When she returned with it, and sat down to pour out, Noor said, "Of course, my mother does not know that I am here. None of my family know where I am. If I am killed, I do not want my mother ever to know that I have been to Suresnes. It would upset her very much to know that I have been back here. She might feel it was because of the house. Will you promise me never to tell her I have been to see you, or that you know I have been in Suresnes?" Madame Pinchon promised.

Noor relaxed a little and showed her her French identity card, which she explained had been forged in London. Madame Pinchon read the name Jeanne-Marie Regnier, which she committed to memory. She saw that the birth-place of this person was given as Bordeaux. Later Noor commented on this.

"I have obtained a little room at Neuilly," she said, "and I am wondering whether, since I have become a tenant I shall have to register at the Town Hall."

Madame Pinchon was not certain, but thought that she would.

Noor was distressed to hear this. "I don't like having to do it," she said. "I don't like having to present this card. It says I was born in Bordeaux, and I don't know Bordeaux. Perhaps I should take a trip there first, and have a look round the town, in case they should ask me questions about it."

She said she was very glad to have got the room at Neuilly. It made her feel independent, and was useful for some purposes, though not for wireless transmission: "I need trees."

Madame Pinchon said she was sorry to have to send her away. "But you can see that this is not the place for you. Is it not imprudent of you to have come at all to Suresnes, where everybody knows you, and where it is full of soldiers?"

"I don't mind soldiers," Noor answered unexpectedly. "I don't feel them as hostile. It is only the Gestapo whom I feel as enemies."

Madame Pinchon suggested that if she were bent upon establishing a post in Suresnes she should try calling on Madame Prénat, whose house was a little less near to any barracks.

Noor said she had already thought of that, and would do so as soon as she had finished her cup of tea.

This visit, says Madame Pinchon, was on a Thursday; but she cannot say on what date. It was in the morning.

She herself never saw Noor again, though her husband saw her once cycling along the Champs Elysées. She did not see him, and he did not stop her.

It seems that immediately after leaving the Pinchon's house Noor called at the home of the Vanlaère family, also in the rue de l'Hippodrome, only a few doors away. Here she learned, however, to her disappointment, that Geneviève was still living away.

It was probably only a few minutes after she had left the rue de l'Hippodrome that Noor arrived at the Prénats' house, a little farther up the hill.[1] Madame Prénat answered the door.

She was surprised, and yet not surprised, to see Noor. What affected her most was that Noor went into the house in such a natural way. She walked straight into the sitting-room, as though she were entering her own house and had been out for an afternoon. It was as though she had been living just round the corner all the time, and not that she had been to England and come back again.

Noor put down her case, explained that it was a wireless transmitter, and said she would like to make transmissions from here if Madame Prénat would allow her.

Madame Prénat found herself agreeing to the use of her house as a base for wireless transmission, as though this were something perfectly normal and to be expected. It was as though she had become infected with Noor's naturalness. Noor had obviously never considered for a moment that she might meet with a rebuff. Within a few minutes of her arrival they were going over the house together, estimating the relative advantages and disadvantages of all the different rooms. Noor decided, after they had completed the tour, that the front living-room would really be the most suitable, and said she would install her transmitter on the dining-table. Without more ado, she lifted it up and put it there.

Then she said, "Will you please give me some clothes-pegs? I shall take the aerial through to the back garden, and hang it up between two trees. If I am carrying a basket of clothes-pegs, anybody who sees me will think I am helping you put up a line for the washing."

She showed Madame Prénat the aerial. It was extremely fine, and painted leaf-green, so that it did not show when it had been put up amongst the leaves.

When Noor had fixed the aerial to her satisfaction they came back into the living-room and experimented with the curtains.

1 Conservations in this chapter taken down from Madame Prénat and Raymonde, according to their recollections.

They found a way of drawing them so that Noor, seated at her transmitter, could see the front-garden gate, through a slight space left between them, without being herself visible from the outside.

"If you see anybody come while you are working," said Madame Prénat, "just get up and run out at the back. Don't worry about your machine. I'll pack it up and push it somewhere."

As soon as Noor was ready to work, she went out and left her in peace.

The 'tick-tack' was naturally audible throughout the house. She reflected, however, that as the houses were detached it was probably not audible in those on either side.

Later in the afternoon, when Noor had finished her work, they had tea, and Noor told her the history of her family and herself since they left Suresnes in 1940.

Raymonde was away from home at the time of Noor's first visit. On her return she was filled with emotion at meeting again her closest friend of the years gone by. She was very happy indeed to see her, and be able to talk as in the old days; at the same time, she was very frightened for her.

Noor transmitted at different hours, sometimes in the afternoons at five o'clock, but sometimes also between 2 a.m. and 3 a.m. In either case, she used generally to come at about mid-day and spend the rest of the day with them. Madame Prénat liked to see her eat a good lunch and dinner on these occasions, as she suspected that she did not feed herself very well. One day Noor brought as an offering two fresh eggs, which she said had been given her by a friend who had a house in the country.

She never informed them in advance when she intended coming. She would just arrive with her machine. Madame Prénat told her that if they should be out when she came she should install herself just the same. On one or two occasions she informed them she had transmitted in their absence.

She expressed herself as very satisfied with the conditions for transmission and reception at their house. "At Grignon," she told Madame Prénat, "they had devoted infinite pains to obtaining the proper conditions, and yet the interference was sometimes so much that I could not hear a thing. But up here, there is the most perfect silence."

She told them the story of her escape from Grignon, on the afternoon when she had called to find it occupied by the SS.

Raymonde, unlike her mother, used always to stay in the room with Noor whilst she was transmitting and receiving. Noor showed her her machine, explaining that it was a transmitter and a receiver, made in one. The case, says Raymonde, was 'wonderfully arranged' inside, with pockets for all kinds of parts, and even for small personal belongings.

One Sunday afternoon, Noor asked her if she would like to assist in deciphering the messages she received from London. She explained her code. Raymonde was surprised to learn what a very slow and complicated business it was to decode a message.

Raymonde never knew any of the detail of Noor's work. Although she helped to decipher these messages, their purport remained obscure to her even when they had been reduced to plain language. She never knew, either, the names of any of the persons with whom Noor worked; Noor said that most often she herself did not know their real names, but only their code-names and their cover-names. These precautions were all for additional security.

"If ever you meet me outside," she said, "call me 'Jeannette'"

Sometimes she would put up her aerial from the roof. Raymonde, who watched her climb, was amazed. "She was like a cat. She climbed with such a suppleness, and moved along the gutters so quickly and with such a sure balance."

It was the nocturnal transmissions which Raymonde felt as the most frightening. Because of the silence of the night, they would draw the shutters as well as the curtains, and then fill up all the cracks with towels and blankets, and seal themselves in as nearly hermetically as possible. But sitting in the room, the 'tick-tack' sounded so appallingly loud that it would bring her heart into her mouth.

Noor told her a little about her training in England. She said that she had been arrested once by a police constable on the charge of being an agent operating for the Germans, taken to the local constabulary, and questioned. She had been very embarrassed to explain herself out of it without giving away too much about the school. "Afterwards" she said "I learned that the whole thing had been 'framed' as a test. I passed it, and they let me come to France."

Raymonde was always oppressed by the thought of what might happen to Noor if she were caught. "I am so terribly afraid," she said, "that they will torture you to obtain information."

"If I am caught," Noor replied, "I shall have great suffering."

Raymonde was awed, as she said this, by the quietness and calmness of her voice.

Noor did not avoid discussing this subject. Talking to Madame Prénat once, she said that she had been told the Gestapo had a house in Paris where members of the Resistance who were captured were plunged into ice-cold baths,[1] and in some cases kept in

1 Plunging in cold baths was certainly carried out in the rue des Saussaies, the rue de la Pompe, and elsewhere (whether there was any experimental side to it I have never heard). In general the members of French Section were spared the more bestial kinds of treatment to which members of the 'RF' and Resistance were subjected. Déricourt told me he was fascinated to learn from my book (in its first edition) that Madeleine knew about duckings in cold baths. He made the point

cold water for long periods whilst a doctor in attendance made observations, for the purposes of medical research, on their physical resistance. She could not know if this was true, but tossed her head slightly and said, "It doesn't matter! They can do what they like with me. I don't mind. I shan't tell them anything."

Madame Prénat says she never had the slightest doubt that this was true, "I knew Noor-un-nisa, and I knew she would keep her word."

Raymonde and her mother both used to feel that Noor ran a very big risk in coming to Suresnes, where everybody knew her. "All the shop people[1] must recognize you, and all the families who have houses on the rue de la Tuilerie, or in the roads near."

Madame Prénat remembers that Noor smiled at her most serenely. "Of course they all know me," she exclaimed. "And they know what I come to do, too. But I don't mind. There is nobody here who would give me away. No one in Suresnes would betray me."

Then, as though to assure them, she added: "But I always make wide detours after crossing the river so as not to bring the Gestapo out from Paris into this place. I always feel safe in Suresnes. I do not even mind the soldiers who are stationed up here. I do not feel them as hostile."

One day she said, "The day that I am followed, I shall know it."

Raymonde did not immediately understand: "Do you mean you think you know what they look like?"

Noor shook her head and explained that she felt herself to be developing a kind of sixth sense by which she knew when she was in danger. Her first experience which had made her think this had

that these did not belong to the domain of public knowledge until after the war. For him, it meant that Madeleine had been, unawares, in conversation with some member of the Bony-Lafont gang who had to do with these. He, himself, had been charged with relations not only with the Germans but with members of this gang of French traitors, who (doubtless in the hope of saving themselves from the death penalty) had made very full statements to the DST before their conviction and execution, from which it appeared, amongst other things, that they had had the job of trailing agents arriving by Lysanders at the field near Angers where they were received by Déricourt. While I might think what I liked about that, he was very sure he never talked to Madeleine about cold baths, and passionately wanted to know who did. Some member of that gang not only trailed her but spoke with her, pretending to be a member of the Resistance, and mentioned these baths, momentarily oblivious that only a member of the gang would know; of that he felt certain.

[1] Madame Pinchon tells me that the laundress, Madame Ruffin, of the laundry in the rue de la Tuilerie, just above 'Fazal Manzil', told her after the war that she had met Noor-un-nisa in the summer of 1943. Madame Ruffin said, "You know that she returned here and worked as a spy all through the summer." I was not able to establish contact with Madame Ruffin. She was out on the occasions when I called, and did not reply when I wrote. I have thought that Noor may have bound her under a promise of secrecy, as she did other people, and can only respect her continued honouring of it.

been at Grignon. "The place was occupied by SS," she said, "on that day; but I did not see anything of them immediately. I just *felt* they were there, and withdrew. Afterwards I realized it was correct." Since then, she said, she had trusted in this sense to warn her when she was walking into danger, and was sure it would not let her down. "I shall know as soon as I am in danger. I shall feel it. I know there is no danger in Suresnes."

"It was," says Raymonde, "as if she had antennae." Raymonde wondered whether the teaching she had received from her father had not conduced to the development of this intuition.

Noor became really agitated only when she spoke of her mother. She hated to think that her mother might suffer any anxiety about her. In case she should be killed, she asked Raymonde and Madame Prénat never to tell any member of her family that they had seen her, or knew that she had been back to Suresnes during the German occupation.

"I died for my country," she said. "That is all I wish should be made known. My mother's health[1] could not support anything in the nature of details."

She explained this a little more, saying, "It will be a very great shock to her to learn that I am dead; but I think it is better she should not know how it happened, or any of the history which led up to it. If she knew I had been back here it would provide a point upon which her imagination could focus. She would go over and over it in her mind, and perhaps feel that it was because we had lived here that I had come back. The letter of notification which she receives from the War Office will be quite impersonal, and short, and it is better it should rest at that."

Noor told Raymonde and her mother that she had a room in one of the big white blocks on the Boulevard Richard Wallace. To nobody else did she give so precise an indication of where it was. She did not mention that she used it only as a depôt, and they supposed that she lived there.

One day Noor told Raymonde a story which terrified her. She said that she had had urgent reason to transmit in the evening. Rather than come up to Suresnes so late she had decided to take the risk of working from her room on the Boulevard Richard Wallace, and to use the tree which grew on the pavement in front of her window. It was dusk, and she hoped nobody would notice her going out. She installed her transmitter on the table, opened

1 Only because the Begum had died did the Prénats speak to me of Noor's visit, which they had not mentioned even to the Inayat Khan family during the five years since the war, so strong was their loyalty to Noor. Even so Madame Prénat said, "If you had not seen Raymonde first, if you had come to me and asked if Noor-un-nisa had been here during the war, I should have said 'No'." Naturally, only since the Begum's death in 1949, has it been possible to write this biography.

the window, and dropped the aerial out, then went out herself, picked it up, and carried it over to the tree which grew on the outside of the pavement next to the kerb. The branches were rather high, and she had to stretch up on tip-toe in order to take hold of it and fix the aerial at the same time. She was wrestling with leaves and twigs and the aerial when she heard a step just behind her. Her heart almost stopped. She heard herself addressed.

"Mademoiselle!"

She spun round and saw, standing in the gloaming, one of the German officers who lived in the building.

He asked, "May I help you?"

Mastering her astonishment, Noor replied, in as level a voice as she could produce, "Thank you. I should be glad if you would."

She handed him the aerial. He took it without a word, and fixed it into the branches of the tree.

Then he bowed slightly, said, "At your service, Mademoiselle," and turned and went into the house.

Noor, trembling a little, went in also, after him, and regaining her room, immediately began her transmission to London.

Raymonde was petrified by this story. Not only was she horrified, she could not understand it. "Why did he help you? Why didn't he arrest you?"

"He must have thought I was using it for entertainment purposes only."

"But people aren't allowed to use a wireless—even for entertainment."

"I know. But I expect some people *do,* despite the regulation. He probably thought I wanted it just to listen to music—or even to listen to the BBC. He decided to be sporting about it. After all, he would never think I could be an agent transmitting to London—in such a place and in such an open manner!"

"But you will leave?" urged Raymonde. "You can't stay there after such a thing. He is perhaps only giving you rope to hang yourself, and will watch you now to see everything you do."

But Noor did not think this was the case, and would not be persuaded to leave. She said she was very comfortably established in that room, and laughed gaily.

She had one other dreadful adventure, which she recounted to Madame Aigrain, to Dr. and Madame Jourdan and to Raymonde and Madame Prénat.

She was travelling in the Metro, and carrying, as usual, her transmitter in its black case when she became aware that two German soldiers, standing a little farther along, were scrutinizing both it and her. There was no way for her to get out until the train came to the next station, and she felt hot and cold all over.

She saw them speak to each other, obviously about her, and

171

presently they both came up and one of them asked her gruffly, "What have you in that case, Mademoiselle?"

She replied, "A cinematographic apparatus."

There was a moment's pause, then he asked, still suspiciously, "May I see it?"

She replied, "Certainly." Terribly conscious of the beating of her own heart, she undid the locks and raised the lid slightly.

He could not, perhaps, see the whole of the machine, since as she was holding the lid, it still cast a shadow.

He stood looking at it, and his companion also. She realized they did not understand the parts which were visible to them. She said, with a slightly impatient edge to her voice. "Well, you can see what it is. You can see all the little bulbs."

Still they both stood looking at it. At last he said, "Excuse me, Mademoiselle. I thought it might have been something else."

Noor was almost hilarious when she recounted this to Raymonde and her mother. "The great thing," she said, "is not to lose one's head if anything like that happens. I knew that only somebody who was familiar with wireless would be sure of what it was. You see, he thought at first it was a transmitter, but he didn't know what he should expect it to look like, because he had never seen one. And then he didn't like to expose his ignorance, and so my bluff succeeded!"

She lived perpetually on the *qui vive*. She was leaving them once at about eleven o'clock in the evening, wearing only a grey tailor-made, and as it was raining slightly Raymonde offered her the loan of a waterproof cape.

She shook her head. "It would be better not. If I should find I was being followed and have to run I should have to throw it off. It would hinder me. I cannot have anything which would hinder me in running."

Raymonde was able to persuade her to accept a navy blue scarf, which she could wrap round her head like a turban. Watching her twist it up over her forehead, she was struck by her profile, as though she had never seen it before. She exclaimed, "When I see you in a turban, I realize that you are an Indian. It is extraordinary how it brings out the features."

Noor smiled.

III

For the August moon, a massive or double aerial operation was being organised. Colonel Buckmaster's second in command, Major Nicholas Bodington, and his wireless operator, Major Agazarian, had been landed by the July moon, with a mission to investigate the extent of the 'Prosper' disaster. Agazarian had already been

172

arrested, but Bodington, who Déricourt—who had received them both—kept under the same roof as himself, was to be picked up in August. During the time that he had been with Déricourt, as he was later to witness in court, Déricourt had confided to him that he had relations with the Germans; he therefore understood that Déricourt was playing a skilful double game, but had confidence in him. Together with Bodington, were to go back 'Antoine'. Benoist, Lise and Claude de Baissac and a number of other agents of importance.

One would have thought this was the massive evacuation concerning which Lise de Baissac came to speak with Noor, as Déricourt's radio contact with London. But then she could not have spoken just afterwards with 'Antoine'. Actually Déricourt told me that 'Antoine' went back by the August moon, with the de Baissacs, but this is not so. I wrote my earlier books solely from information pieced together from those who had taken part in these operations, having no access to official records. In 1973, however, the late Baroness Ward prevailed upon the Parliamentary Under-Secretary for the Foreign Office to allow for me to put some questions to Colonel E.G. Boxshall, which he would endeavour to answer from their files.

To the best of my knowledge, I am, apart from Professor Foot, the only author to whom this privilege has been granted. Colonel Boxshall told me 'Antoine' was brought back to London by Lysander on the night bridging 19/20 July. On 15/16 August, Bodington and the de Baissacs were brought back by Lysander, and on 18/20 August, ten people by a Hudson. The July operation was from Soucelles, the August ones from Pont-de-Braye and Soucelles again. On 12 September, 1973, Rémy Clément drove me to see all the fields on which he had assisted Déricourt with these operations.

Why did 'Antoine' not insist on Noor's returning with him to England and safety? He was her direct chief in the field. Moreover, they had become personally attached. This is a delicate matter, which I did not mention in the earlier editions of this book in case it caused pain to anyone who was attached to either of them. Yet the omission has caused some to reproach me with having left out an important part of the story. Moreover, I have been assured of it by so many people—

[1] Baroness Ward remarked to me that the award to Lise de Baissac after the war, for this and a subsequent mission, of an M.B.E. seems pitifully inadequate. See **F.A.N.Y. Invicta,** Irene Ward (Hutchinson, 1955), p. 217. The French awarded Lise de Baissac a Croix de Guerre.

including Déricourt—that I am forced to consider it. After all, she and the Mauritian Major had been thrown together from the moment of her arrival. First of all, they were both in the Garrys' flat. When that was raided, they both took refuge in Madame Aigrain's flat. Together they went under Déricourt's escort down to Angers for the July moon, with Benoist; together they came back with Benoist and stayed with him in his home until that was raided; and then together they went back to Madame Aigrain's — for Noor only used the room at the Boulevard Richard Wallace for an occasional address. Had no bond of sympathy and affection formed between the fugitives, it would almost have been unnatural. Some of their friends thought they intended, after the war, to marry. Yet Noor had, just before leaving London, become unofficially engaged to someone who was going to be sent to Norway, and 'Antoine' had, though nobody in the Resistance seems to have known it, a wife, a very long way away, and also a very serious attachment of the heart to London. It may have been a sense of duty, in more senses than one, which decided Noor to remain at her post, letting the Channel divide them.

After the war, I was in conversation with an officer of the Sûreté (D.S.T.) when he said to me that one of the mysteries of the 'French Section' was why Madeleine did not go back with 'Antoine'. Why had not 'Antoine' taken her with him? She would have wanted to be in London with him. Her having remained in France seemed to him not only against common sense but against nature. I told him of her previous attachment to someone who was being sent to Norway. He thought about this deeply for a moment; then said, "If this was serious, it could have been in order *not* to be with 'Antoine' in London that she remained."

It was probably in the mailbags carried back by the August moon that three letters by Noor, to her mother, to Vilayat and to Miss Atkins travelled. The one to her mother is remembered by Ernest of the Sicherheitsdienst as having been photocopied by the Gestapo, and one need not doubt that the other two little letters were similarly treated. To let the Germans borrow the mail which would be carried on the aircraft was almost certainly part of the price Déricourt had to pay for being allowed to put so many major agents on home-bound aircraft.[1]

I do not find the letter to her mother amongst the papers Vilayat passed to me.

[1] Ernest, in a handwritten statement which he made for me at his home, on November 13th, 1954 (quoted in full in my **Double Webs** [Putnam, 1958], pp. 41-43), stated that "Gilbert" [Déricourt] was permitted by the Germans to receive and despatch British aircraft without interference in return for keeping them informed of the time and place of operations and lending them the mail, so that they could photo-

The letter to Miss Atkins, [1] which is written in pencil on grey paper, and is undated, reads:

> Dear Miss Atkins,
>   Your bird has brought me luck!
>   I remember you so often cheered me up so sweetly before I left. Lots of things have happened, and I haven't been able to settle down properly. Still my contacts have started to be regular, and I'm awfully happy. The news [2] is marvellous, and I hope we shall soon be celebrating! In fact, I owe you a date!
>
> Lots of love,
Yours,
Nora.
>
> (Excuse pencil)

Her letter to Vilayat is also undated:

> Box 574, GPO,
Wimpole Street, W.1
>
> Brother dearest,
>   Do let me know about yourself. I was so disappointed not to have been with you on your birthday—it is more than your birthday anyway, a day we shall never forget and never regret.
>   And now you will be in your new uniform—I am longing to see you. When will that be, I wonder?
>   I expect you are frightfully busy at present. I feel so awfully proud of you. I guess I will be quite conceited soon.
>   Till we meet again, brother dear. Such a lot of things we shall have to tell each other. Good luck to you and tally ho! [3]
>
> Babuly.

"Such a lot of things we shall have to tell each other." Rarely perhaps have such simple words, written from a sister to a brother, covered such startling matters. The whole little letter becomes

---

copy it, before it was put aboard. Déricourt, though considerably vexed by Ernest's statement, which I brought to Paris for him to read in the original, in 1957, at least agreed, significantly, that there was absolute certainty no one would be arrested while being taken by him to board an aircraft.

[1] Kindly given me by Miss Atkins.

[2] The North African victories, and invasion of Sicily by the Allies.

[3] 'Tally ho!' was the word which Vilayat's flying instructor used to give to the 'boys' in training before they went up. Vilayat says that it had sometimes been used between him and his sister as a word of encouragement when either of them was embarking upon some new adventure.

almost unbearably poignant when read in the light of the terrible background against which it was written. For despite everything, and despite the enthusiasm of the letter to Miss Atkins, written upon the crest of General Montgomery's victories, now that the last English-speaking person had departed Noor must have felt a little desolate. For she, through whom all the arrangements for the evacuation had been made, was now the only British officer in the Paris field.

In August, also, Dr. and Madame Jourdan went out of Paris for a month to give the children a holiday in the country, and so Noor's circle was further depleted. To Madame Jourdan she wrote a simple letter, as little suggestive as the others of the desperate action in which she was engaged. It is undated, and in French.

> My dear Madame Jourdan,
> So happy to receive your letter. A thousand thanks! I hope the frightful rain we are having here is not spoiling the beautiful country at Florac. Thanks for the card also! Don't worry about me. I am very well. Everything is going well, moreover, and you will find me looking much better on your return. I hope to see Françoise and (illegible) with beautiful rosy cheeks, and well browned too. Give them a kiss for me.
> My most affectionate regards to you, Madame, as well as to the dear Doctor.
>
> Jeanne.
>
> P.S.—I shall have such a lot to tell you when you come back!

On August 15th, the same day that Antoine left, the Garrys returned to Paris from Le Mans, and their reappearance on the scene must have contributed in some measure to relieve Noor's feeling of isolation after the big operation, and to preserve a sense of continuity.

Lieutenant and Madame Garry now took a furnished apartment in Neuilly—not very far, therefore, from Noor. Garry's sister Renée still lived with them.

Noor became a frequent visitor at the Garrys' flat. Between the young couple and herself there had always existed a natural sympathy. Both the Garrys had the greatest admiration for Jeanne-Marie.

Lieutenant Garry, now that he had returned to Paris, was, like X, dependent upon the Post-Madeleine for his communications with London. These generally concerned, on his side, specifications as to the types and quantities of arms, explosives, and other commodities required by different networks of the French Resistance, and on the London side, notification where the parachute cargoes would be dropped. Frequently there would be some discussion concerning the matters, and the Post-Madeleine was kept working steadily. If any important acts of sabotage had been carried out the Poste-Madeleine would also inform London, as it would receive any instructions regarding sabotage to be attempted.

As Madeleine had to call frequently at the Garrys', for the purpose of consultation and arrangement, she sometimes used their rooms in Neuilly for receiving and transmitting, also, since it was possible to dispose of an aerial from their window. Madame Garry used often to sit with her whilst she was doing this work and assist her in deciphering the messages she received from London. They enjoyed these hours together, and discussed many things. Madame Garry was touched to discover how Jeanne-Marie (who, doubtless, was sensible in her turn of the sweetness of her friend's character) considered her happiness in the difficult conditions under which they were all living, and attempted in some ways to shield her.

Although she had now these places from which to transmit, Noor needed yet another. This was because it had always to be supposed that the wireless transmission-detecting machines at the disposition of the Gestapo were trained upon her operations. These machines were installed in cars which used to patrol the streets very slowly. The only thing which protected the wireless operator from discovery by them was that they could only indicate, in the first instance, the general area from which the transmission was emanating; then, as the car neared the spot, a slow process was involved of fining down the search to the more precise district, the street, and the house. If the transmission did not last for more than half an hour, this would probably be insufficient to allow a detecting car to trace the point of emanation. Nevertheless, if an operator worked continually from one locality the detectors could gradually come to define it more and more precisely. For this reason it was always desirable for a wireless operator to change his place of operation as often as possible. Noor had operated now from Marly-le-Roi, from Suresnes, from her room in Neuilly, from the Garrys' rooms in Neuilly, as well as from various places to which Y and Vaudevire had taken her out in their cars. Still, she had worked perhaps too much at some of these places, and it behoved her to find another.

It was Vaudevire who introduced her (at what date is uncertain) to Madame Peineau, having arranged beforehand with this lady that she should allow Noor the use of her house for wireless transmissions. Madame Peineau was the half-proprietress, with a Monsieur Durand, of a small iron-foundry in Bondy, an industrial suburb to the east of Paris.

Madame Peineau agreed not only that 'Jeanne-Marie' might use her house as a regular base for transmission, but also that she might sleep there, in the front bedroom, and thus be spared a

177

long journey back to Paris in the evening. The house was situated at the end of a quiet cul-de-sac, and nobody, said Madame Peineau, would notice her comings and goings.

After this a new regime began for Noor, more regular than any she had enjoyed before. She would arrive at Madame Peineau's house every afternoon shortly before 5, install her machine on the table in the kitchen, and work from 5 until about 5.30. Once, when she exceeded the normal time, and transmitted for three-quarters of an hour without stopping, the machine became so hot that it scorched the kitchen-table. [1] Then she would come into the living-room, seat herself at the *escritoire,* and begin deciphering straight away the message she had received from London. Whilst she was doing this Madame Peineau would be preparing the supper in the kitchen. When ready, she would bring it in and set it on the dining-table so that Jeanne-Marie could sit down to it as soon as she had finished her deciphering. She took care always to put a good plate in front of her, and to insist upon her eating it. She suspected that Jeanne-Marie did not eat very much at any other time.

"When do you eat during the day?" she asked once.

"When I have time."

"And I suppose you allow yourself five minutes?"

After they had finished the meal they would sit talking for a little while, and then Noor would go early to bed. She had the bedroom just over the living-room. She would set her alarm for an early hour, and after a brief breakfast would be gone from the house by 7 in the morning.

On the first morning when she came downstairs Madame Peineau scolded her. *"Ma petite,* what do you think you left on the kitchen-table last night? Your note-book, containing all your decoded messages—lying flat open!"

Jeanne-Marie apologized, but said, "I didn't think anybody went into the kitchen, that's why I didn't trouble."

"What do you mean, you didn't think anybody went into it? *I* go into it!"

"You?"

"Yes. What reason have you to suppose that I am to be trusted?"

Thus taxed, Jeanne-Marie was a little perplexed, and stammered, "Well, I—I was introduced to you by Monsieur Vaudevire."

"Ma petite, you are very wrong. How do you know that Monsieur Vaudevire is not mistaken in me? That I am not a German agent? I might be a double-agent. I might be appearing to Vaudevire and to Y to be working in their network and yet be

[1] Madame Peineau has shown me the mark, with pride and sentiment.

doing this, in fact, as a spy for the Germans. How do you know that this is not so? You do not know. And therefore you should regard me with suspicion, and conduct yourself, when in my house, as though you were in a place where you might be under observation by the enemy. And in such a place you would never allow any of your papers out of your sight for an instant."

As Jeanne-Marie was still looking confused, she said in a more motherly way, "*Petite,* there are some things which I must tell you. You must never trust *anybody*. It does not matter how good are the credentials with which they have been presented to you. Sometimes it is the person to whom you have been introduced with the best testimony by the most reliable member of your own organization, who is a double-agent. It is the person who is closest to you, and whom you would least suspect in the world who is the traitor. That is why, even with those with whom you are working the most intimately, you must never disclose any information beyond the minimum which is necessary for the conduct of operations. This is a discipline which we have to learn in our relations—and it does not harm them. Let it be so, also, between us. Believe me, it is better."[1]

Then she added, "Even for myself, and for my own protection, I am not happy that this note-book should have lain in a place where I could have seen it whilst you were not present."

Despite—or perhaps because of, this beginning, the two became firm friends. "I felt to her," says Madame Peineau, "as if she were my own child."

On the first evening when Jeanne-Marie had come in, Madame Peineau, remembering that she was an English girl, and thinking to make her at home, had made some tea. Whilst she was pouring it out, Jeanne-Marie had exclaimed suddenly, "Oh, you pour out tea just like my mother. It is so nice to see you!"

She discovered that Jeanne-Marie was very fond of her mother. One day she came in very happy and excited because she had received (perhaps by a 'plane at the September moon) a letter from her. She was clutching it, and kept on reading it over and over again, and in the end she must have known it by heart. She said, "It is so wonderful to see her writing. It feels quite incredible to be receiving a letter from her here." She explained that her mother thought she was in North Africa. With the letter was also a tin of sardines. Jeanne-Marie was so affected by the thought that these had been bought and packed up by her mother that she could hardly bring herself to eat them; she seemed inclined to keep them intact because they were something which had come from her mother.

1 Conversation as dictated to me by Madame Peineau, from her memory.

She told Madame Peineau her true name was 'Nora Baker' and that she lived in Taviton Street, London. She said that her brother was in the Navy, her sister in the Army, and her fiancé also in the Army. She said that she had said good-bye to him in London a few days before she came to France, and that if she came alive out of the war they were going to be married when she returned to England. She seemed quite sure they were going to be happy, and told Madame Peineau, who felt he must have been very nice, how she used to look forward to the things they would do together.

She wore under her blouse a small, greyish-white stone on a string. When Madame Peineau asked her what it was she replied, "It's a talisman. It will keep me safe and bring me luck." [1]

To Madame Peineau Noor seemed a most lovable and wonderful girl, an extraordinarily hard worker, extremely conscientious, and devoted to her duty, even when she was physically exhausted. She could never bear to fail in the smallest obligation or let anybody down.

It was unfortunate for her, in one way, that Bondy, a suburb to the east of Paris, was so far from Neuilly, to the west. From the Pont de Neuilly—the nearest Metro station to the Boulevard Richard Wallace—to the Eglise de Pantin was a journey of twenty-nine stations, with a change at Bastille; and from the Eglise de Pantin it was necessary to take a bus to Bondy. As she continued to keep all her personal effects in the room on the Boulevard Richard Wallace, she was obliged to make this journey twice in every twenty-four hours. And if, from Neuilly, she went on to Suresnes to see Raymonde and her mother she had to take a further bus from the Pont de Neuilly.

Sometimes, says Madame Peineau, she would be so tired that her eyelids would be practically closing as she ate her supper. She had the impression that Jeanne-Marie spent her whole day in rushing from one point of call to another, charged with numerous obligations to different people, and that she never had a moment in which to relax.

It was particularly the fortitude and loyalty with which she maintained her circuit of obligations that impressed Madame Peineau. She would not subscribe to the remarks of one or two people [2] that Jeanne-Marie was foolhardy. "She was not foolhardy," she replied. "She was very, very brave, and did sometimes things which were almost incredibly audacious, but there was always a reason which justified the risk. For me, she was without fault."

As Noor's days were now organized, she had four regular points

<hr/>

1 This may have been the scarab I gave her.
2 Which I mentioned to her.

of call, Madame Peineau's house in Bondy, the Garrys' rooms in Neuilly, her own room at Neuilly, and, in the centre of Paris, the bench opposite the Tuileries where she met X, Y, and Vaudevire. Besides this, she still went to Suresnes to see Raymonde and Madame Prénat, and to Auteuil to see Madame Aigrain.

Madame Aigrain had become deeply fond of her, and was glad when Jeanne-Marie still came back to see her now that she had moved. To Madame Aigrain, also, Noor said that her true name was 'Nora Baker', and that her father had been 'a professor of Philosophy.'

The question arises why Noor concealed her real identity even from those who were closest to her in the Resistance, and whom she trusted most. Probably it was a measure of extreme care lest either of her brothers should be held a hostage against her. Hidayat was somewhere in France and Vilayat might return. [1] She and he had talked so often about the possibility of returning to France to work that she had to suppose he might still do so. Noor was always quite ready to credit the Gestapo with the basest methods of extorting information, and very likely feared that they might threaten her with the murder of her brothers, or of Hidayat's children, as a means of bringing pressure to bear on her. It was this fear which had caused her, even in England, to keep secret from those who did not know the fact, that she had a younger brother still in France, and it would seem that, from the beginning of her mission, she had deemed it prudent to suppress entirely her connection with the Inayat Khan family.

At the end of August a big secret meeting was held in a building off the Place de l'Alma, when the Chiefs of the Central Committee, recognized by General de Gaulle, assembled to choose the President of the National Committee of the Resistance. Noor was present, and Maître Y.

Monsieur Bidault was elected to be the President.

Afterwards Noor was established in the kitchen of the premises, and transmitted the intelligence to the Headquarters of General de Gaulle in England.

In September several members of Garry's network were arrested; as they knew his address in Neuilly, the Garrys left this, as a matter of routine, and found themselves accommodation in a studio near the Porte d'Orléans.

In September also Lieutenant Garry obtained for Jeanne-Marie the use of another room for occasional transmissions, in the flat of a friend, 'Solange', the directress of a *parfumerie*. This room would also serve him as a post-box where he could leave and pick

---

[1] In fact, Vilayat was posted some time after being commissioned, to Enemy Occupied France. He never had any contact with his sister, or heard anything of her, whilst in the field.

up messages. It was at 98 rue de la Faisanderie—not very far from the Avenue Foch, seat of the Headquarters of the Gestapo.

'Solange' had known the whole Garry family for a long time, and when he asked her to serve as a 'letter-box' she agreed with all her heart, hoping that she would be rendering a service which, if not glorious, would at least be useful. Her flat was on the first floor, and the kitchen opened on to a little terrace, surrounded by walls and by the roofs of houses. It was not very high, and Noor had only to climb on to the walls in order to reach the roofs, from which she could have found a way of escape in case of need. 'Solange' still remembers her when she came to study the layout of the flat, climbing among the walls, so frail and yet so resolute.

The transmissions proved difficult because the building was made of reinforced concrete. She came and went when she pleased, and always with discretion. The few nights when she slept in the flat 'Solange' heard her alarm clock ring very early in the morning, and the sound of her departure soon afterwards.

AUTUMN DRAMA

About this time, Noor received from London radio instructions to go to the Café Colisée, on the Champs Elysées, and make herself known to the cloakroom attendant in the basement, who would put her in touch with two Canadian agents of the "French Section." Following instructions to the letter, she found the Café Colisée, went down into its basement cloakroom and disclosed herself to the cloakroom attendant, who indeed put her into contact with two men, who gave their code-names as 'Bertrand' and 'Valentin'. They told her that the mission with which they had been sent from London was to organise a network in the north of France — "le Nord" — but that they had missed contact with the person, a certain Monsieur Despret, with whom London wished them to work. Noor replied helpfully that she could put them in contact with someone who knew this Monsieur Despret, and they arranged to meet her the following day at the Etoile, when she presented X to them. This was to have repercussions that were to prove far-reaching, and the reverse of any Noor could have foreseen.

It was one day when her wireless set went wrong that Vaude-vire, who was in his normal life Director of the Societé Française Radio Electrique, introduced Noor to Monsieur P. Viennot, the administrative secretary of the firm, who worked regularly with him, and X and Y.

Viennot thinks that this was about the middle of August. He

mended her wireless set; and this was the beginning of a loyal comradeship.

Viennot was a young man, very French, very lean, very vital—and, more important, one of those rare people who know human nature very well on its underside without being exactly cynical about it. A player in some of the dirtiest games associated with the Resistance, he retained a large human charity and respect for persons.

His activities were multifarious. First, as the Administrative Secretary of a firm officially engaged upon work for the Germans, he enrolled on its staff members of the Resistance. Secondly, and in the same capacity, he penetrated the Avenue Foch, and other foci of the German police in Paris, and also visited Germany, where he mixed freely in business and official circles. From these visits he learned much. Thirdly, he had contacts in the Paris underworld, and organized bands of gangsters—mostly recruited from the Corsican 'settlement' in Montmartre—to combat, on the lowest level, other bands of gangsters who worked for the Gestapo. For underneath the regular warfare between the Sicherheitsdienst and the 'recognized' organizations of the Resistance there ran another, as between gang and gang of organized Paris bandits.

These people—the modern descendants or replacements of the older and poorer Apache—might be in 'regular' life traffickers in contraband commodities, proprietors of licensed establishments, or big jewel or fur thieves. Mostly accustomed to the use of the revolver in peace-time, when they were occupied in inter-gang warfare, they had, with the advent of the German Occupation in 1940, turned largely to new activities. Some worked for the Gestapo, and others for the Resistance (this division corresponding in many cases to ancient feuds).

Viennot was confident in the loyalty of the persons from this world whom he had drawn into his own organization, and which formed, as it were, its basic muscle. He used them occasionally to bring off a coup requiring physical force, such as the rescue of a prisoner from the hands of the Gestapo, and several times they had engaged successfully in street encounters with the SS. He had so organized his circuit that in case of need he could, by telephoning, obtain very quickly the services of a band of these people at any hour of the day or night.

From the same milieux he drew a number of professional ladies, whom he groomed until they lost the appearance of what they were. In some cases he chose suitable clothes for them and installed them in discreet apartments. Then he presented to them German officers desirous of making acquaintances in French society. Generally speaking, when they tried to make lady-friends for themselves, those they found were always more or less professionals, and they wanted to be introduced to good French society. In effect, Viennot procured them women—but in such a way that they did not realize that the introductions were not purely friendly or that the women were prostitutes. They had to think they had made the conquest of a superior woman, and so it was above all necessary to get rid of any appearance of the professional. When they were ready the women worked as spies in the old tradition. It was slow work, and demanded very much patience, but it yielded results which made it worth continuing. The Germans talked—not always, but sometimes. They would like to show how much they knew.

Viennot himself was lunching with Germans four or five days in the week, and managed to know personally SS Sturmbahnführer Kieffer, the Commandant of the Counter Espionage Service of the German Security Police. Kieffer did not seem to suspect him, and they lunched on several occasions. Viennot describes his personality as "Not disagreeable. He appreciated beautiful motorcars, beautiful properties, and beautiful women. He gave the impression that he wanted to be accepted as an ordinary person."

Through all these intricate manoeuvres he moved with a zest, and at times a devilish merriment, probably possible only to a Frenchman. "It was a dirty game," he says, "but one played with everything one had!"

He was often in possession of intelligence of considerable interest, which he used to disseminate through the French Resistance networks. Now that he had made the acquaintance of Noor he asked her if she would care to relay it to the War Office also. She said that she would do so.[1] He had no connection with the French Section, but told her that she might, in order to make the matter 'regular' from her point of view, give his code-name with the Resistance to her Chiefs in London, since she must explain the source of her intelligence. Therafter, when he learned anything of interest, it passed over the 'Poste-Madeleine.' He came to know Noor well, and felt great friendship and admiration for her.

She was introduced to him as 'Rolande', but afterwards she told him that her code-name with the French Section was Madeleine, and that she lived in Paris under the cover-name of Jeanne-Marie. She told him also that her true name was Nora Baker.

Her courage and her integrity impressed him. "She was very young," he says, "but I always had the confidence that if she

---

1 The transmission of intelligence was no part of Madeleine's job. As has been mentioned before, the business of French Section was not espionage. In transmitting Viennot's occasional intelligence to London she was, strictly speaking, exceeding her duties. It does not appear, however, that any reproof came from London.

184

were captured she would not speak, and never had any anxiety on this score."

Nevertheless, from the point of view of security three things caused him concern: the note-book in which she kept her messages, her personal appearance, and her English accent.

The note-book, like the transmitter, she carried everywhere with her. It was an ordinary exercise-book, such as school children use, and she used to turn it sideways so as to be able to write across the length of the pages, which were squared, as for mathematics. He was a little more familiar with its appearance than he liked to be, because she was always opening it when they met. It contained all the messages which had ever passed between herself and her Chiefs in London since she had come to France.

"That is a very dangerous document," he said. "Anybody into whose hands it should fall would be able to work out your code from it."

"I know," she said. "That is why I carry it about with me everywhere."

"But this means that if the Germans capture you, they capture this on you!" "Yes; but there is nothing I can do about that."

"But do you have to keep all these messages?" he asked "Can you not burn each one as soon as it is done with?"

She told him her instructions were to keep the messages carefully. He was concerned about this and said that if she cared to put all responsibility on him, he would burn the notebook and if there was trouble about it she could tell her chiefs in London he had done so without her permission, and he would sustain that. She was, he lamented, "too honest to accept this solution", and as he "saw that it did not lie with her to change the system" and did not really like to seize the notebook violently, he let the matter drop. [1]

1 Miss Atkins has asked me to say in any subsequent edition that it was not on instructions from London that Noor kept the back-messages. Quite on the contrary, it was always stressed they should be destroyed as soon as possible. She could not think how Noor had so misunderstood her instructions, and did not know of any other agent who had made this mistake. The author of the official history SOE in France (H.M. Stationery Office, 1966, p. 339) does however reveal that Noor's personal file in London contained an instruction in these words "We should like to point out here that you must be extremely careful with the filing of your messages." As to who wrote this, there was no indication, but the same instruction was found on two other agents' files. Professor Foot suggested that the word "file" was used "in the special sense it carries for journalists", meaning no more than that her messages should receive sequential numbering. I can only say that this use of the word was unknown to me, and that if I were told I had "to file" papers I would suppose I had to place them within covers and keep carefully. If Noor was expected to know the special jargon of a profession to which she did not belong, it seems very thoughtless. One could only wish that after her conversation with Viennot she had queried the point with London; but probably the instruction seemed to her so clear as to render this needless.

Her appearance caused him a good deal of cogitation. She wore most often a grey tailor-made, and in the wet weather, which was frequent, a very light coloured mackintosh, almost white—a sort of trench-coat—which could only have been bought in England.

He felt that everybody who saw her in this mackintosh must think, "There is an English girl!" She seemed to him typically English, in her walk, in her manner, in everything. And the mackintosh brought it out. Walking in the street with her, he had always the feeling of walking with an English girl.

Her hair, when he met her, was an ugly and unbecoming yellow. This would not have mattered, except that it contributed to make her conspicuous.

He would have liked to see changed both the hair and the mackintosh, but for some time hesitated to say so to her.

About her English accent there was nothing to do. When sitting with her in a café he would sometimes ask her to keep her voice down, being afraid lest her accent, coupled with her markedly English, and slightly peculiar, appearance, should attract the attention of people at the tables near them.

One day he was walking with her on one of the Boulevards when he saw coming towards them a relative whose sympathies were strongly Pétainist, and who naturally did not know of his association with the Resistance. If they met he would have to introduce Jeanne-Marie, and he was sure that the relative would recognize that she was an English girl. He had to find a way of avoiding the encounter. He knew that the relative had already seen them, so he had to use his ingenuity.

He put his arm round her, and leaned his head a little towards her, as though they were taking a sentimental stroll. Then suddenly he appeared to see the relative, straightened, took Noor brusquely by the elbow, and began walking away very quickly with her, and whisked her round a corner—as though he were annoyed at having been seen with a woman, and did not wish, for personal reasons, to have to introduce her.

She was a little startled, but intelligent enough to cooperate in the manoeuvre, and he explained to her the reason when he had got her round the corner.

The stratagem proved successful to a degree. When he arrived home a little later he found that the relative had preceded him and was already engaged in recounting to his wife the story of the treachery in which he had caught him. Very much to his embarrassment, he was obliged to sustain his role of culprit until the gentleman's eventual departure. It nearly caused a quarrel!

He was never able to introduce Jeanne-Marie to Madame Viennot—who was herself an active worker for the Resistance. They had young children, and knew that a child may always talk, without understanding. He did bring her back to their flat in the Quartier Latin once or twice, but during a short period when Madame Viennot had taken the children on holiday. Otherwise he met her regularly in cafés.

Their meetings were nearly always rushed, and their conversation limited to the business in hand.

He had a friend, however, who went sometimes to the house of Madame Peineau. This friend told him on one occasion that he had spent a whole evening there in the company of 'Rolande'. She had told him she had a fiancé and that he was an Englishman, working for the War Office, who moved about in Norway and Denmark. He supposed therefore that her fiancé must belong to an organization similar to the French Section, which operated in Scandinavia. They intended, she said, to be married in England after the war, if they both survived it.

Early in the morning of September 30th, Viennot had some business with Jeanne-Marie. She told him she was uneasy about X. She had had a rendez-vous with him the previous afternoon, and he had neither turned up nor telephoned during the evening— as he could have done—to explain the reason. She wondered if he had been arrested.

It was about 10 a.m. when she told him this, and they were driving together in his car.

"There's only one way to find out," he said.

They stopped the car at a place between the Porte Maillot and the Porte Champerret, and went together into a public phone box.

Jeanne-Marie dialled the number of X's flat. She was answered by a man whose voice she did not recognize (nor Viennot, either, who was listening as closely as he could).

She said, "Can I speak to X?"

He said, "Hold on. I will give you X."

After a moment X spoke to her. Viennot also recognized his voice.

She said, "It's me. Can I see you?"

He said, "Of course. But would you mind coming to my apartment? I am not very well, and would prefer not to have to go out."

She had never before been to his apartment.

She was already suspicious, and so she replied that it was a little out of her way, and that she was pressed for time and would not come.

He answered, "Never mind, I will come out, then. Will you meet me at eleven o'clock, at the corner of the Avenue Mac-Mahon and the rue Tilsit?"

Viennot did not like the sound of it. As they came out of the box, he said, "The Gestapo were perhaps standing behind him with a pistol. You cannot keep that rendez-vous."

They got back into his car, and drove, shortly before eleven o'clock, to the Etoile. Here he put her down, under the Arc de Triomphe, and said, "Wait here. I will come back for you."

So she waited, with the Unknown Warrior.

From her slightly elevated position she could see down the whole length of the Avenue MacMahon.

Viennot drove in the car down the Avenue. At the corner of the rue Tilsit he saw X sitting on a bench. It was one of those benches which have a 'back' down the middle and a board to sit upon on either side. With his back to X, and sitting a little farther along, was another man. At each corner of the cross-roads was standing a man. There were six men in all, in addition to X. They were all big men, all wearing mackintoshes, and most of them horn-rimmed spectacles. All were quite still, as though they had been cut out in cardboard.

He drove straight through the 'frame' and down to the bottom of the Avenue. There he turned, made a detour, came back to the top of it again, and drove down a second time. All the men were still there, still keeping the same positions.

He went down to the bottom again, turned, and came back to the top, and drove down a third time. The situation was unchanged. There could be no possible doubt that it was an ambush.

He went to a telephone box and rang up a friend who had a key position in his gangster circuit, explained the dilemma, and said he wanted at once a sufficient number of men to rescue X. He did not think that X had willed, in the profundity of his spirit, to betray his comrades; he thought only that he was helpless.

The friend said he could not muster the men and send them to reach the spot in less than half an hour. He would move as quickly as possible, and could promise that they should be at the Etoile by about 11.45.

Viennot drove back to the Etoile, got out from the car, and joined Jeanne-Marie where she was waiting under the Arc de Triomphe. She had seen everything, and was pale. The rest they witnessed together.

Viennot had a watch, and looked at it every now and then.

At 11.40 exactly a Citroën drew up at the corner of the Avenue MacMahon and the rue Tilsit. The six men and X all moved forward from their positions to converge upon it. They got into it together, and drove away.

Viennot and Jeanne-Marie still had to wait, because he had called for a team of gangsters. Exactly five minutes afterwards, another big car drew up, bringing the 'friends' for whom he had asked. There was nothing to do now but to thank them and tell them it was too late.

Viennot and Jeanne-Marie walked together to a café on the Avenue de la Grande Armée, where they were accustomed sometimes to meet.

Here they sat down and ordered coffee.

Jeanne-Marie was shaking like a leaf. She was totally unable to take in what she had seen a few minutes ago—it was as if she just didn't believe her own eyes.

She had always felt that X was one of the pillars of the organization, and kept saying. "I couldn't have believed he would do it! I would never have believed it could be possible! I didn't think he would do it!" She was crying and trembling, and the tears were running down her cheeks so fast that she could not drink her coffee.

Viennot said, "I will make myself responsible for informing Y and Vaudevire, so that they can take what steps they think necessary for their security."

Jeanne-Marie recalled suddenly that she had given X the telephone number of her room in Neuilly. "They will be able to get the address from the Exchange! I shall have to leave there in case there is a raid!"

"You will also have to change your personal appearance," said Viennot. "You must get rid of that mackintosh, in which you have been seen about Paris, and of that tailor-made. You must have entirely new things, and discard any clothes which you have worn since coming to France. You must also change the colour of your hair."[1]

She was very upset and said she had not the money.

He said he would be responsible for the money. At the moment when he promised this he did not know where he would obtain it; he would have to borrow, but he did not tell her this. Since she would have been described to the Germans as a peroxide blonde girl he thought that her hair was the most urgent thing to change.

"This afternoon I'll take you to a hairdresser," he said.

They had separate engagements immediately, and parted, agreeing to meet again after lunch.

In fact, though Noor still did not know it, she herself had been the innocent agency through whom X had been arrested. For the two men with whom the attendant at the Café Colisée had put her in contact were not the two Canadians 'Bertrand' and 'Valentin' but two Germans of the Sicherheitsdienst, Placke and Holdorf; both spoke fluent English and French. The two real Canadians, Pickersgill and Macalister, had been arrested on June 21st

[1] Conversation dictated by Viennot according to his recollection.

189

(only three days after having been parachuted). Their radio-set had been played-back to London by the Germans; London had accepted the messages as genuine, and had radioed instructions to them and to Noor to meet each other, thus putting Noor into ˙contact with two Germans who impersonated the two Canadian prisoners. Carried away by their eagerness to make important contacts in the north, they had let her slip from view after she had served their purpose by introducing them to X, had played along with him until through him they had met others more important, when, on September 30th, they arrested him. He may, in fact, have felt annoyed with Noor for not having detected that the two to whom she introduced him were Germans, and as it was from him I first heard the story, I at first doubted it. Much later, I read Placke's deposition made after the war to the French D.S.T., and realised that it was true.[1]

II

It would seem as though it must have been on the same day, after she left Viennot, that Noor met Madame Salmon for the last time.

Madame Salmon had an appointment with her at a café on the Rond Point du Champs Elysées. She had just heard that the Germans were installing dictaphones in all the principal cafés, for the purpose of recording any conversations capable of interesting the Security Service; therefore she did not sit down at a table, but walked up and down within a short distance of the café, ready to intercept Noor when she should arrive.

Noor was unusually late; three-quarters of an hour passed without her appearance. Madame Salmon became anxious lest something had happened to her, and was almost giving her up when she saw her suddenly come running out of the Metro George Cinque.

She was very agitated, and whilst apologizing for being so late explained that something in the nature of a major catastrophe had occurred that morning in the network to which she belonged. She had been going to see an important member of her organization, so Madame Salmon understood, in his house, when she discovered this to be occupied by the Gestapo, and he and his family prisoners in it. Afterwards she had had some very narrow escapes from capture in the street. She and one other person[2] had

---

[1] Deposition of Placke to the Departement de la Surveillance du Territoire, April 1st, 1946. Quoted in full, in my translation, in my **Double Webs.** (Putnam, 1958) pp. 81-6.

[2] Madame Salmon understood her to say, 'her Chief'; nevertheless, the correspondence of several points of this narrative with the events of 30th September, as told by Viennot, is so close as to leave little doubt that what Noor told Madame Salmon related to the events of this day.

escaped, but must consider themselves in danger. The coup was so shattering that they did not know how it would be possible to carry on.

They accomplished their business as quickly as they could; Madame Salmon told her what she had just heard about the installation of dictaphones in the cafés. Noor thanked her, and they parted, making an appointment for a future date.

Noor never kept this appointment, and Madame Salmon supposed she had been arrested.

In the afternoon Viennot again took charge of Jeanne-Marie.

"I have had my hair made a different colour so many times since I came to France," she said, "that it has become all brittle and looks horrible."

"Yes," he said, "but perhaps a good hairdresser will be able to do something about it."

He took her to a good hairdresser, and said, "I want her brunette." [1]

He explained to the lady in charge that he wanted her hair to be a natural brown, 'French brown' or some unremarkable tint which would tone harmoniously with her eyes and complexion; above all, he wanted her to get rid of the brittleness and of the 'dyed' look.

When it was done the result was a tribute to the lady's skill. She had succeeded, by the application of oils or lotions, in getting the stiffness out of the hair, and now it rippled supply and was a light brown.

He told Jeanne-Marie to meet him early the next morning and they would go shopping.

The next morning October 1st, he took her to good shops and chose some clothes for her—not without a certain pleasure in fashioning her new appearance. He bought her a navy-blue suit, a jumper knitted in a fine grey wool with a rolled polo collar, some accessories to match, and finally a navy-blue hat. She had not had a hat before, though sometimes he had seen her with a navy scarf tied round her head when it was raining.

With her new and more soberly coloured hair, and these new clothes, she looked to his eye like a French girl, and he was pleased with the achievement.

She promised she would wear the hat; and said also that she would call herself Marie-Jeanne instead of Jeanne-Marie to complete the assumption of a new personality. He thought it was a good idea, and said he would call her this.

A matter had been occupying his mind all the morning while they had been buying these things. At last he spoke of it "Marie-Jeanne," he said, "we have now taken all the measures of which we

[1] Conversation dictated by Viennot according to his recollection.

can think for your safety. It still remains that you are in great danger, and may be arrested within the next few days. You may find that the Gestapo already know my code-name and your connection with me, and will wish to use you to bait a trap. If they ask you to telephone to me and invite me to a rendez-vous you can do this; I don't mind, but there is one thing I will ask you. If you are in such a situation, will you give me as a rendez-vous the Underground station of the Pont Levallois?"

She was looking at him with startled eyes.

He explained. "I should like you to wait for me with your 'companions' on the 'Entry' platform. You will have to persuade them there is some reason why it must be on this platform—you can say it is a place where we have met before. I shall come to the 'Exit' platform. As it is a terminus[1] there is no barrier to get in one's way. It should be possible to walk straight through—in at one end and out at the other—and so to reconnoitre the position without too much danger. I should hope to be able to rescue you, with the aid of some of my gangster friends; but before rushing into the middle of things I should like to see how you are placed, how many people are guarding you, and just where they are all stationed—for they will be sitting or standing around trying to look like ordinary people. That is why I have thought that the Underground Station, with its two platforms, is the best place for such a rendez-vous."

She was troubled. She said it sounded very dangerous, and she was afraid that if something went wrong with the arrangement he would be captured.

He insisted, saying that the gangs had sometimes succeeded in rescuing a prisoner from such a situation. "Above all, don't be uneasy on my account. I assure you, I shouldn't approach the place without the utmost caution."

After they had talked about it for a little she agreed. "If the occasion arises, I may do it."

"Tell no one what we have arranged," he said. "I shan't, either. For security, this should remain between ourselves."[2]

III

The exact date when Noor returned for the last time to the Boulevard Richard Wallace appears impossible to ascertain; probably it was immediately—either October 1st or October 2nd.

Madame Jourdois recalls that Jeanne Regnier suddenly came running in and deposited a portfolio with her, saying, "Will you

---

[1] On the Paris 'Metro' tickets are presented for punching as one enters and are not required as one goes out. At the 'Exit' platforms of terminal stations there are therefore no barriers.

[2] Conversation dictated by Viennot according to his recollection.

192

keep this for me for a few minutes? I will be back almost at once."

She went away, and came hurrying back after two or three minutes, saying she would like to settle the rent to date.

Whilst Madame Jourdois made out the bill she said, "Madame, I shall not see you again. I am going away now and shall not come back. I have to move because of my work."

Madame Jourdois did not immediately understand. She had come to feel affectionately towards her and said, "But you will come back from time to time to see me, won't you? Come in and have a cup of tea when you are passing. I should like to know how you are."

Jeanne shook her head. "This place has become unsafe for me; I have come only to settle the rent. I am afraid there will be a raid here by the Gestapo within a day or two."

She had never said openly that she worked for the Resistance, yet she must have supposed that Madame Jourdois knew it, for she added, speaking more rapidly, "I have been taken by the Gestapo twice[1] already, and I have a feeling I shall not escape a third time."

Then, as Madame Jourdois gazed at her in astonishment, she added, "Don't worry about me! We have between us twelve apartments which we use like this one. It confuses the Gestapo and makes it more difficult to trace us."[2]

With this, she squeezed her hand, and taking up her portfolio ran away.

A day or two later three or four men came from the German Police. They asked Madame Jourdois for Jeanne-Marie Regnier, and entered and searched the room she had occupied.[3]

I believe that it was now, rather than earlier, that Déricourt's courier 'Claire' found for Noor the second flat, on the corner of the rue Berlioz and the rue Pergolèse. In one of his longest letters to me, twenty-six pages, Déricourt first gives the date as in the first week of August, well before the aerial operation of the August moon, but, on a later page, as at the end of September, or after the Germans had raided the flat at the Boulevard Richard Wallace,

---

[1] Ernest thinks she must have said, or meant to say, 'nearly taken'. She had not been captured at this time.

[2] Conversation dictated by Madame Jourdois according to her recollection.

[3] Ernest confirms this, and says he brought the party. He had obtained the address, 3 Boulevard Richard Wallace, through the Telephone Exchange. Kieffer gave him the number, Sablons 88.04, on one of the first days of October, telling him it was the number of the apartment which 'Madeleine' occupied under the cover-name of Jeanne-Marie Regnier, and that she shared the use of it with a young man who acted as her courier and liaison agent. He (Kieffer) had learned this from a Frenchman. This was the first time Ernest heard the name Regnier and, he thinks, the first time Kieffer had heard it.

making necessary a new one. Moreover, by a curious wording, he makes quite clear that he is aware of the ambiguity or self-contradiction which he is creating and means me to prefer the date he suggests at the end to that which he states at the beginning. The difficulty, for him, was that he did not wish to appear as having had any knowledge of Madeleine as late as this, since, if he could maintain that neither he nor 'Claire' so much as heard of her after about August 10, this would absolve him from responsibility in respect of a statement made to me by Madame Aigrain, [1] that a report by a colleague of hers concerning an event which took place in September, which she gave to Madeleine to give to 'Gilbert' (Déricourt's code-name) who took charge of the mail for London, was after her own arrest shown to her in photostat by Ernest of the Sicherheitsdienst. Déricourt was, I believe, trying to give me the facts in a way that would not lay him open to accusation in respect of this. Afterwards, he says, there was an apparent burglary in the new Berlioz-Pergolèse flat. Everything was turned upside down; but even Madeleine—whom he insisted was not usually perceptive where security was concerned—realised that it was not an ordinary burglary and that it was the Germans who had paid a visit and camouflaged their break-in to look a burglary. He did not know where she went to after that.

The Jourdans had now returned from the country. Describing to Madame Jourdan the evacuation of her premises at Neuilly, Noor said, with a wry little smile, "All I regret is the pot of gooseberry jam you gave me."

"The pot of gooseberry jam!" exclaimed Madame Jourdan, laughing despite herself. "But I gave it to you a month ago! Why didn't you eat it?"

Noor's answer was rather pathetic. "You made it from the gooseberries at Marly, and whilst I had it to look at, I didn't feel so far from friends." She said ruefully, "I know it's still on the window-sill, but I can't go to get it because the Gestapo will be there."

She told the Jourdans the story of the rendez-vous which X had given her with the Gestapo, praising the gallantry of the friend who had driven in his car "ever so slowly past the place where X was waiting surrounded by them." She spoke of what had happened with a complete lack of malice towards X.

Noor told the Jourdans she found it impossible to believe he had acted only in order to save his own life. "They were in occupation of his house," she said, "and probably they held his wife and son also prisoner. Supposing they had threatened to shoot his son?"

She was very much upset, but she did not want to harbour

[1] See my **Double Webs** (Putnam, 1958) pp. 119-20, 201.

hard feelings against somebody with whom she had worked in good comradeship until this happened. "I won't think he did it *against me*," she said, *"but for his son.* If we meet after the war I won't hold it against him."[1]

Madame Aigrain was also struck by the very generous attitude of Jeanne-Marie in this matter. She knew X, and was furious when she heard the story of the 'frame' on the Avenue Mac-Mahon. She cried out, "It was a most gross betrayal! It was a shameful thing!"

Jeanne-Marie stopped her, with the exclamation, "Oh, no! We must not say that. We don't know what happened."

"But we *do* know! That is what is so revolting."

"We do not know *all*. We don't know if it was for himself alone. Perhaps it was for his son. We must not judge."[2]

This she repeated every time the subject was mentioned. "We must not judge."[3]

In the Prénats' house, however, she revealed herself as very distressed. To Madame Prénat she said, "I am so afraid he will tell them everything he knows." Then, beginning to speak very quickly, and raising her small clenched fists in a gesture that was characteristic of her when she was excited, she cried out, "It's useless to try to strike a bargain with the Gestapo! It's so silly, and quite useless. They will shoot you just the same, in the end."

Suddenly she burst into tears, and burying her face in her hands exclaimed, "I wish I were with my mother!" She wept bitterly for several minutes.

Madame Prénat tried to comfort her, and told her that she could stay in their house and not go out any more if she was in fear of being captured. She could regard their home as her own, and at any time retire to it as a refuge. Noor shook her head. She thanked her, but said that she had obligations in Paris she could not desert. Besides, she said, there was another man, belonging to the same network, who was rendering her very loyal assistance. "I know that I could rely on him in any circumstance. I would trust him with my life."[4]

Although she would not give up her work, yet the incidents following upon the arrest of X had made a deep impression on her. Madame Jourdan felt that she was not the same girl after-

[1] Conversation dictated by Madame Jourdan according to her recollection.

[2] Conversation dictated by Madame Aigrain according to her recollection.

[3] I found Viennot not alien to this charitable attitude. When I referred to 'the treason of X' he said, "You are harder than I am, Mademoiselle. I have not called it that."

[4] Conversation dictated by Madame Prénat according to her recollection.

wards. She grew thinner in the course of a few days, seemed to feel herself pursued, and had a hunted look.

One day she came in saying that she had been going with a friend through the gardens behind the Trocadero when they had realized they were being followed by two men. They believed them to be agents of the Gestapo and had had to make many twists and turns before they succeeded in eluding them.

Shortly after this there occurred an incident of considerable dramatic force. Noor called in the afternoon at six o'clock and found nobody at home but Françoise.

She said, "This evening I have to do something which is very dangerous. I am going to leave my transmitter and my papers here. Will you give your father a message for me when he comes in?"

"Yes."

"Will you tell him that if I am not back here by nine o'clock this evening I wish him to assume that I have been captured, and to burn my papers at once, and bury the transmitter at Marly-le-Roi as soon as he is able?"

"Yes," said Françoise, feeling herself go a little white.

When the doctor returned at dinner-time she delivered the message.

The family dined in the utmost gloom and nervousness, and afterwards all sat watching the clock, as the hands crept round from 8 to 9. They had actually touched 9 o'clock, and the chimes were beginning to strike, when the Jourdans heard steps on the stairs.

Madame Jourdan hurried to the door and opened it. Noor staggered in, panting terribly.

She could hardly speak for a moment or two, and when she did it was to explain, "I have been running! I was afraid I would not get here in time and you would have destroyed my papers."

Her teeth were practically chattering in her head. They made her sit down. Madame Jourdan went out and made her a hot drink and something to eat.

She was trembling and feverish, and could not immediately eat. "I have done my duty," she said, when she regained control of her breathing. "But it nearly cost me my liberty. There was a moment when I thought that I was taken."[1]

They never asked her questions concerning her work, and did not, on this occasion either, think it proper to ask her what had happened.[2]

[1] Conversation dictated by Madame Jourdan according to her recollection.

[2] Professor Balachowsky says that whilst he was in Buchenwald a fellow prisoner who had been captured later told him something of a shooting incident in Paris in which Jeanne-Marie had been concerned.

She was obviously in no state to go out into the streets again that night, and Madame Jourdan persuaded her to stay and sleep at their flat. In the morning she did not wish to let Noor go. She felt like a mother to her, and told her she could stay with them as long as she wanted. Whilst she remained in their flat she was completely safe. Unless anybody had seen her come in the Germans could never have found her there.

Noor thanked her, but explained—as she had to Madame Prénat—she had obligations in Paris she could not desert. There were certain persons whom she met every day, and who would suppose her to be arrested if she did not come.

After this they saw her a few times more.

On the last occasion when she worked from Marly-le-Roi, Madame Jourdan was sitting with her in the room whilst she deciphered the message which had just come through from London. When she had finished putting it into plain language, it was found to end: *May God keep you.*

Noor was very much affected. She said, "I didn't think they ever said things like that. I thought I was just a cipher to London. We have to learn to be quite impersonal in our work, as if we allowed our feelings to interfere, it wouldn't do." It seemed as if she was fighting for her self-control, and this unexpected address as a human soul almost undid her.

During the days which immediately followed the arrest of X, she had some words with Y. He said she must leave Paris. He would arrange for her to go to a farm in Normandy, where she would be received and given sanctuary. She objected that she did not want to go; she wanted to continue working in Paris.

He said, "You must go. You are known now by the Gestapo. There is no question of working any more. We have to stop work. Later, perhaps, it will be possible to start again. Now, we have to lie low."

She was obstinate. She repeated that she did not want to go.

"It is folly!" he said.

He arranged with the farm in Normandy to take her, and presented her with the *fait accompli*. "You must go," he said. "The Gestapo know you and will follow you to all the people whom you meet, until they have every one of us."[1]

Against this argument she was powerless.

With Vaudevire, he accompanied her to the station of St. Lazare, bought her ticket, and gave it to her, and they conducted her together on to the platform and saw her into a carriage on the

The Professor thought this must have related to the occasion when she was arrested, but the evidence of Ernest (see next Section) makes it plain this was not so. Was it on this evening?

[1] Conversation dictated by Y according to his recollection.

197

train. They both waited on the platform until it went out, she in it. This, says Y, was about October 5th.

Two days later he was furious to catch sight of her again in Paris. Immediately she returned she got in touch with Viennot, explaining what had happened. They talked over the situation together. Garry was away again, and Noor had, in fact, only Viennot now with whom to talk. It seemed to them both that there was now no work for her to do. With X arrested, and Y not wanting to work with her, there remained no more network. So far as Viennot was concerned he was not a member of the French Section, his organization was independent, and whilst he had been pleased to send intelligence through her to London this was not an interest from his point of view. They agreed, therefore, that she ought to return to England. She said she had not wished to vegetate on a farm in Normandy, but if she returned to London perhaps they could give her another assignment.

Vaudevire, although he had joined with Y in seeing her to the station, was willing, when he learned of her return, to resume contacts and even to work with her until she could be repatriated.

He went with her—either on the same day or the day after—to a rendez-vous near the Porte Maillot. They were to meet here, in a café, a man with whom they would speak of the means to have her returned immediately to England. They had not met before, and knew only his code-name and some signs by which they were to recognize him.

Vaudevire and Marie-Jeanne approached the café together and identified a person corresponding to the description they had been given. Some feature of the situation[1] struck them as abnormal; they stopped, took counsel with one another, and decided that they had very nearly walked into a trap. They thought they should separate—in order to divide any agents of the Gestapo who might follow them—and walked, with as natural an air as possible, towards different Metro stations.

Both got home safely.

It must have been one day during this week that Noor went to Suresnes to say good-bye to the Prénats.

"I am going to England," she said. "When I see you again it will be after the war." She had brought Raymonde a gold powder-compact as a parting gift.

So they said good-bye, both deeply moved.

Her last contact with Viennot was dramatic. This was on Saturday, October 9th, at about 9.30 in the morning. He had just come into his office and sat down when the telephone rang.

---

[1] Viennot, who is the source for this story, does not remember further details. It was told him by Vaudevire.

198

He took off one receiver, and his secretary, Mademoiselle Simone Truffit, took off the other.

Marie-Jeanne spoke, asking for Viennot, under his code-name in the Resistance.

As soon as she heard him speak, she said, "I need to see you at once! Please come quickly! To the Pont, as usual."

Before he had time to reply, she had rung off. She had sounded very agitated.

They had never met at any 'Pont'. He thought immediately, therefore, of their pact concerning the Underground Station at the Pont Levallois. Nevertheless, there was something he did not understand. He had told her to give him this rendez-vous if she were already a prisoner in the hands of the Gestapo; but in this case he would have expected her to do so in a voice which pretended to sound natural. Her words gave the impression that she was still free, but felt herself in danger.

He said to Mademoiselle Truffit, "She is *perhaps* with the Gestapo. Will you take my car and go immediately to the Metro Pont Levallois? Go down on to the 'Exit' platform, look across the line and see if she is on the other side, and whether she is alone or 'accompanied'. If she is alone, bring her back here in the car immediately; if 'accompanied', phone and tell me by how many. I will be phoning a friend to have men on the ready."[1]

Mademoiselle Truffit was a young member of his network whom he introduced recently to Marie-Jeanne.

She went immediately, and after a little while phoned back to say that she looked where he had told her, but there was nobody there at all. He went also to the Pont Levallois, and joined her. It was true that there was no Marie-Jeanne—'accompanied' or otherwise. It was a rule between Viennot and Marie-Jeanne never to wait for one another at a rendez-vous longer than half an hour. On this occasion, he waited with Mademoiselle Truffit three quarters of an hour on the platform. Then they went back to the office, Viennot completely perplexed.

This was the last he ever heard of her.

Mademoiselle Truffit had had an appointment that afternoon to meet Marie-Jeanne and Vaudevire, to perform an act of sabotage. They were going to blow up a building in which were housed instruments used in submarine warfare. It was an act which would be of some importance in the Atlantic war. Vaudevire turned up at the rendez-vous, but Marie-Jeanne did not. This seemed to confirm that she had been arrested.

Yet she had not been arrested. What had happened will probably never be possible to ascertain.

During the evening of that day she called at the Jourdans' flat

[1] Conversation dictated by Viennot according to his recollection.

199

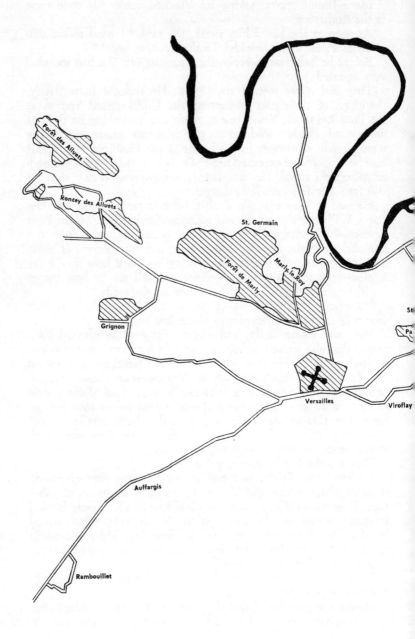

Trempley

Seine

Bondy

⑤

Pantin

Noisy

④ Neuilly

⑩ Montmartre
Nord

⑨

③ ⑥ ⑦

St. Lazare

Est

⑧

⑪

Bois
Bologne

⑫

⑬ ⑮

Auteuil

⑭

Eiffel Tower

⑯

Jardin du Luxembourg

⑰

⑱

Seine

Marne

Sceaux

Frèsnes

Wissous

1. Suresnes/Fezal Manzil
2. Rue de la Tuilerie
3. Bvd. Richard Wallace
4. Pont de Neuilly
5. Pont de Levallois
6. Avenue de la Grande
   Armée
7. Place de l'Etoile
   Arc de Triomphe
8. Avenue Foch
9. Porte Maillot
10. Porte de Champerret
11. Av. des Champs-Elysées
12. Place de la Concorde
13. Tuileries

14. Notre Dame
15. Place de la République
16. Place de la Bastille
17. Place de la Nation
18. Porte d'Orléans

and told them that something had happened which made it unsafe for her to be about in Paris any longer. Madame Jourdan repeated her offer of sanctuary. Noor said she intended to accept it, but could not do so immediately.

"I shall come to you," she said, "on the evening of Thursday the 14th, and take shelter with you, without going out, until a person comes to tell me where I have to go to meet the plane which will take me back to England. There is nothing further for me to do here."

"You cannot stay with us immediately?" asked Madame Jourdan, not liking to let her go out into the streets again.

Noor shook her head. "No. I wish I could, for I am in danger. But there is a job which I have to do first. I have worked it out, and I cannot come before Thursday. I shall come on the 14th, if I have not been arrested before then."[1]

On Sunday, the 10th, she failed to come to Madame Peineau. Madame Peineau was extremely anxious, because Marie-Jeanne never missed her transmissions. She waited up until late in the night for a phone call, but none came.

The next morning Marie-Jeanne phoned. She did not explain her absence of the previous evening, but asked, "Is Monsieur Vaudevire keeping well?"

Madame Peineau understood that she must have some reason to fear Vaudevire had been arrested.

She replied, "As far as I know."

Marie-Jeanne said she was glad, as she had been afraid he might have been taken ill; then she rang off, without giving any explanations.

Madame Peineau never heard anything of her again.[2]

On the evening of the same day Madame Aigrain received a visit from Jeanne-Marie. She said she had just come in to say good-bye and to thank her for the support which she had given her. She was going to England on the 14th[3] and would come again to see her after the war.

[1] Conversation dictated by Madame Jourdan according to her recollection.

[2] From Ernest's evidence (see next Section) it would appear that she had taken refuge with Solange in the rue de la Faisanderie.

[3] There is some mystery about this. Miss Atkins told me emphatically that Noor did not ask to be brought back and no arrangement was made for a plane to bring her back. On the other hand, Prof. Foot writes in SOE in France (H.M. Stationery Office, 1966 p. 338) "She was offered a passage back to England by Lysander; characteristicaly, she refused until she had an assurance about her relief. The arrangements were about to be settled, in the second week of October, when without explanation she went off the air for ten days. When she came up again she had missed her aeroplane." On the other hand again, Déricourt told me that two aeroplanes did leave by the mid-October moon, from Amboise and from Angers, but that he received no instruction to meet Madeleine and include her in the party to be shepherded aboard either. What did happen?

On the following evening, Tuesday the 12th, Madame Aigrain was surprised when Jeanne-Marie telephoned again. She sounded rather agitated and asked, "May I come to see you again?"

Madame Aigrain realized that something must have happened to trouble her; yet, as she had guests who did not belong to the Resistance, she replied, "I have people with me whom it is better you should not meet."

She spoke more truly than she knew; half an hour later, men from the Gestapo entered her flat suddenly and took her away under arrest.[1]

THE AVENUE FOCH

The Avenue Foch is a broad and magnificent way, running through the best part of Paris, from the Arc de Triomphe to the Bois de Boulogne.

It is composed of large private houses, so many of which had then been taken over by various German organizations that it had gained, among the French, the nickname 'Avenue Boche'. In particular, three adjoining buildings had become the seats of notable headquarters: No. 82, Gestapo, under Sturmbahnführer Boemelburg, and Nos. 84 and 86, Sicherheitsdienst (Security Service) under Sturmbahnführer Kieffer and Dr. Schmidt respectively. All these were directly responsible, through a Colonel Dr. Knochen, to SS General Oberg, chief of both the Gestapo and the Sicherheitsdienst for the whole of France. These last two, Oberg and Knochen, did not have their offices in the Avenue Foch but on the Boulevard Suchet. It is No. 84 Avenue Foch with which we are concerned in this story, for it was to Kieffer's department that captured French Section agents were brought.[2]

No. 84 is a five-storied, rather grandiose building in the eighteenth-century style. All the rooms have very high ceilings, so the total height is considerable.

The first three floors were mainly occupied by various Services which do not come into Noor's story; it is the fourth and fifth floors with which we are concerned. Here the broad marble main staircase of the house stopped before a door giving access to the office and personal quarters of SS Sturmbahnführer Kieffer. First there was an ante-room, laid with a plain puce carpet and furnished with Louis Quinze chairs. From this two large rooms gave on to the front of the house. The biggest of them, which contained a

[1] Deported to Ravensbrück: returned 1945.
[2] Readers of The White Rabbit (Evans, 1952) are reminded that the experiences of the British secret agent Wing-Commander Yeo-Thomas relates to Schmidt's department, as do those of all members of 'RF' section.

magnificent hanging chandelier, Kieffer had adapted as his office. The other room was his secretary's office. Leading from the ante-room towards the back of the house were Kieffer's bedroom and a kitchen.

Just outside Kieffer's bedroom a fragile-looking little wooden staircase ran up to the fifth floor. This consisted of seven small, rather dark rooms, formerly maids' bedrooms, which had been converted into cells; two slightly larger and lighter rooms, both looking on to the Avenue Foch, one of which was the guard-room and the other the office of the interpreter, Ernest; a bathroom and two lavatories, one of them used by the prisoners. The bathroom and lavatory windows gave on to adjacent sides of a small interior courtyard.

It was in the seven converted cells that a few prisoners were housed. In the beginning it had been the custom to keep captured agents in outside prisons, at Fresnes and elsewhere, only bringing them to the Avenue Foch when they were required for interrogation. However, captured agents housed in these other prisons had sometimes found means of communicating with other prisoners, who had subsequently been released, and in this way information had leaked back to the Resistance and London. In order to reduce the risk of such leakages it had been decided to keep prisoners interesting the Sicherheitsdienst in private houses. Most of the agents of the French Section were taken to a house on the Place des Etats-Unis: and a smaller number, limited to the accommodation available, were kept in the seven cells at the top of 84 Avenue Foch. Those selected for this distinction were naturally the most important.

Kieffer had been an official of the police since before the rise of Hitler. He was a Karlsruhe man, and was for a long time in the Counter-Espionage Department of Karlsruhe. After the Anschluss in Austria he directed this service in Vienna; and in 1940 he was appointed to Paris.

Ernest, whose testimony forms so important a part of the coming pages,[1] was a civil auxiliary. A native of Baden, and Swiss on his mother's side, for fourteen years before the war he had lived in Paris. In September 1939 he was interned by the French: he was released when the Germans came in 1940, and because of his knowledge of French and English was placed under Kieffer in the capacity of interpreter. He was never an official, and had not the right to give orders to anybody; on the other hand, nobody except Kieffer could give him orders. Since June 1943 he had been conducting interrogations by himself, in his own office on the fifth floor. This was because it had been discovered that better results were gained this way than when he acted as a third party

[1] And which I have already cited passim.

between an official and the prisoner. Kieffer was pleased with his work, and only the most important agents, mainly the principals of the French section were given to him to examine. He had not the right to make arrests on his own initiative, but made them when instructed by Kieffer; he was then always accompanied by an official—but if the official knew less than he of the affair, it was only a formality. (In principle, Kieffer's service did not make arrests—it instructed subsidiary services to make them; only when a case was, as it were, presented to them on their doorstep, or when the chase got very hot, would Kieffer let his own men go out.)

Dr. Goetz, before the war a schoolmaster, was the specialist of the Radio service which occupied the second floor. He spoke good French and English, and interrogated only the most important wireless operators of the French Section on the technical side of their work. On paper, Goetz was simply the interpreter of his immediate chief Otto, the head of the Radio department; but because of his superior knowledge, it was Goetz who did nearly all the important work.

It was a remarkable feature of Kieffer's service that all his best interrogators were auxiliaries—amateurs—and had not been through the SS schools. It was perhaps because of this, and because they were, therefore, new to the work and able to bring to it a freshness and suppleness of mind beyond that of officials, that they were so successful. Kieffer recognized their value, and let them work very much in their own way.

Assisting wherever he was needed was Pierre Cartaud, called by his wish Peter (pronounced as in German), a young Frenchman in his middle twenties, dark and rather handsome. He had started in the Resistance, but after he was captured had agreed, to save his life, to work for his captors. He did this with a fidelity that distinguished him from the common run of traitors—at first under surveillance, but later with complete liberty, being even allowed to go to Toulouse and back by himself to complete a 'job'. In the end he became one of 'the most active agents of Kieffer's service. He had a flair for any kind of adventurous mission involving impersonations, and when set on a trail would follow it with such excitement as to be unable to eat or sleep, and with an imagination, resource, and even audacity which in the end commanded the slightly puzzled admiration of the Germans. He lodged at the Avenue Foch and received a small salary; after the war he hoped to be allowed to become a German citizen. During the short period when Ernest was in hospital, after being wounded by the British agent 'Hercule', he assisted the attenuated staff by taking over some of the interrogations. But it was generally agreed that in this 'job' he was not a success. His mercurial temperament did not lend itself to such a slow work; he was impatient, and when the prisoners would not answer he would become excited and slap their faces or box their ears, minor brutalities which only sufficed to put their backs up and ensure that they would not say a word.

II

(Ernest's testimony)[1]

One day in the first half of October, SS Sturmbahnführer Kieffer informed Ernest that he had received a telephone call from an unknown Frenchwoman, telling him she had an important proposition to make, and asking him to send a man speaking French to .the gardens behind the Trocadero. He had arranged with her that the man who came to keep the rendez-vous would introduce himself by the name of 'André' and would have an illustrated review under his arm; she would introduce herself as 'Renée', wear a flower, and be dressed in a certain manner. He told Ernest to keep this rendez-vous, and sent Otto to follow him at a distance with a revolver. Naturally, Ernest also took one.

When he arrived he saw a woman who answered to the description he had been given, went up to her, and said, "André".

She replied, "Renée."

She told him she had need of money, and would give him Madeleine for a price.

He was surprised, because Madeleine was the code-name of a woman radio operator, and would be known normally only to the French Section.

To be sure that this was really the person of whom she was talking, he asked, "Who is Madeleine?"

She replied, "Phono's radio operator."

He knew that 'Phono' was the code-name now being used by Garry, and so was assured about Renée's *bona fides*.

He promised her a sum between 50,000 and 100,000 francs if she enabled his service to make the arrest.

As a proof of her good faith, Renée gave him immediately the cover-name of Madeleine, Jeanne-Marie Regnier (which he knew already), and her address, care of a certain Solange, at 98 rue de la Faisanderie.

She asked him not to arrest Solange. He promised not to do so, on condition that she would allow him to arrest Madeleine at this address in the absence of Solange, or else just outside the house. It was arranged that Renée should telephone Ernest on a day

[1] Although, to cooperate with me in preserving the narrative form of the book, he refers to himself in the third person, the whole of this section, pp. 206-216, is in Ernest's own words.

when the flat was empty, or when Madeleine was there alone.

The next day she telephoned to ask him to meet her in a café. When he came she told him that Madeleine and Solange were both out, and proposed that he should go with her to their apartment and she would show him Madeleine's transmitter. When they arrived she showed him first the place where the key was hidden, so that he would be able to let himself into the apartment at any time he liked. Then she took him in and showed him the transmitter in the kitchen.

A day or two later, Renée telephoned to Ernest early in the morning to tell him that Solange had gone out for the day and that Madeleine had also gone out but would be returning in the course of the morning. He thinks this was on Wednesday, October 13th; at any rate, he is certain it was on one of the middle days in the second week of that month.

He referred the matter to Kieffer, who told him he should take Pierre Cartaud (Peter) and lock him into the apartment, where he could arrest Madeleine on her return.

At about 9.30 or 10 a.m. Ernest conducted Peter to the flat in the rue de la Faisanderie, took the key from the place he had been shown, let him in, and locked the door again. Then he replaced the key and went back to the Avenue Foch.

Peter hid himself behind the door. Presently Madeleine came in. He seized her immediately by both wrists. She struggled violently, and as she could not get her hands free bit Peter's wrist. He could not release it without loosening his grip on her, and cried out, "Let me go!" She would not, but drove her teeth deeper and deeper into his wrist until it bled.

They were thus at a deadlock. Eventually he released her hands suddenly, pushed her on to a sofa, and tried to put on her the handcuffs he had brought with him. She fought with so much strength that he was unable to do this. In the end he drew a revolver from his pocket, said, "Stay where you are, or I shoot!" and whilst covering her with it with one hand, with the other took the receiver off the telephone, which stood on the table, and called SS Sturmbahnführer Kieffer, to whom he explained the situation and asked for help.

Kieffer came into Ernest's office and told him to go to Peter's assistance, taking with him two or three other men. When Ernest arrived he found the situation still as it had been when Peter telephoned.

The spectacle was really funny.

Peter was standing covering her from the farthest possible corner of the room; and Madeleine, sitting bolt upright on the couch, was clawing the air in her frustrated desire to get at him, and looked exactly like a tigress.

When they came into the room she turned on them, calling them *sales Boches* and a stream of other insulting names. She was trembling with rage and her eyes were flashing. In all his experience he had never seen such fury.

She exclaimed passionately, "This would happen at the last moment! Another few days and I should have been in England!"

He noticed that Peter's wrist was bleeding considerably.

He tried to calm Madeleine without coming too near, telling her she should go with them quietly, since if the people in the house were to be disturbed he would be obliged to arrest Solange as a security measure.

She consented eventually, and was escorted down the stairs by all four, her hand on Ernest's arm as he told her. They brought with them her radio-set and the note-book and papers found in the drawer of her bedside table.

They had left the car in which they had come on a corner where it could not be seen from the building so as not to attract the attention of the inhabitants. They brought her back in it to the Avenue Foch. Here Ernest took her straight into his own office on the fifth floor for interrogation.

She said, without waiting for him to ask her any questions, "You know who I am, and what I am doing. You have my radio set. I will tell you nothing. I have only one thing to ask you. Have me shot as quickly as possible!"

He said, "Oh no, I will not have you shot." He then tried to persuade her to answer some questions. She would not answer any of them; and after about an hour, seeing that he could get nothing from her, he told her he would take her to her cell and leave her in peace until the afternoon.

She asked him if she might be allowed to take a bath.

This seemed to him rather an odd request, in the middle of the day and in such circumstances; but it was in his interest to humour her, since it was his only hope of procuring any co-operation. So he replied "Certainly, and anything else you like."

He told one of the guards to take her to the bathroom, and to let her enter alone to use it.

When a prisoner took a bath—as did sometimes happen—the guards had orders to allow the door to be almost, but not completely, closed, a small brick being inserted to prevent its shutting. Through the crack which was left, the guard could see the window of the bathroom.

When Madeleine saw this brick she became furiously angry and demanded that it should be removed. The guard, who understood nothing, [1] called to Ernest to come and see what was the matter.

---

[1] The guards were mainly Rumanians and Russians (prisoners of war) and could hardly speak a word of German, let alone French or English.

208

She explained to him that she wanted to take a complete bath, to undress entirely, and that she could not possibly do this unless the door were properly closed. Ernest told the guard to take the brick away and let her close the door.

The guard said, "On your responsibility, then?" since it was against his orders.

Ernest replied, "Yes," but as he did not feel very happy about it, he went into the lavatory, which gave on to another side of the same courtyard as the bathroom. Standing on the seat, he could see from the small, high-up window across to the bathroom.

When he looked out she had already climbed out of the window and was standing on the narrow gutter which ran beneath the roofs of the attic windows. She was walking along it, touching the tiles with her hands to give herself a little support.

Ernest was horrified. The gutter was only a few inches wide; she might easily lose her balance and fall to the stone courtyard five stories below. It was not even very strong, and might break beneath her.

He was afraid that if he called out the shock might cause her to overbalance; but observing her patiently he perceived she was coming towards him. He realized that there was only one way in which she could hope to climb from the gutter up to the flat top of the roof, from which alone she could escape, and that was by mounting on the triangular roof of the lavatory window, where he was standing—and it was, indeed, towards this that she was making purposefully.

She must, therefore, come to him.

When she was almost directly in front of him, he said in a very quiet voice, "Madeleine, don't be silly. You will kill yourself. Think of your mother! Give me your hand."

She froze, hesitated, and for a moment he thought she was going to overbalance. Then she grasped the hand he was holding out towards her. He caught hold of her shoulders and dragged her head-foremost through the window of the lavatory. He took her straight into the cell already destined for her reception. She sat on the small folding bed and began to cry.

She accused herself passionately, now, for having accepted his hand. "I am a coward!" she wept. "I ought to have let myself fall." She could not forgive herself because, only an hour before, she had asked him to have her shot, and now, when the opportunity had come to her to kill herself, she had not taken it. She blamed herself furiously for being so weak-willed. "When I looked out on that gutter" she sobbed. "I said to myself,

It was very difficult, even for the Germans, to make them understand anything, and the staff were always anxious lest a mistake should occur because the guards had not been able to follow their instructions.

'It's death or escape, one or the other'. I don't know what I took your hand for. It was just because you held it out."

He tried to comfort her, but she was inconsolable.

Reflecting that she was acquainted with Archambault, who was still a prisoner on the premises, he fetched him from his cell and brought him to her, asking him to try to calm her and to persuade her it was not necessary to commit suicide. Archambault said what he could, and she became a little quieter. After about five minutes Ernest took Archambault back to his cell and left Madeleine alone.

Going to the bathroom, he discovered that she had bolted the door on the inside before climbing out. This was the cause of some annoyance; in order to open the door they had to break the lock. [1]

At midday Madeleine refused lunch, which was brought to her in her cell by one of the guards.

In the evening Ernest ordered dinner for two to be served in his office with English tea and English cigarettes. He told Kieffer this preparation was for Madeleine. At about 8 pm he fetched her from her cell into his office and invited her to dine with him. The things he had ordered were brought in, but so far as he remembers Madeleine did not eat. She accepted the tea, however, and the cigarettes, which she smoked furiously all the evening.

He talked practically all the time. He showed her papers on which a member of the staff had already submitted, completely deciphered, all the messages in code found in the notebook in her drawer, a photographic copy of a handwritten report she had sent by 'plane to her chiefs in the French Section, and also a photographic copy of a letter she had written to her mother and sent by the same mail. When she saw the copy of the letter she had written to her mother she was very much affected and the tears began to run down her cheeks. Then he told her he knew quite a lot about the French Section. He knew the head of it was a Major Buckmaster, who had his offices in London, at Orchard Court, and the names also of several of his principal collaborators in London, which he recited to her. He told her, further, that she had had her physical training in a place in the west of Scotland called Arisaig, her security training in a place called Beaulieu in Hampshire (this looked to him like a French name, but he had been assured by Kieffer that it was in Hampshire, England, and that he must pronounce it Biooly, and from Madeleine's reaction when he did so, he was sure that it was not a mistake) and that

---

[1] After this they did not have another lock put on the door, in case of a similar incident; if he remembers rightly they even had bars put across all the windows of the fifth floor, including the bathroom and the lavatory.

her parachute training was at Ringway, near Manchester; and showed her aereal photographs of some of the schools.[1]

Madeleine was aghast at all this. She exclaimed, "But you know everything! You must have an agent in London!"

He said, "Perhaps."

He continued talking to her until about midnight, but did not get any information from her. At last he said, "Well, I am going to bed now. I shall take you to your cell, and advise you to do the same. I hope you will sleep well and reflect about everything before we meet again."

The next morning he began again. He drew her attention to a number of names figuring in both her decoded messages and her report, and asked her who these persons were and what they did.

She replied, "I won't tell you."

He said, "Madeleine, some of these are perhaps not members of the French Section, or of any Resistance organization—simple people, who have perhaps rendered you some small service, such as giving you lodging for the night or allowing you to use their houses for some purpose, out of their friendship for you, and for no other reason. If you will not tell us enough to enable us to distinguish we shall be obliged to arrest them all—for we shall find them all in the end—and those who have done so little, and perhaps hardly understand in what they have been assisting, will suffer with those who are important. If, on the other hand, you tell me which of these people are responsible agents of the French Section or of any French Resistance organization I will promise you that none of the others will be touched."

He saw that he had troubled her by this; she obviously saw and was struck by the point he had made, and for a moment he had hopes he might be going to get somewhere. At length, choosing her words very carefully, she gave him some bits of information

[1] On Ernest's advice, I omitted the names, Arisaig and Beaulieu from the original edition of this book. He was — rather touchingly — apprehensive lest by disclosing details which might be classed as Official Secrets in England, I get myself into trouble. Moreover, Messrs. Gollancz and their solicitor shared his view, that if neither Colonel Buckmaster nor Miss Atkins nor anybody in the F.A.N.Y. had told me the locations of these schools, they were British Official Secrets. Though this seemed to me a case of "locking the stable door after the horse had gone", I did not insist, in the face of so much advice. Also, I could not be absolutely sure the information Ernest had given me was correct. On one point, he was mistaken; Noor had received no parachute training. That he was right concerning the names of the places where the schools were and what was taught in them, I did not know for certain until I met Colonel Spooner, in 1954 (which was after my book was out). When I told him what Ernest had told me, he confirmed that it was correct, and displayed some curiosity as to how Ernest — or Ernest's chief, since Ernest had the information from Kieffer — knew. Ernest's one slip, based on the assumption Madeleine had been parachuted, is interesting as it shows that Déricourt, though he may have told the Germans quite a lot, in addition to letting them see the agents' mail, had not betrayed to them Madeleine's landing by one of "his" Lysanders.

211

in this sense—bits that were rather aggravating than interesting, because she had selected them in such a way that he could not see how they were useful. They brought him no nearer to seeing how he could make any arrests.

Later in the morning the radio specialist, Dr. Goetz, came to collect her from Ernest, and took her downstairs to his own office, to question her concerning the technical side of her work. Perhaps one or two hours later, he came back with her to Ernest, saying, "She will not tell me anything. She won't trust me. She has a certain confidence in you, and perhaps if you go on with her, you will get something." Then, in sudden anger, he exclaimed, "She is impossible! I have never met a woman like her!"

Ernest took her in hand once more. He talked to her all through the afternoon. He talked of all sorts of things, about things unconnected with her work or, sometimes, even with the war, trying with infinite patience to get her to relax.

Later in the afternoon Kieffer came in and asked Ernest, "Well, how far have you got?"

Ernest replied, "Nowhere."

Kieffer had in his hand a document, and asked her to explain something in it.

Madeleine regarded him fixedly for some moments, then replied very deliberately, "To you I will tell nothing— even less than to him. I don't trust you. You are false, and are trying to set a trap for me. I can read it in your eyes."

Kieffer reacted with some anger, and exclaimed to Ernest, "Why don't you give her a slap?"

Ernest replied, "Because afterwards she would tell me nothing at all."

Ernest said to Madeleine, "Why did you do that? It was not necessary to make the Chief angry."

She retorted, "It's all one to me. I don't care."

He continued talking to her until late in the evening, when he took her back to her cell. She had been interrogated during the whole of this day, since the early morning; all he had learned was that her name was Nora Baker (he believed this the more completely because the letter to her mother of which he had a photocopy had been within an envelope addressed to Mrs. Baker and was, therefore, the more surprised to learn from me that her name was Inayat Khan) and that she was a Lieutenant in the RAF, information that was of no interest to his Service.

Ernest wishes now that she had told him her real name and about her family. In his opinion she could well have used her titles as an Indian, and if she had not been so ferocious with Kieffer and the other Germans, perhaps she would not have been killed. But she was too honest to play with her captors.

212

For the next five weeks [1] Ernest interrogated and talked to her every day, sometimes for an hour or a couple of hours at a time, sometimes only for twenty minutes. He had, naturally, other things to attend to, and could not give all his time to so unprofitable a subject. In all his career at the Avenue Foch he never encountered a prisoner who made so much difficulty. He fitted her in with his other work, and took her into his office whenever he had nothing else to do.

He noticed that she was always studying him. She would look right into his eyes, as if she would read his thoughts, her own eyes very wide. She would look at him quite steadily.

Sometimes she would say, "What have you in your mind? You ask me questions which sound quite harmless, but I don't answer them because I don't know where they are leading. I ask myself always what you can be trying to find out."

Once, with a movement of impatience, she exclaimed, "What can you be trying to know, with all these questions? You talk round and round, and it infuriates me because I do not know what you are trying to get at. Will you not tell me at once what you want to know? Since I will not tell you in any case, it would make no difference."

She told him one day she was surprised she had not been tortured.

She had always believed, from the moment when she accepted this mission, that if she were caught she would be tortured for information. During the first week she had expected this every time she had been taken from her cell.

She asked him how his Service had learned the address at which he had arrested her. He replied, "I cannot answer that question. That is a question I never answer to a prisoner."

He was impressed by her steadfastness and her self-control, and the way in which she behaved like a good English woman.

After she had made up her mind she was not going to be tortured she lost her fierceness. She had never at any time shown any fear of him, but now he could see she let herself relax to some extent. When he brought her into his office she would sit down at her ease at the table. She talked in a natural manner about a number of things unconnected with the war, and became almost friendly. It was as though she had acquired a certain confidence in him.

She spoke to him a little about her mother. She said she had asked her chiefs in London not to inform her mother if she were missing, but only if she were known with certainty to be dead. It was some consolation to her, in her present predicament, to know that her mother was unaware of it, and would be receiving

[1] Until he was wounded on November 19th and taken to hospital.

213

from the War Office the usual bulletins to the effect that she was well. Her mother, of course, did not know that she had come to France, or even that she worked for the Intelligence. Ernest realized how deeply she loved her mother.

During all this time the quality of his admiration for her was gradually changing. He admired her first for her wildness, her frankness, and her courage when she insulted her captors after her arrest. Later on, when he knew her better, he admired her for her cleverness, her bravery, and her kindness.

She was always asking for things—he had never known a prisoner ask for so much. On one occasion she asked him to have a man sent back to the rue de la Faisanderie to collect for her a change of clothing and some other effects. She wrote a note to Solange asking her to make up a parcel and give to 'bearer'.

It occurred to him immediately that he might be able to use this note to some purpose, so he told her he did not mind having it taken for her, but she should not mention in it her place of detention.

She believed, evidently, that Solange knew she was a prisoner, and so it did not strike her that this reserve could open the door to any developments.

He thought that since her note did not betray her position there would be no harm in sending Peter with it, with instructions to present himself to Solange as a member of the Resistance and Madeleine's liaison agent, and to see what might come out of that.[1]

On another occasion she asked him for eau-de-Cologne, scent, face powder and other toilet preparations.

He said, "Will you, then, write another note to Solange? Since she is the directress of a *parfumerie,* she can obtain these things for you."

He was glad she had asked for these things, since it gave him the pretext to send Peter to Solange a second time. Again, he did not know what might come out of it, but it was always interesting to maintain the contact. He did not tell Madeleine that Solange had not realized she was a prisoner.

One day she asked for writing materials and plenty of paper. After that, she was always writing in her cell, and always asking for further supplies of paper.

He asked, "What is it you are writing? Is it a novel?"

She replied, "Well—a story."

"May I read it?" he asked, smiling a little.

"No," she replied, "because it isn't finished yet. I don't like people to read my stories before they are finished. When it is finished you may read it if you like."[2]

[1] With the result told in the following chapter.
[2] Since the first edition of this book appeared, I have several times

214

One evening she accepted an invitation to dine with him in his office. She was quite friendly, and told one or two anecdotes, and at some moments they even laughed together. She did not, however, let slip any word which could afford him any information concerning the operations in which she had been engaged, or the identity or whereabouts of her comrades.

He tried to draw her out about herself, and she owned that she loved music, and from the way she spoke of classical composers, Beethoven and Bach, he perceived that she was a considerably educated and cultivated girl.

After they had finished eating, she fell silent, and he noticed that there were tears in her eyes. She had become so nearly relaxed and natural, that he was distressed. In the early days, when he had been interrogating her until she was fatigued and he knew she must have been under great strain, he would have understood if she had broken down; but on this evening he had not been interrogating her.

He asked, "What is it, Madeleine? Have I said something to hurt you? Unknowing? I didn't mean to hurt you. What is it I have said?"

She shook her head. "It isn't you. It's just everything. I was thinking of my mother."

He got up and stood by her, and gathered her against his chest, and stroked her hair. She made not the slightest movement. He became suddenly frightened in case she should trust him and led her back to her cell.

At the door of her cell, he said, "I am your enemy, Madeleine. Never forget that I am the enemy."

She said, "Thank you."

He gave her one kiss, on her forehead, and closed the door, with the key.

It troubled his conscience.

On another day, but it may have been before this, he asked her: "Don't you feel it is a pity you have come on this mission, Made-

been asked what became of this story. It should be appreciated that the fact she wrote one, whilst at Avenue Foch, is known only because I saw Ernest, after the war, and he told me she passed the time by writing and told him what she was writing was a story. I did ask him, without much hope, if he knew what happened to it. Naturally, he did not. Anything written by a prisoner would have formed part of the papers of the Sicherheitsdienst. In the days preceding the German retreat from Paris, he told me, Kieffer and his staff went through every piece of paper, file or drawer of papers that they had. Every scrap of paper at 84 Avenue Foch was looked at and considered by them; and they divided the papers into three piles: to take with them in their retreat, to destroy, and to leave so that the Allies might find them. Noor's story, having no interest from the point of view of their service, would probably have gone into the pile for destruction, but in fact he could not remember its coming up for consideration, and thought it likely it had been destroyed before that, probably when her cell became vacant.

leine? It seems to me such a waste. You are an exceptionally intelligent and gifted girl. If you had not accepted this terrible mission you could have done at home so many interesting and valuable things."

She shook her head. "If I had to make the choice again, I would make it the same way."

"Even although you have seen how things are here? You realize that we have the French Section three-quarters mopped up, and that your sacrifice will not have counted for much."

"It does not matter," she said "It makes no difference. I have served my country.. That is my recompense."[1]

[1] On November 16th, 1949, Renée Garry was tried before a French Military Court at the Reuilly Barracks, on a charge of intelligence with the enemy in having sold Madeleine to the Germans. The witnesses for the prosecution were Ernest (at that time a prisoner in French hands), Madame Garry (widow), Madame Aigrain and Vilayat Inayat Khan. Of these, the only witness of substance was Ernest. The defence at no time challenged his good faith, only his identification of Renée Garry with the Renée of whom he spoke. Asked if he had had any dealings with her after the arrest, he replied that she had telephoned again to the Avenue Foch and asked him to come out and meet her once more. When he did so, she asked him for the balance of the reward promised. He had not been given it to take with him, and told her she would have to come to the office of his service for it. She was upset, and accused him of not keeping his promise. He replied that the balance of the sum promised would be paid, but that she must come, to collect it, to the office of their treasurer, who would require her to sign a receipt and show her identity card. She said she did not see why such formality should be necessary and seemed reluctant to come with him to his office. He said she was not obliged to come. In the end, she accompanied him back to the Avenue Foch, and he took her into the treasurer's office. He saw that the identity card which she produced was made out in the name of Renée Garry. Renée Garry said, "That man is mistaken. What he says may be true, but it was not me." The President of the Court, recalling Ernest, asked, "You maintain it?" ("Vous maintenez?") Ernest replied, "I maintain it" ("Je maintiens.") He agreed, however, that when he had been confronted with Renée Garry in the office of the Judge d'Instruction, he had not at first recognised her. She had changed a lot. "She has fattened."

Madame Garry said Renée was a possessive sister and thought Lieutenant Garry accorded too much importance to Madeleine, and told her it would be better if Madeleine were not so much with them. Renée Garry said she was in love with 'Antoine.' He had liked her, but never noticed her after Madeleine came. Madame Garry, asked by the defence whether she thought Renée Garry would have wished to send her brother to his death, replied, "No." The sole witness for the defence was X. He said Madeleine did not need anyone to betray her, being herself imprudent, and in any case in contact with double agents. He told something of the story of the two supposed "Canadians" who were Germans from the Avenue Foch to whom she had introduced him as the result of the radio-game. The advocate for the defence produced a letter from Colonel Buckmaster written to Renée Garry shortly after the end of the war, thanking her for her assistance to members of his organisation, and asked the panel of nine military judges, "Which are you going to believe, this German or the English Colonel Buckmaster?" Renée Garry was acquitted by five votes to four.

I should have considered I ought to see Mademoiselle Garry, to give her the opportunity of saying anything she might wish to a biographer of Madeleine, but I was told she had not returned to her flat after the

216

III

(Madame Garry's testimony) [1]

At the time of Madeleine's arrest the Garrys had been in the country. It had been arranged that Lieutenant Garry should visit England, and as it was expected that he would be away some time he and his wife had gone to spend a few days with one of his sisters, so that he could say good-bye to her. As soon as the Garrys came back to Paris from the country they learned of the arrest of Madame Aigrain. They thought it more prudent, therefore, not to return to their apartment near the Porte D'Orleans, [2] and went to stay with Madame Garry's sister until the 17th; then on the evening of the 17th they went to the apartment of Solange, 98 rue de la Faisanderie, where Jeanne-Marie sometimes stayed. (They did not realize she had been arrested—neither did Solange.) Lieutenant Garry expected to find here a message fixing exactly the date of his departure for London, which was to be some time between October 20th and 25th.[3] They passed the night in this apartment—for the first and only time.

In the morning they were taking breakfast with Solange when a young man called.

It was Peter.

He said he was an Englishman, and a friend of Jeanne-Marie She was, he told them, now working in the country, and as she expected to remain there for some time she had sent him to fetch some personal effects of which she had need. He gave Solange a letter from her. Madame and Lieutenant Garry both read the let-

---

trial, and had left no forwarding address. Vilayat, who telephoned her lawyer to ask whether he would forward a letter to her, told me the lawyer regretted he did not, at present, know, either, where he could get in touch with her. Neither has anyone ever told me where it would be possible for me to do so.

[1] I call this a testimony, though it is not so in quite the same sense as Ernest's; for whereas Ernest, who knows English, composed with me the words of the preceding chapter, what follows is my summary of what Madame Garry told me during an interview at which I took notes, particularly of the conversations she related. However, I translated the whole into French for her before publication, and she went over the draft carefully, adding some lines.

[2] Ernest says that this address was, however, not known to his Service.

[3] But Déricourt told me the Garrys were not on his passenger-list for the October moon, any more than was Madeleine. He always received from London, by radio, a little before each full moon, the names of the persons he was to put aboard aircraft coming when the moon was full, and instructions for meeting these persons. Neither did London, after the October moon, reproach him with having boarded three persons too few. The question remains, were Madeleine and the Garrys expected in London, and if not, what had given them, all three of them, the impression that they were?

ter, as well as Solange, and they both recognized the writing of Jeanne-Marie.

Solange and Madame Garry went together into another room to pack up the things for which Jeanne-Marie had asked. Whilst they were doing this Lieutenant Garry conversed with Peter, who offered him some English cigarettes.

Solange came back and gave Peter the parcel which she and Madame Garry had made up; and he went away with it.

They all finished their breakfast. Solange had then to go out straight away, but the Garrys had no reason to hurry. They were still in the apartment when Peter returned with Ernest and three other men.[1]

Ernest placed them under arrest. "He was not brutal," says Madame Garry. "Peter was young and liked to show his strength. I was glad we were not left alone with him, as I had the feeling he might hurt us. But with Ernest, I felt always that he had a human respect."

He conducted them back to the Avenue Foch without handcuffs, and took them up the fifth floor, where he put them in different cells.

Madame Garry received a meal at midday, and in the evening dinner. She was not interrogated. At the moment of their arrest Lieutenant Garry had immediately cleared his wife, saying that she knew nothing of the details of his work.

The next morning, after some coffee and rolls had been brought to her, Ernest unlocked the door and came in.

He said, "I have just come to see how you are. I hope you slept well."

"I have slept a little. But I am anxious about my husband. What have you done with him?"

"You need not be anxious, Madame. He is quite well." After a pause, he asked, "Is there anything you need... anything which is lacking to you in this cell?"

"Thank you, I don't need anything."

"If there is anything I can do for you, I hope you will tell me. You can at any time knock on the door, to call the guard, who is not very far away, and tell him you wish to speak with me."

"I only want to know the truth about my husband. I am afraid he must have been tortured."

"He has not been tortured, Madame. He has been interrogated, naturally, but he has not been tortured."

She found it almost impossible to believe him, and stood

[1] Ernest confirms. The Garrys, he says, were arrested on Monday, October 18th. He sent Peter early in the morning with Madeleine's letter to Solange. A little while later Peter came back in a great state of excitement, exclaiming, "Phono's there with his wife!" Kieffer said Ernest should go back with Peter, taking some other men, to arrest them.

looking into his eyes, searching them to know if he were telling the truth.

At last, he said, "I will allow you to see him. Then you will be able to see for yourself. He is having some breakfast now. In a little while I will fetch you and take you to see him. He has been asking about you this morning, too."

After, perhaps, half an hour he came back, fetched her, and brought her face to face with her husband in his office.

He said, "I am afraid I cannot leave you alone together. I shall have to stay in the room, and must ask you not to talk about anything very much. I have brought you together for a few minutes because I thought it would be of some comfort to you to see each other." Turning to Madame Garry, he said, "You can see, Madame, he has not been tortured. He is perfectly well. You can ask him to tell you how he has been treated."

Her husband told her he had been interrogated throughout the night, and was a little tired, but that he had not been maltreated. She could see this was true.

After they had spoken for a few minutes, Ernest told them they would have to finish, and turning to Madame Garry, he said, "You see that what they tell you about the Gestapo is not always true." Then he took them back to their cells.

After they had been for two days at the Avenue Foch they were transferred to the Place des Etats-Unis. Ernest, who came with them in the van, on this occasion put handcuffs on her husband, but not on herself.

Madame Garry adds that she has an appalling memory of the Germans, having seen what they did in the prisons and the concentration camps, but that she owes it to truth to say that Ernest showed himself human in his relations with her husband and herself, treating them certainly as the enemies of his country, but without brutality.

Lieutenant Garry was executed at Buchenwald in September 1944. Madame Garry returned in 1945 from deportation to Ravensbrück Concentration Camp.

IV

Solange confirms Madame Garry's account of the first visit of Peter, when he presented himself to Lieutenant and Madame Garry and herself and collected a bundle of clothes on behalf of Jeanne-Marie.

She had at this time noticed the recent absence of Jeanne-Marie, but without paying special attention to it, even though it was longer than usual, since Jeanne-Marie came and went irregularly. Nor, after Peter's visit, did she see the Garrys again. But as their

219

visits were occasional she did not find their absence more abnormal than that of Jeanne-Marie.

Some time later Peter came back with another note from Jeanne-Marie. Solange remembers the beauty products, including an ochre-rose shade of face-powder, for which she asked, and which she packed up with some things she thought Jeanne-Marie would like.

She gave these preparations to Peter, and he took them away.

V

At about 11 o'clock in the morning of October 30th Vaudevire and Y were arrested together in front of the Palais de Chaillot, when SS, armed with truncheons, had converged upon them from all points.

Viennot heard about the arrest from the son of Vaudevire.

He thought it likely they had been taken to 84 Avenue Foch, where he supposed Jeanne-Marie was also. As all his comrades in this network were now probably in this building, he resolved to try to make contact with them inside.

He bought two double agents, whom he knew as such, both French, a man and a woman, and told them he required to meet a person having access to the prisoners on the fifth floor of 84 Avenue Foch. They introduced him to a German; he bought this man also, and told him he required to see Vaudevire privately.

The German took him into 84 Avenue Foch, conducted him up the stairs, and showed him into an anteroom on the first floor. Here he brought Vaudevire in to see him, and then went out and left them alone together for half an hour.

Vaudevire told him everything that had happened since he and Y had been arrested. He had not been badly handled. He had been confronted once with Y in an office upstairs, but not with Jeanne-Marie. It was his impression that the Germans had not realized the connection of Jeanne-Marie with Y and himself, and it was obvious she had not betrayed their relations with her.[1] He did not, in fact, know whether she was on the premises, for he never heard her name mentioned.

When the interview was over the German reclaimed Vaudevire, and let Viennot out.

He considered afterwards what he had learned from this episode. It occured to him that since he had been able to see Vaudevire it might in the same manner be possible to obtain a meeting with Vaudevire and Y together; and then, instead of

[1] Ernest confirms: "It was not Madeleine who was responsible for the the arrest of—[Y] and Vaudevire. She told me nothing of them, nor of Viennot. I do not know how or why these men were arrested. If they had been arrested as a result of information given by Madeleine, they would have been questioned about their relations with Madeleine."

waiting for the German to reclaim them, to walk out with them through the front door. He had observed that on certain days—whilst the coal was being delivered—there was not a guard on the front door. Even if there was a guard, this man would have seen him come in with the German, and if he saw him walking out with two other persons would suppose it was for some authorized purpose.

A question which troubled him was whether or not he should attempt to include Jeanne-Marie in this scheme. Because of their connection in the same firm, he had been able to represent to the German a business reason for wishing to speak with Vaudevire; and since Y was associated with Vaudevire in the minds of the Germans, perhaps he could extend this reason to cover Y. To mention the name of Jeanne-Marie or Madeleine would, however, be to disclose a relation of which the Germans were ignorant, and also to reveal his own connection with the network. This he did not care to do to a German, even to one who had accepted a bribe. Very reluctantly he came to the conclusion that he would have to leave her out, as to attempt her inclusion in the scheme would be to jeopardize the rescue of the other two. With this he determined to proceed.

He was not, unfortunately, in a position to do so immediately. He had to go through the same channels as before, and they were expensive. It took him a little time to collect the necessary amount of money; and when he obtained a meeting with the German for the second time he learned that both Vaudevire[1] and Y[2] had been sent to Germany.

A question which still remained with him was whether he should attempt to see Jeanne-Marie. If she was still on the premises she would be on the fifth floor. He had had on some occasions to present papers to Ernest, and knew the way 'up the little white staircase' to his office at the top. He could invent a pretext to go and see Ernest again.

It would, however, be pure chance if he should see Jeanne-Marie whilst he was there. Moreover, there would be a certain danger attached to an encounter with her, which she would not be expecting, in the presence of Ernest. He had complete confidence in her loyalty, yet if the unexpected sight of him should cause so much as a flicker in her eyes it might be sufficient to betray their connection.

He feared the perspicacity of Ernest, whom he had always considered to be the most intelligent person in the Avenue Foch. Certainly, he was the most intelligent man whom Viennot ever met there, though he did not get to know him on such a 'friendly'

[1] Died in Buchenwald.
[2] Sent to Mauthausen; returned in 1945.

221

basis as Kieffer and some of the others. When he had been to see Ernest about something, the latter dealt with the matter in hand without entering into unnecessary conversation, and he was never able to suggest a lunch out, or anything. Viennot did not think he was brutal, and had the impression that he was quite polite to the prisoners. In view of the observant character of Ernest, he decided it would be better not to attempt to see Jeanne-Marie on the fifth floor.

Viennot himself was arrested by the Sicherheitsdienst on January 12th, 1944, and was taken to their premises on the rue des Saussaies. It did not appear to him that the Germans were aware of his connection with Y or Jeanne-Marie—though they knew, of course, of his business connections with Vaudevire, and had now discovered that in his capacity of Administrative Secretary he had with open eyes been enrolling members of different Resistance organizations upon the staff.

At one moment the man interrogating him asked him if he knew a person called Jeanne-Marie. He replied, "No." The interrogator did not press the point. He had the impression that the interrogator had tried this question as a random shot, since he also asked him about a number of other persons of whom he had in fact never heard.

He was not sent to the Avenue Foch. He was very severely beaten—largely, he thinks, in revenge for the social side of his activities—and then sent direct to Mauthausen Extermination Camp. However, he was not exterminated, and returned in 1945.

THE ESCAPE

(Starr's testimony)[1]

At the time when Madeleine arrived two prisoners, whose stories were to become closely interwoven with hers, were already being held on the fifth floor of 84 Avenue Foch—Colonel Faye, a Frenchman, and a British officer, Captain John A. R. Starr.

Starr, before the war a poster artist living in Paris, had in May been dropped (on his second mission) into the Jura Mountains, for service in the Dijon area. Here he was betrayed, and after five weeks' detention under revolting conditions at the local HQ of the Gestapo at Dijon, sent up to Fresnes, whence, a fortnight later, he was brought to the Avenue Foch for interrogation.

Here he was questioned by Kieffer, through the intermediary of Ernest. A map of France was put before him on which were

[1] In Starr's words from beginning to "sent up to Berlin" p. 223, line 39, thereafter in mine from notes taken during our interviews, read and corrected by him.

marked the operating areas of the officers of the French Section already captured. There were twelve such areas. He was asked to draw in his own area, which he did, giving it a rather generous contour, and to fill in his code name, 'Bob', and the number 13. Inevitably the hand of the artist revealed itself.

Kieffer was delighted with the elegant appearance of the entry, and showed it off to Ernest with the exclamation, "Prima! Prima!"

Ernest asked, "The Sturmbahnführer wants to know how you come to print like this."

"I am a poster artist. My profession involves lettering."

Kieffer and Ernest talked to each other for a few minutes, then Ernest said, "He asks if you will copy out the whole map for us in the same style."

Starr said he would think about it.

Ernest told him he would be taken back to Fresnes, but would be fetched again.

When he got back to his cell at Fresnes, which he shared with three other prisoners, he told them about his visit to the Avenue Foch. It had occurred to him that if he did do the copying which Kieffer asked him he might later be given other documents to copy which would reveal in further detail what knowledge the Germans had of the British networks. In order to have him work regularly, Kieffer would be obliged to keep him at the Avenue Foch, and from there it might be possible to escape—since it was only a converted private house—and to carry to London the information he had been able to gather. His three companions agreed with him, and gave him their moral support.

When he was brought back to the Avenue Foch he told Ernest he would do the copying.

He was now kept in one of the cells on the fifth floor, from which he was brought out when required for work and installed at a table in the guard-room. As he had expected, when he had finished the map other documents were presented for him to copy: most frequently 'family trees' of the British networks, which the Germans knew about. These displayed the relations between the different operating officers in each team, together with their photographs. The written matter was unsuitable for typing, because of the amount of setting-out involved, but Kieffer liked to have it printed in a neat hand, since the whole sheets had afterwards to be photographed and sent up to Berlin.

When there was no copying to be done they created employment for him, requesting him to draw greeting cards for various purposes, and portraits of themselves. Kieffer asked for a serious portrait of himself which he could send home to his wife for a Christmas present. As he could spare only a little time for sitting he left a photograph with the artist from which to work, and came up from time to time to inspect the progress of the picture. As this was a fine pencil-drawing it occupied some weeks. When it was finished, Ernest asked for a portrait also.

Thus, with one thing and another, Starr was in the guard-room most of the time. From his table he had a vantage point from which he could see much of the life of the place. He could, if the door was open, see the stairs. Prisoners brought in from outside prisons for interrogation were conducted in the first place into the guard-room, to wait until the officer dealing with their case was ready to receive them. And the Germans often came in.

The establishment was entirely SS, but the Germans wore, as a rule, plain clothes; Kieffer generally wore a lounge suit, though on occasions he appeared in the normal uniform of the SS.

On Sunday mornings Kieffer would come up to the fifth floor and go round the cells, opening the door of every one in turn, and offering the inmate sweets and little biscuits out of a paper bag. Along with the confectionery, he usually proffered a few genial remarks in his limited French.

He had a certain sense of humour. Starr drew one day, to amuse himself, a couple of cartoons representing the SS Sturmbahnführer in situations scarcely becoming to his dignity—and left them inadvertently on the table in the guard-room. In the middle of the night he was woken up when Kieffer himself unlocked his door, put on the lights and demanded blusteringly, "Did you do these?" He was holdings the cartoons in his hand.

Starr said, "Yes."

Kieffer grinned hugely, exclaimed, "Prima! Prima!", wished him good night, and locked him in again.

He learned afterwards that there had been a big banquet somewhere outside. When Kieffer appeared he came face to face with these cartoons pinned up on the wall. Somebody had found them on Starr's table and put them where he would see them.

Humour—of a sometimes surprising kind—was not, in fact, lacking in the Avenue Foch. Starr tells a story which was repeated by one of the SS in French, for his benefit.

Goebbels had just died. He went to the gate of heaven, where he found St. Peter waiting with his keys. St. Peter allowed him to look through the gate, and saw a number of rather sanctimonious-looking persons playing harps. He did not quite know what he would do amongst them, and felt self-conscious.

St. Peter said, "Of course, there's always the place down below."

Goebbels looked down and saw Hitler and Goering comfortably installed before a roaring fire, with a bottle of wine between them and a box of cigars.

He said, "I think I'd rather go down and join my old colleagues. I'd feel more at home."

As if by magic, he found himself transported below; but when he got there, the place seemed quite changed. The bottles of wine and the cigars had disappeared, the comfortable armchairs in which his friends had been reclining had become metamorphosed into mean little benches, there was no proper light, and the place resembled nothing so much as a prison.

He felt he had been deceived. He filed a protest and demanded to see St. Peter. Due to numerous regulations, he found great difficulty in contacting the saint again. At last he got put through to him on the telephone and indignantly demanded an explanation.

"Propaganda," said St. Peter blandly, "propaganda."

Starr first became aware of the arrival of Madeleine about breakfast time one morning, when he heard her brought in and taken into Ernest's office.

Von Kapri who came into the guard-room said that they had had unusual difficulty in making the arrest. She had fought most ferociously. At one moment he had put his hand over her mouth to stop her shouting. She had bitten his finger on the inside, and had so clung on to it that he had had difficulty in freeing it from between her teeth. He showed it to Starr, who saw that the flesh was really seriously chewed. He said she had also pulled his hair and kicked him. He expressed the opinion that she had created such a storm that the neighbouring tenants must have been aware of the arrest, and the flat would be useless as a trap for other members of her group. He thought she had done it for this purpose. He did not conceal his very high admiration for the spirit she had shown.

Later in the morning there was a sudden commotion in the passage. Starr did not know precisely what had happened, but he gathered from the guards that she had climbed out of the bathroom window. Afterwards, she was put into a cell opposite that which he occupied at nights.

Later, Ernest gave Starr a slip to copy, with her particulars: *Nora Baker, Royal Air Force.* He heard she had refused to answer any questions.

Later he had his first glimpse of her as she was taken down the passage. After this he saw her every day as she was taken into Ernest's office or to the bathroom. He had the impression that she was a French girl. All the time that he knew her he remembers her in navy-blue slacks, a light grey woollen jumper with a rolled polo neck, and plimsolls. She must have had other clothes, because, with Ernest's permission, he had had a man sent back to the lodgings where she had been arrested to fetch a jacket and some other things; but he cannot remember having seen her wear them. Her hair he remembers as 'light brown with some red lights.'

He does not think she was badly treated. "They all had an admiration for Madeleine—and so had I." Since he saw her every day he would have been bound to be aware if she had suffered ill-treatment.

Living conditions were not bad. The cells were perhaps a little gloomy, since they were very high in proportion to the floor space, and had no windows in the walls (being in the interior, so to speak, of the house). In the middle of the ceiling of each was the square aperture to a sort of funnel. Across the base of this aperture were placed, in every case, three iron bars. At the top of the funnel was a dormer window, opening on a rod. The light which penetrated was obviously not very considerable.

There was no furniture except the bed. This, in Madeleine's case, was an iron one which folded up against the wall when not in use; presumably she sat on it in the day-time. In Starr's case, it was a narrow, movable divan. There were grey blankets, quite clean.

Meals were more than adequate. The prisoners received the same as the Germans, and the portions were very ample. By a curious irony, they were served here with things that the population outside could not obtain, eggs, butter, and an occasional chop.

There was a small library in the guard-room, and prisoners could always borrow a book. These were mostly detective stories and some volumes belonging to a popular series of romances, 'Les Cahiers de la Masque'; there were also some novels of Alexandre Dumas.

Starr saw Madeleine sometimes at closer quarters when she came into the guard-room to choose a book from the shelves. She could do this as often as she liked. On one occasion she said some friendly words to him, but it was impossible to have private conversation, as there was always a guard present.

After she had been there for a little time she asked for writing materials, saying she was bored with having nothing to do. The request was presumably referred to Ernest, and he allowed it. She asked for considerable supplies of paper, and must have spent most of her time afterwards in writing. From the Germans he understood that her compositions were mostly little poems and stories about animals and children, apparently written to be read by children.

II

In the day-time, whenever Starr saw her, Madeleine appeared perfectly calm and self-possessed, but after the lights had been turned out she used very often to cry by herself in her cell.

On one occasion she sobbed all through the night. He wished he could comfort her. If their cells had adjoined, he could have tapped through the wall; but hers was opposite to his, and if he had called this would have brought the guard. As he could not sleep either, he spent most of the night trying to think of a method by which he could get a word to her. It was not till daylight that the sound of her weeping ceased.

When he saw her a little later, from the guard-room, as she passed to the bathroom, she appeared as usual dry-eyed and self-possessed, but he felt that he must communicate with her.

There was only one place, apart from their cells, in which either of them was ever alone; and that was the lavatory. This, then, would be the apartment most appropriate to use as a 'posting-box'. He considered the facilities it offered for the concealment of messages. Besides the lavatory-pan, there was, against the wall, a tap from which a can might be filled. There was a little basin beneath it to catch the drips, and a pipe to take the water away. The under-surface of this basin was naturally convex, and where it fitted to the wall there was consequently a crevice. The whole affair was set rather low, so that one could not see under the basin without stooping, and it was dark beneath. Altogether, the crevice seemed to be a suitable place to conceal notes.

The question was how to make contact with her in the first instance, in order to suggest the use of this repository. If he could manage to be, for one moment, alone in the passage which ran between his cell and hers, he could slip a note under her door.

After some consideration, he wrote, at the guard-room table, his first message. He started: "Cheer up. You're not alone. Perhaps we shall find a way to get out of here," and went on to indicate the place he thought they should use for the exchange of notes.

The lavatory was situated in the passage which ran at right angles from the one giving on to the cells, and was only a few feet from the doors of his and Madeleine's cells, which were at the near end. He needed a pretext to turn the corner in order to be in the other passage just for an instant.

The door of the lavatory was visible from the guardroom, and the guard on duty did not generally follow him up the passage. On his next journey he took with him the note, and also a pencil, a round one that would roll easily. Just at the door of the lavatory, he dropped the pencil, stooped as if to pick it up, caught it with his foot as if by accident, and kicked it so that it rolled a little farther; then he repeated the operation and kicked it round the corner into the other passage. Being already in a stooping position, it was the work of only a moment to slip the note under Madeleine's door.

The guard perceived nothing suspicious in the manoeuvre.

On his next visit Starr looked under the basin and found there was already an answering note from Madeleine. She said she had been very pleased to receive his, and that they should certainly correspond to keep their spirits up. She was, she said, already in communication with a Colonel Faye, a Frenchman, in the cell next to hers. They had been, for a long while, tapping through the wall to one another in morse code, and had by this means exchanged much information. Like herself, the Colonel had obtained writing materials to amuse himself, and would join them in the correspondence through the lavatory.

The question of a triple escape now became uppermost in all their minds.

In Starr's cell a rectangular wooden frame had been fitted under the aperture in the ceiling—that is, at the bottom of the 'funnel'—and it was upon this frame that the three iron bars had been laid and fixed down with screws. He could tell, from underneath, the manner in which they were fixed, and realized that if he could find the means to climb up to the frame, with a screwdriver in hand, he could get the screws out in a few minutes. What was lacking was something to climb upon, and a screwdriver.

He enquired of Madeleine and Faye if their bars were fixed in the same manner; they replied that they were not, but were inserted at each end into the wall itself. To remove them would obviously be more difficult.

Just at this moment luck played into Starr's hands. There was a young woman, Rose-Marie, who cleaned the floors at the Avenue Foch. One day she knocked on the door of the guard-room to say the carpet-sweeper had gone wrong. None of the guards showed any interest, but Starr jumped up and said, "I understand carpet-sweepers!" As nobody demurred, he took the sweeper from her, brought it into the middle of the guard-room, turned it upside-down, and began taking it to bits in a knowledgeable manner. All the dust and fluff fell out on the floor. The Germans became restive, because it was irritating to the nose. Eventually, one of them commented, "It seems to be a long job!"

Starr retorted, "It might be less long, if I had some tools to work with!"

A German told Rose-Marie to fetch from the scullery the box in which she kept her oddments. She did so. It contained some nails, miscellaneous instruments, and a screwdriver. Starr would have liked to retain the screwdriver after he had reassembled the sweeper, but the Germans were watching him too closely.

His repair to the sweeper did not, however, last very long. He had not intended that it should. After a few days, Rose-Marie knocked again on the door of the guard-room to say that the sweeper had broken down once more, and to ask if she might bring it and the tools back to Starr. The Germans said she might, and Starr found himself once more before the sweeper and the box.

This time they did not watch him so closely, and he decided to take the risk of retaining the screwdriver. He thought it unwise to take it straight to his cell, since if Rose-Marie noticed it was missing she might come back and ask for it. Instead, he found a hiding-place. Before the fire-place was a metal screen, and in the middle of this was set a panel that could be slid up to reveal the grate, or down to hide it. Since he was working with the sweeper near to the hearth he was able, without attracting attention, to lift the panel slightly and push the screwdriver underneath it.

If it was missed, and subsequently discovered in this place, he could plausibly deny all knowledge of how it got there. Why should he have wished to put the screwdriver in the fireplace?

A few days passed, and Rose-Marie did not report the loss of her screwdriver. He retrieved it, took it to the lavatory, and left it, stuck by its point, under the basin, for Madeleine and Faye. (A file would naturally have been preferable, from their point of view, but he thought they would be able to use it to mine the walls round the base of the bars.)

As their task would obviously be longer than his, it was agreed that they should keep it between them, to begin with, using it on alternate nights—passing it backwards and forwards, always through the lavatory—and let him have it when they had nearly finished.

They agreed that, in each case, it would be sufficient if one bar of the three were removed. This would leave an aperture big enough to crawl through.

Whilst the other two were working Starr had to solve the problem of how to reach his bars. He was not very tall, and it would be necessary for him to use both the bed and a chair. He had no chair, and the bed was not placed under the skylight. It was at the side of the room; and if he moved it into the middle, this might cause suspicion.

He decided that a series of steps would be necessary.

One evening, he moved his bed from the side where it was to the other side.

When the guard came in next and saw the change he looked very astonished, and gesticulated as though to ask the reason.

Starr said, "I moved it to change the view."

The guard did not appear to be satisfied. He went out, and after a few moments came back with Ernest.

Ernest asked, "Why have you changed the position of your bed?"

Starr said, "I got tired of seeing the room always from one side. Now I shall be able to look at it from the other. It is just to make a little change."

The room was very small and nearly square, and since it had no furniture in it but the bed, presented practically the same view from whatever angle. Starr felt sure that Ernest must think it either silly or suspicious. He watched his face: it showed no sign of distrust. "That's all right," he said, and went out.

A few days later Starr moved his bed again, this time to the wall opposite the door. The guard, when he came in, stared at it once more with the same astonishment; but this time he did not fetch Ernest. After that the bed suffered a number of moves before it eventually came to be stationed in the middle, under the sky-light. By this time the guard was no longer interested.

His next step was to obtain a chair. In a moment when no one was looking he took one from the guard-room into his cell. When the guard came in he stared at it with some disapproval.

Starr said, "It's to hang my clothes on," and tried to show what he meant.

The guard went and fetched Ernest.

Ernest asked, "Why have you taken a chair out of the guard-room?"

Starr explained again. "I have nothing to hang my clothes on at night, and it isn't doing them any good. I thought nobody would miss one chair out of the guard-room."

Ernest said, "That's all right. You can keep it."

For Starr, the problem of how to reach the bars was now solved.

He did not know how Madeleine and Faye were managing to reach their bars. Faye was taller than he, but Madeleine was a small person. She did not, however, post any appeal for assistance, so he supposed she must have contrived a way of reaching them.

One night, some time after lights had been put out, there was an alarming crash in her cell. He realized she must have been standing on the rim of her folding bed, whilst this remained folded up against the wall. From this position she must have had to lean very much forward to reach the bars in the middle of the ceiling; and the bed must suddenly have come down, and she with it.

The guard who was on duty came running, opened her cell, switched on the light, and exclaimed as though he were trying to understand what she had been doing.

She said she had been trying to hang herself by the blankets from the bars in the ceiling.

Luckily he did not think of looking up at the bars, or he would have seen the sockets where she had been mining round them. Neither did he see the screwdriver she had been using. He grumbled a bit, but eventually she pacified him, and he went back to the guard-room.

As the mining of the bars progressed, so the holes round them became larger and more conspicuous. At first, Madeleine and Faye used to fill these up with bread; but the bread was too dark in colour to match the walls well. Madeleine asked Starr, in a note, whether he could not obtain for them a spongy substance the colour of the walls.

He replied, Try face powder, mixed with the bread.

Madeleine had no powder, so she asked Ernest to obtain some for her. So that he should not be suspicious at this sudden request, she asked him at the same time for other toilet preparations, creams, a lipstick, eau-de-Cologne, and scent. He allowed her to have all these things, and somebody was sent out to obtain them.

She had told Ernest the exact shade of powder she required, and when it was mixed with the bread it matched the walls very well. She shared it with Faye, passing it in little twists of paper through the lavatory. With the remainder of the things she made herself look nice.

In the pockets of the jacket she had obtained from her former lodging were rolls of bus and Metro tickets. [1] These she now shared out with Faye and Starr. Once they escaped into the streets the possession of tickets would facilitate a speedy getaway.

Faye was the first to report that his bar was completely free. He passed the screwdriver to Starr, who unscrewed the screws with which his bar was held down, and left it simply lying upon the frame. Then he passed the screwdriver back to Madeleine, and she retained it from this time onwards.

During the days that remained, while Madeleine worked with the screwdriver Starr occupied himself with another problem. The lights in the cell were controlled by switches in the passage. Thus, it was always the guard on duty who came round to put them off at night.

For three people to climb out simultaneously would be bound to create a noise that would be audible in the guard-room. He himself could always stay up late and find some noisy occupation to cover the sounds of the other two; but if he waited till they were free and then asked for his light to be turned off, and afterwards noises were heard from his cell, the guard would think it suspicious and come to investigate. And if he did not ask for it to be extinguished the guard might nevertheless come round to know whether he wished it to be put out. He used to do this. He would have allowed him to read all night if he had liked, but came round, at fairly frequent intervals, knocked on the door,

[1] On the Paris Metro the holder of a 'book' of tickets can go straight down to the trains.

231

and expected to hear an answer, Yes or No. If he came at the moment when Starr was engaged in climbing out this would be embarrassing. He could not fail to reply, and a reply from near the ceiling would betray his position.

One day he saw a piece of flex, with a switch attached, lying on the floor in the guard-room; he took it into his cell. He was trying to fix it when the guard came in and seeing this gesticulated, full of indignation.

"I thought that if I could rig up a switch inside my cell, then I could turn my own light out at night, and you wouldn't have to keep coming round." He tried to show him what he was talking about.

But the guard went and fetched Ernest.

Starr explained. "This piece of flex was lying on the floor in the corner of the guard-room. It didn't look as though anybody wanted it for anything. I thought, if I could rig up a switch inside my cell, then I could be independent of the guard."

Ernest saw the point immediately, and replied, brightening as though he thought it a good idea. "Oh, yes! He wouldn't have to keep coming round."

The last trophy was in the nature of a windfall. One of the guards left his cosh lying on a chair in the guard-room. Starr took it and hid it in the fireplace. He was not decided in his mind whether it would be good to take such a weapon. If they should find themselves, after their escape, near enough to the Germans to have occasion to use it, it would probably be all up with them. He consulted Faye, who said he fancied having it. So Starr transferred it from the fireplace to the lavatory, where he left it for Faye.

Their preparation for climbing out of their cells was now complete, but it remained to consider that this was only half the task before them. When they had extricated themselves from the skylights they would find themselves upon the top of a five-storey building. And they would have to find a way down. They did not know what the lay-out of the roofs might be. They would certainly need ropes; and it was only from the blankets that they could make them. Blanket material was not the best from which to make ropes, because of its tendency to tear. Sheets would have been preferable, but they had no sheets. They would have to be prepared, moreover, to tear the blankets into strips, since a number of descents would be necessary. It was a question of how thin they should risk tearing these, to have an adequate number. They decided in the end not to tear them until they were on the roofs, and could estimate their position.

They believed that the houses on either side of them were also occupied by the Gestapo, and that it would be advisable

232

to make, therefore, across the roofs of those which ran back at right angles from the Avenue Foch, flanking a big courtyard. From one of these it should be possible to find a way down.

Finally, Madeleine signified that she was ready. They decided they would go at midnight that night, as soon as the guard had extinguished the lights. Since they would have to carry their blankets, they would wear their shoes about their necks, to leave their hands as free as possible.

Starr put together the notes he had taken.

III

Starr sat up in the guard-room until late, working upon Kieffer's portrait. At about midnight the guard went and extinguished the lights in the cells; then he came back. Starr went noisily to the bathroom, whistled while he washed, came back, and began to pack his affairs noisily.

Scraping sounds from within the cells went on for some time, audible to him as he was listening for them, but the guard did not notice. At length they ceased. Starr said he was going to bed, and the guard came and locked him in.

He climbed up, removed his loose bar, drew himself between those remaining, and stood on the frame, from which he reached up the 'funnel'.

Faye was already on the roof, and leant down to give him a hand out.

"Where's Madeleine?" he asked.

"I don't know," said Faye. "Something must have happened to her."

They picked out what must be the skylight of her cell, and groped their way towards it.

It was still closed, and when they opened it they discovered, to their dismay, that she was still imprisoned below and working at her bar with the screwdriver. They could not know what had happened, and could hardly ask since she was too far down to make speech wise. Presumably, she had not liked to take the bar out of its sockets in order to test whether it were really free, in case she should not be able to get it back again. Whatever the reason, there was still some plaster holding it at either end.

It was difficult to assist her, because the bar was so far down. Faye, by reason of his longer arms, could reach the more easily. They worked for a long time, more than an hour, perhaps a couple of hours. It was difficult to get under the ends of the bar. The screwdriver grated continuously against the iron, and they were all dreadfully conscious of the sound.

At last Faye got the bar out, removed it, and pulled Madeleine out—and in his enthusiasm, seized her in his arms and kissed her.

They picked up their blankets, adjusted their shoes about their necks, and began hurrying across the roof.

The line of roofs which ran back from the Avenue Foch at a right angle gave, on the one side, on to the courtyard of No. 84, and on the other to a street intersecting the Avenue Foch. All these roofs had flat tops but slanting sides, and from where they were, with access only to the slopes on the side of the courtyard, there was no way of getting on to the flat tops. On the far side of the courtyard—the side facing the back of No. 84—they could, however, see some slightly lower houses with totally flat roofs. If they could once get on to these houses it should be possible to find a way down from them.

To reach these flat-roofed houses at the back, they had, naturally, to traverse the whole length of one side of the courtyard. Instead of the normal gutter there ran beneath these attic roofs a strip of roofing which had a slight slant *downwards*. They had to walk along this; and at five storeys from the ground, carrying blankets, it was not a pleasant walk. The strip was only a few feet wide, and if they had slipped there was nothing to break their fall. Fortunately, the roofs were dry.

At the end of the first, very long reach of the roofs was a raised, circular projection. They had to climb on to this, for it completely blocked their way. To get on to it, with their blankets, was a delicate performance.

From the top of it they could now look straight down on to the flat roofs which had been their goal. The drop, on this side, was considerable, and would necessitate a first use of their blankets. There was, on the circular disc on which they were standing, a vertical projection. This would serve as a staple. They estimated the number of lengths they would require in order to make the drop, tore the strips, knotted them, and tested their knots, all the time talking excitedly. They fixed their rope to the staple and slid down it, Faye first, then Madeleine, and finally Starr.

Now that they found themselves upon the flat roof at last, Faye was almost irrepressibly jubilant. "We've done it!" he exclaimed. "We're free! We're away!"

At this moment there sounded the wail of an air-raid siren. Their hearts sank, because they knew that whenever there was an air-raid the guard came round the cells. Their absence would be discovered immediately, and all available men sent out to search for them.

Their only hope was to hurry. They had to abandon the rope by which they had descended, but had still sufficient blankets left from which to make another.

234

Anti-aircraft firing started from the Bois de Boulogne, and searchlights began to sweep the sky, Suddenly they realized that the roofs were also being swept by long-range torches, pointed from one of the windows of the Avenue Foch. They all fell flat on their faces, hoping that, lying down, they would be invisible. The torches were being shone from one of the lower floors, so that it was possible their forms would not show against the sky-line.

After a few moments the torches ceased sweeping over them, so they jumped up and hurried on across the roof in the direction of the street. They had to climb by some iron steps on to a higher piece of roof before they could look down and search for a means of descent.

From the top they surveyed a drop of four storeys to the pavement. The only intermediate projection upon which they could come to light was a small piece of roof, perhaps three or four feet wide, jutting from beneath a window one storey beneath them. It slanted, unfortunately, downwards, and was scarcely a thing to stand on. Nevertheless, if they could lower themselves to this ledge, by means of another rope, they should be able to break the window and descend the stairs.

They began to tear up their remaining blankets to make a rope. Whilst they were doing this Starr thought of the notes which he was carrying in his pockets concerning what he had learned at the Avenue Foch. If they were to be recaptured—as seemed now very probable—to be found in possession of these notes would make their offence graver. At the foot of the iron steps were some flower-pots. He went down, and buried in one of them as many of the notes as he could.

The second descent was much more hazardous than the first. If the blankets should rip under the strain—the strips were not very thick—the one who was on the rope must fall to the street and be killed.

They tested the knots, and tied one end of the rope to a piece of iron. Faye went first. As it was impossible for him to take his cosh, whilst clinging to the rope, he had to leave it, regretfully, on the roof. [1] Reaching the ledge safely, he broke the window with his elbow and climbed through. Madeleine and Starr followed him.

They found themselves now standing on a landing. The house was in total darkness. They felt that the noise of the falling glass must have wakened the occupants, and were expecting a light to be switched on. Yet this did not happen, and they could hear nobody moving. They crept down the stairs as quickly and quietly

[1] It was found the next morning by one of the guards, and used on Starr.

as they could, reached the hall, opened the front door cautiously, and looked out.

There was nobody in the street, but they saw, to their dismay, that it was a *cul de sac*. It had been originally an ordinary street, but an enormously high brick wall had been built right across it, and the house through which they had descended adjoined the obstacle.

Across the open end of the *cul de sac*, they could see SS guards passing and repassing. It was obvious that a cordon had been put round the block, and they were trapped.

The question was what they should do. Whatever they did now, they were almost certain to be recaptured. They could go back into the house, and wait until it was invaded, or they could make a dash for it. Faye was for making a dash for it. They might be able to break through the cordon, he thought. The other two agreed, and followed him. They went in single file, Faye first, the other two at distances of about a couple of feet, keeping in the shadow of the wall, their shoes still about their necks.

When they reached the corner, Faye made a sudden spurt forward. There was immediate firing from automatic weapons, and SS guards seized him from all sides and took him away.

Madeleine looked back at Starr, as much as to say, "What shall we do?"

He plucked her sleeve, and said, "Come back."

They retired a little farther into the shadow. As there seemed nothing to do now, they began walking back together towards the house. When they reached it the door was still open, and they went in again. They went—a little aimlessly—up the stairs. On the first floor, they tried a door. It opened, and gave on to a sitting-room.

They went in, groping their way round the furniture, and sat down on a couch. They began talking—about what, he does not remember now, except that they were probably exchanging information, in case one or other of them should be able to escape on another occasion. Suddenly they realized there was a woman standing looking at them, from over the banisters. [1]

[1] Madame Esmerian recognized Starr, when he and the author called on her on January 3rd, 1950. She then told the history of this night, as she remembered it.

She was awakened by the noise of anti-aircraft firing from the Bois de Boulogne, and then heard a crash of glass, as one of her windows fell in. She thought a piece of flak had come through, until she heard footsteps. She got up and listened at the door, and realized that some persons were descending the stairs, but did not like to come out, in case they might be thieves who would attack her. At last she heard the front door creak, and knew that they had gone out. Then she heard firing in the street, and understood that they must have been prisoners who had escaped over the roofs from the Avenue Foch.

A few minutes afterwards she heard the front door creak again. She remained behind her door, listening, and realized that people

She asked sharply, "What's going on?"

They had no time to answer. At that moment the door swung open into the hall below and a troop of SS surged up the stairs, putting on all the lights. They came straight into the sitting-room, seized Madeleine and Starr, and marched them down the stairs.

They had traversed about half the distance back to the Avenue when the SS began to belabour their two captives with blows and kicks as they walked. [1]

In the vestibule of No. 84 everything was in commotion. Kieffer was downstairs, in a towering rage, shouting orders and accusations in all directions. Even the Germans were trying to keep out of his way, for his anger seemed ready to break upon any person who crossed his line of vision. Faye was standing between guards.

As soon as Madeleine and Starr were brought in Kieffer marched over to them and said, "You're all three going to be shot!"

He ordered the SS, "Take them upstairs to the fourth floor and stand them up against the wall!"

The whole party trooped up the stairs and into the ante-room of Kieffer's personal apartment. Here, at the foot of the little white staircase, the recaptured fugitives were arranged in a row for execution.

Kieffer stood glowering at them, looking from one to another of their faces as though bursting with overmastering passion.

Faye spoke suddenly: "I have only done my duty!"

One of the guards struck him on the mouth.

There was silence, the SS waiting with their automatics.

The tension was broken when one of the guards had to go upstairs to fetch something. When he came down he said he had looked into the three prisoners' cells, and that Madeleine had drawn a V sign and a RAF device on the wall. Kieffer made no comment.

During this time the guards had been searching the prisoners. One of them found in Starr's pockets the photograph which Kieffer had given him from which to work at the portrait. He handed

were now coming up the stairs. She did not know whether they were the same ones who had passed through before, or loafers who had come in from the street, seeing the door open.

She came out from her room and, without putting on the lights, crept down the stairs very quietly. She saw the sitting-room door was open, and, leaning over the banisters, could discern a man and a girl sitting on a couch.

She called out, "What's going on here? Are you thieves?"

They both started and looked round at her.

The girl answered, "We're not thieves! We're escaped prisoners!" She was crying.

At that moment the front door opened and the SS men came pouring in.

[1] Witnessed by the Concierge du Square, who had been peering from a window since the firing began.

it to the Sturmbahnführer, who asked, "What were you taking my photograph away for?"

"A little souvenir."

Kieffer's face twitched into the ghost of a smile upon one side, then straightened again.

There was a long, heavy silence. Kieffer was obviously fighting a battle within himself. It was painfully visible—visible in every muscle of his face—that he could not make up his mind whether to give the order to shoot. The longer he delayed the more difficult it became for him; his blood was not now so hot. He knew them personally, and perhaps it began to feel like murder. He kept looking from one to another of the three faces before him; and the three against the wall watched his.

At last, as though he got control of himself with difficulty, he said they should be taken upstairs again and he would come to see them later.

During this ordeal nobody, Starr thinks, had spoken directly to Madeleine, and she had not said anything. [1]

IV

Immediately following the recapture of the three fugitives Kieffer visited Madeleine that same night in the cell to which she had been taken.

He asked her to give him a written declaration that she would make no further attempts to escape. If she gave him such a declaration he promised her that he would continue to keep her at the Avenue Foch, under the same conditions as heretofore; if she refused it, he would be obliged to resort to the severest measures.

She refused to give him the declaration for which he asked, telling him she would consider it her duty always to seek and to take any possible way of escape, and to resume her hostile activities.

In the face of such a statement he felt it impossible to continue keeping her on the premises.

He immediately sent a telegram to Berlin saying that she was a desperado, that 84 Avenue Foch was not a stronghold, that he was unwilling to accept further responsibility for her safe custody, and that he requested permission to have her transferred to Germany. He received the authorization by return telegram, and had her sent away without delay.

He transferred her to Karlsruhe, because he was himself a Karlsruhe man and had a cousin who was a member of the Karlsruhe Gestapo. His idea was that this cousin could visit and inter-

[1] Starr's testimony ends here.

rogate her in prison and keep him informed by telephone of anything which he might learn from her without their conversation
having to go through official channels.

She was the first British agent to be sent to Germany.

Madeleine and Faye (who had also refused the option of
parole) were sent together from Paris to Germany later in the
very day the early morning of which had seen their recapture,
November 26th. In Germany they were separated; he was sent
to Bruchsal (where he was kept with hands and feet in chains) [1]
and she to Pforzheim.

Starr was kept at the Avenue Foch until July 1944, when he
was sent to Sachsenhausen Concentration Camp, and from there
to Mauthausen Extermination Camp, from which, after frightful
sufferings, he was eventually able to escape. As I have told the
story of Starr fully in my second book, *The Starr Affair*, I do not
want to go into it here.

In 1947, Kieffer was put on trial, together with Knochen, his
direct chief, before a British Military Court at Wuppertal, on the
charge of having passed on an order (which came from Berlin and
which had been passed down to him by Knochen) for the execution of a party of uniformed paratroopers captured in Normandy
in August 1944. This was the sole charge, and we have it on the
authority of Miss Atkins (Intelligence Officer to Lt.-Col. Buckmaster, she was the officer charged after the war with tracing
the fate of the missing agents of the French Section and represented the Section at the War Crimes Trials held at Wuppertal
and Hamburg) that if his responsibility in this matter had not
come up he would be walking about a free man today since "we
had nothing else against him."[2] Kieffer asked for Starr as a
witness, and he was called through the Judge Advocate-General's
office. Speaking under oath in answer to Counsel, and choosing
his words very carefully, he said that he had not been ill-treated
himself and that to the best of his knowledge and belief no
member of French Section had been ill-treated whilst in Kieffer's
department at 84 Avenue Foch. Of what might or might not
have happened further afield he could obviously say nothing.
Asked by Counsel whether he could state that he had seen all

---

[1] Colonel Faye was executed, ultimately, on January 30th, 1945, at
Sonnenburg, but I am indebted to Madame Marie-Madeleine Fourcade,
OBE, his collaborator in **L'Alliance**, for showing me copious notes in his
hand which were, after the war, found behind the radiator in the cell
he had occupied at Bruchsal, folded into an infinite number of small
pleats, to escape detection by the guards. They included an account of
the triple escape, or rather attempt to escape, which confirmed Starr's,
down to the delay caused by Madeleine's unfortunate failure to remove
her bar, and the order which the three of them made their way across
the roofs and descended by the blanket-ropes.

[2] In speaking to Vilayat and me, not in court, but in her flat, on
November 17th, 1949.

239

prisoners who were brought to the Avenue Foch, he replied, "No." Kieffer was executed.

V

There is one extraordinary episode related by Raymonde, who says that on a Thursday in the latter part of November (she thinks on the 25th), at about 8.30 in the morning, Noor appeared suddenly at the front door. She was very much out of breath, excited, and for the first time was empty-handed.

Raymonde was amazed to see her and exclaimed, "Noor! I thought you were in England!"

"No, no no!" She made a frantic little gesture with her hands. "I haven't been in England. Something else happened."

"Where have you been?"

Noor was still very much out of breath, and had obviously been running for a long way. She would not reply to Raymonde's question, but brushed it aside with another little gesture: "I'll tell you later. I haven't time now. I must transmit from here this afternoon. At three o'clock. It's very, very important."

Raymonde did not understand why she had come empty-handed: "Why haven't you brought your transmitter!"

"I can't tell you the whole story now. I will come with it this afternoon. You will be in, and ready for me when I come so that I can start at once?"

"Yes, yes, of course."

Noor ran away down the path.

This was the last time Raymonde ever saw her.

She had an appointment that morning in Paris, to be fitted for her trousseau, having recently become engaged. She went to it, but thought of nothing all the morning but Noor's strange reappearance. She supposed that she must have been in the provinces for these six weeks, since she said she had not been in England. But she had looked so wild and agitated. Raymonde was troubled, and arrived home from the dressmaker's by 1 o'clock. She waited in the whole afternoon, but Noor did not come—then or ever.

Ernest knows nothing about such an escape as Raymonde's story would suppose. He was in hospital at the time, but is positive that if Kieffer, Goetz, or any of the others had known of it, they would have told him. Kieffer came to see Ernest in hospital, and told him Madeleine, Starr and Faye had got out on to the roofs.

It is always possible that the escorting party lost her as they were taking her to the station. If this had happened, and they had been able to recapture her in time to put her on the train—

Noor

Noor in
WAAF uniform

Avenue Foch, 84

The FANY memorial
at St. Paul's Church, Knightsbridge, London,
Corps Commander MacLellan laying the wreath after
the unveiling by H.R.H. Princess Alice on May 7th, 1948.
The author, who was at the ceremony,
laid among grander tributes a small bunch of lily-of-the-valley,
thinking of Noor.

Memorial plaque in Suresnes to Noor
(a similar memorial plaque has been placed at Dachau)

RAF Memorial at Runnymead
unveiled by Her Majesty the Queen - October 17th, 1953.
As Noor's next of kin, Vilayat received an invitation for two to
the unveiling and took the author as his fellow-guest.
After the ceremony they made their way through the vast crowd
and moved slowly around the edifice until at last
in the fading light they found among the many names
N. Inayat Khan G.C. in the stone.

by luck—it would be understandable that they should not have mentioned the matter on their return to the Avenue Foch. The evidence in Germany shows that she arrived in Pforzheim on Saturday, November 27th, having spent one night in Karlsruhe. She had travelled from Paris on the 26th. This puts out of court Raymonde's date of the 25th for Noor's strange reappearance, though curiously enough it was on the night of the 25th/26th that the triple escape was attempted. Noor would have been meditating upon it at the time Raymonde thought she saw her.

GERMANY

Pforzheim is a small industrial town on the northern borders of the Black Forest, about twenty miles east of Karlsruhe. Its main business is the making of jewellery. The prison, which is not very big, and is intended only for local delinquents, had not housed military or political prisoners before the winter of 1943. The first political prisoner to be sent to Pforzheim was Nora Baker. According to the records of the Staatsanwaltschaft, she was brought at 2.30 pm on November 27th.

The cells are of a fair size, each furnished with a folding iron bed, or beds, and a chamber-cabinet with a wooden lid. The windows are set too high for it to be possible to see out without climbing, but in spite of this the rooms are surprisingly light; probably because the walls are painted in a very light cream or white. (When I visited the prison in 1950 it appeared scrupulously clean.) Nora Baker was in one of two cells on the ground floor, separated by double iron gates from the main part of the prison.

Herr Wilhelm Krauss, the Governor, now retired (he was seventy-two in 1943) says he was not warned of her arrival.[1] He came into his office one day and was told that men from the Karlsruhe Gestapo had come and put a British spy in one of his cells. They had brought papers with instructions concerning her. These said her name was Nora Baker, that she was a 'very dangerous prisoner' and had to be kept 'under the most severe régime', in chains by day and by night, in solitary confinement, and without the possibility of communication with other prisoners. None of the guards was to speak with her; he was forbidden even to do so himself.

Nevertheless, he went at once to the cell where she had been put. There he found her, sitting on the edge of the bed, her hands in handcuffs, her feet in handcuffs, and a chain from the handcuffs on her hands to the handcuffs on her feet.

1 Testimony of Krauss to the author in 1950.

He was horrified that he should be required to keep her in this condition night and day—even when she ate, which would mean that she would hardly be able to lift a spoon to her mouth. He ordered that when her food was taken to her the handcuffs should always be removed, and replaced when her feeding-bowls were collected.

In all the fifty years of his service he had never known a prisoner to be kept under such conditions, or heard of one so kept elsewhere. He had had murderers in his prison, but had never been required to keep them in chains. But he did not dare refuse, for fear of the Gestapo. Herr Friedrich Fässer, Hauptwachtmeister at the time when I visited Pforzheim prison, told me that each of the chains was about five feet long.

The only person besides Herr Krauss who was allowed access to her cell was Herr Anton Giller, at that time Hauptwachtmeister. The instructions were that she was to be kept strictly segregated from the other women prisoners; even the woman attendant, who normally served in the women's section of the prison, was not to enter her cell. When she arrived at the prison Noor was completely dressed by the woman supervisor, but after that the supervisor was not allowed to see or speak with her. She was never to leave her cell, or to see or be seen by any other prisoners. The cells on either side of her were to be kept empty.

Every morning, before the cells of the women's section were unlocked, Herr Giller brought her drinking and washing water, just as he brought her her meals. Afterwards her pot and tub were emptied and cleaned by a woman, in his presence. Every Saturday before the cells were unlocked, he issued her with a complete set of clothes and underclothes. When he unlocked the cell a little later she would give him back the used clothes. In the same manner he issued sanitary towels to her.

It is impossible to tell how long she was kept completely chained, as at first. That the conditions of her detention were gradually eased emerges from the statements of all my informants, though they naturally do not tally in every detail.

Krauss says he thought at first that she would be left with him only for a few days, but time passed and he became troubled. She could not live in chains for ever. Eventually he took it upon himself to have the chains taken off, and ordered that once a week she should be brought out from her cell and allowed a few minutes' walk round the courtyard.

A few days after he had taken this step he was telephoned by an offical of the Karlsruhe Gestapo, who asked whether he was still following his instructions faithfully, and in particular whether he was still keeping her in chains.

He replied, "No, not any longer, She cannot escape from here. If she does escape, I will be responsible."

He was anxious about the possible consequences of this defiance; but there were no repercussions.

She seems to have been allowed to walk round the courtyard of the prison under the surveillance of Giller, for about three-quarters of an hour on each occasion. Some of this time she spent doing gymnastic exercises. Fässer, the only person still on the staff who knew her personally, speaks of her with an admiration which convinced me as being sincere and deeply felt. "She made a very good impression on me; not only because her conduct gave no cause for complaint, but above all because in spite of her obviously unhappy position she was always frank, open, and friendly. She could speak some German, and as often as the situation allowed we would talk to her. On such occasions she always showed a good spirit and a healthy humour. Her courage made a very strong impression on me. I shall not forget her expressive face, her friendly smile, her athletic figure, and her lively manner. She always had a word of thanks when we stopped for a few moments' conversation with her, or allowed her out for a walk."[1]

Giller remarks how she would sometimes ask him to explain this or that phrase in the German books she read, but he never talked with her about politics or the war. There were two days, he remembers, when she was particularly sad—the birthdays of her mother and her brother.

Krauss came in the end to know her quite well. He used to sit down beside her on the little iron bed. Their conversation was rather laborious, because she did not speak German very fast; nevertheless, she could express most things, and told him something of her history—that she was a spy, and had been captured in France. It was only from her that he learned this, since the papers he had received from the Gestapo revealed nothing of her story and bore no indication that she had been captured in France. She said she had volunteered in London for the Secret Service and had asked to be infiltrated as a spy into German-Occupied France. He was impressed by the courage with which she emphasized that she had chosen this work freely; a less honest type would have said she had been persuaded into it. She said she had been brought to France by aeroplane and had sent back communiqués to England until she was arrested by the Gestapo and taken to their headquarters.

She said that after a few weeks she had escaped and had rejoined some people with whom she had worked prior to her capture. If Krauss remembers correctly this is the one external

[1] Fässer to the author.

243

corroboration of Raymonde's story. I mentioned the unsuccessful triple escape over the roofs, but he said this sounded to him like another story. He was positive that she told him she had reached friends. She said that if she had not been recaptured she would have resumed her communications with England and former work.

One thing perplexed him for some time. His idea of a spy, if female, was a woman who made love to men and drew their secrets out of them. Miss Baker seemed to him so obviously respectable that he could not imagine her doing this. At last he plucked up the courage to ask her. She assured him that she was not that sort of spy!

She told him that she was half Indian, which surprised him very much since she was so fair-skinned he would never have thought it. She said her father had been a kind of priest, and she had spent some time in his country as a child, and had studied Indian literature and philosophy, about which she told him something. He realized she was a very well-read girl and possessed a developed mind.

She bore the conditions of her detention with a great fortitude. He asked sometimes if she had any complaints, but she always said she had not. She never made any comment upon the chains, even at the beginning when the fettering was complete. She seemed to realize that he was not responsible for their imposition, and did not hold it against him.

When she first arrived it was obvious that she was having a great spiritual struggle with herself. She looked tormented, and sometimes her expression was quite wild. She said she had come from Karlsruhe, and he thought she had perhaps had some bad experiences. As time passed she became calmer, and he thought the tranquillity did her good. Her present circumstances, if not comfortable were probably less frightening than the adventures through which she had come. His final impression was that she was a very fine person.

It is remarkable that Noor told Krauss things—that her father was an Indian and a spiritual teacher—which she had kept from Ernest, and even from her colleagues in the Resistance. This was doubtless because, now that her interrogation at the Avenue Foch was behind her, she felt that the great ordeal—the interrogation by the Gestapo, for which she had been braced from the beginning—was over, and that she had nothing more, in a security sense, to fear. Neither does it seem that Krauss in fact passed these details to the Gestapo. He was just an old man, who came and sat in her cell, with whom she could relax, to some extent. But I think, more than that, that her mind was turning back to her father. She had told me, in London, that if ever she found

244

herself with the time to be alone she would try seriously to prac-
tise meditation, and I have not a doubt in the world that in
Pforzheim, in the solitude of her cell, she meditated upon her
father and tried to get in touch with him.

II

In January of the next year, 1944, a group of French political
prisoners was sent to Pforzheim from France. Three of the women
shared a cell, and the only one who has survived has described
to me their life in the prison. Every morning, she says, the
prisoners were woken by a bell at 6.30 am. As soon as it sounded
they had to get up, fold the iron beds against the wall, put the
cell in order, and complete their toilet by the time the guards came
round. Under the surveillance of the latter, they emptied their
slops and refilled their little basins so as to have clean water
during the day. Then the door of the cell closed, and they waited
for breakfast.

Towards 7.30 they would hear the noise of clinking bowls, and
their own bowls were passed to them through the grilles. They
were forbidden to look at the guards who brought the bowls. The
breakfast consisted of coffee, which was more like hot water than
anything else. They were also given bread, which had to last for
the day. Then they waited for the walk, which they were
permitted after the men from the floor above had exercised.

The courtyard was small, and the prisoners walked in a circle,
one behind the other, an equal distance apart so that they should
not talk. They were not allowed to turn round. Several guards
kept watch over them, and also made certain that they did not look
in the little windows of the cells: such an indiscretion was
punishable by the dungeon. Sometimes, while they were exercising,
their cells were searched to make certain they had no pencil,
paper, scissors, penknife, or any other useful object. The walk over,
they were locked into their cells again, and everything relapsed
into silence until the lunch hour.

They were kept occupied with little tasks such as the threading
of tickets of different sizes, which they put together by the
hundred on a knitting-needle—a needle which had its uses.

At midday the serving of the bowls began again: a bowl of hot
water masquerading under the name of soup, and a second bowl
which contained the main dish: swedes, crushed peas unfit for
consumption, or a kind of paste made out of sour cabbage. After
the meal the guards opened the cell to collect the dirty bowls;
and then the women started to work once more.

At 5 pm clean bowls were brought to every cell and the serving of water began again; each prisoner poured clean water into her little basin; then they waited for the soup. In the evening there was only soup, but a little thicker than in the morning.

Again all was silence. At 7 pm they had to go to bed. In the winter there was no light. Sometimes they ate their soup without light. They were not allowed to talk or make any sound whatsoever.

Every day the same monotonous life went on. They heard the guards pass in the corridors, the noise of keys when a cell was opened to let out a prisoner going to be interrogated. Often Herr Krauss carried out an inspection, and the prisoners had to stand to attention.

The women's section, my informant went on, occupied the ground floor, and consisted of twelve cells facing one another, but cell No. 1 was on the other side of double iron gates which closed the entrance to the women's corridor, and was therefore distinctly separated from all the others. This cell never opened, even at the time of the walk.

One day they had the idea of trying to find out whether there was perhaps another prisoner there, not one of the group which had come together from France. So with their knitting-needles they scratched on the bases of the six bowls they had between them: *There are three Frenchwomen in cell No. 12.*

They waited impatiently for the clean bowls to come back at 5 o'clock. When they did, the reply was scratched: *You are not alone, you have a friend in cell 1.*

To and fro the bowls went, after this, with their messages scratched on the bottom. It took a long time, and sometimes the women had to wait several days for the reply, as the bowls might be circulated to other prisoners before they came back.

What is your name?

I cannot tell you. It is too dangerous.

Nevertheless they persisted in the question; and at last she replied: *Nora Baker, Radio Centre Officers, Service RAF, 4 Taviton Street, London.* [1]

They all memorized this address for after the war.

On July 4th, American Independence Day, Noor wrote on her bowl: *Long live the 4th July.* And on July 14th, the French National Fête, she wrote: *Long live free France! May this rally us!* Underneath, she drew two little flags, one English and one French.

The French prisoner says that in other messages Noor wrote that she was very unhappy, that her hands and feet were chained, and that she never went out. She asked if they could give her news of events, and in response the inmates of cell No. 3 sang

---

[1] This is obviously a garbled recollection. 4 Taviton Street was the address of Noor's mother, not of the Air Force or any office.

246

the news to the tune of a popular song. Unfortunately a guard heard them, and Noor was punished for it. On another occasion she had an altercation with one of the guards and, much to the admiration of the Frenchwomen, held her end up bravely. They were both moved and impressed by her refusal to be browbeaten.

One day, as the three of them passed her cell, they said, as though they were talking to each other, "Courage, Nora!"

One afternoon, when everything was quiet, they thought they heard steps in the courtyard. Out of curiosity, they climbed on to the bed in turn, while one of them kept watch in case a guard should come down the corridor, and saw Noor. It was the first time she had come out. As she passed by their cell she raised her eyes and saw the women and smiled. She was still wearing her own clothes.

In other messages she wrote, *Keep me in your thoughts, I am very unhappy,* and *Never tell my mother I have been in prison.* They wrote to comfort her, *The Allies advance, we shall celebrate the victory and drink champagne,* and each of them put her address in France so that they could meet after the war.

They saw her on another occasion when she went out for a walk. This time she no longer had on her own clothes, but was wearing a garment made of sackcloth. As before, she looked up towards their window and smiled. Afterwards they read on the bowl, *Don't look at my clothes. They have taken away my own. Forgive me!*

Her last message was in September, *I am leaving,* written in a nervous, trembling hand. The Frenchwomen were surprised, and much troubled. Where had she gone, they wondered?

This was the last they heard of her.

III

Krauss says he came into his office one day and was told simply that men had come from the Karlsruhe Gestapo and taken Nora Baker away. He never learned any more. Giller thought she was removed because they had lightened the conditions of her detention.

According to the records of the Staatsanwaltschaft, she was fetched at 6.15 in the evening on September 11th, 1944, and taken to Karlsruhe. So ended her stay in Pforzheim of nearly ten months.

DACHAU

Details concerning the last phase are meagre.

In the course of the enquiries which preceded the Natzweiler

Trial, in May 1946, it emerged that on July 6th, 1944, a certain Wassmer, formerly a clerk of the Karlsruhe Gestapo, had, with another man, conducted four women from Karlsruhe to Natzweiler, where they were executed on the evening of the same day; and that this same Wassmer, on September 11th of that year, conducted four other women, of whom Nora Baker [1] was one, from Karlsruhe to Dachau, where they were shot on the following day. [2]

As this was all the information available from official sources, I wrote in 1950 to the United States Resident Officer in Karlsruhe and asked if he could give me the address of Herr Wassmer, as I wanted to write to him about Nora Baker. Six months later his office sent me Wassmer's address, together with a copy of a memorandum from another United States Office, giving the substance of an interview with him by a member of its staff. This contained the following passage:

'On direct orders of a Gestapoleiter Gmeiner[3] (shot in 1947), Wassmer and another Beamter took Nora Baker and three other British agents to Dachau. They travelled by fast train and arrived with their prisoners at midnight. They received receipts for this transport and returned to Karlsruhe on another fast train at 8.30 the following morning.

'... The above is all he claims to know about this affair. He volunteered further that he has been in various internment camps for three years, one year thereof in respect of the Nora Baker affair.'

I wanted something more personal. At the same time, I realized that Wassmer must be weary of interrogations, and did not suppose he would be pleased to be asked yet again for information. After some thought, I wrote him a long letter explaining very fully the matter in which I needed his co-operation. I said I had received his address from the American Office, and was almost sure the renewed questioning to which he had been subjected had been started by my enquiry. I told him that I had been a friend of Nora Baker in private life, and expressly stated that I did not belong to any official service or organization and asked him for his more intimate recollections of the journey to Dachau only in order that I might complete the last chapter of the biography of her that I was writing.

[1] The other three women were Mrs. Yvonne Beekman, with whom Noor had trained at Wanborough when they first joined the FANY. Mrs. Elaine Plewman, and Mademoiselle Madeleine Damermant, all posthumously awarded the Croix de Guerre.

[2] See **The Natzweiler Trial**, 'War Crimes Trials Series', published by William Hodge & Co., Introduction by Anthony M. Webb, p. 21.

[3] This Gmeiner, head of the Karlruhe Gestapo, had received, as in the Natzweiler case, a teleprint message from the Reichssicherheitshauptamt in Berlin instructing him to arrange for the execution of these women in a convenient camp.

My hope of receiving a reply was not very great. Wassmer had had too much trouble to want to be further concerned. I was therefore very moved when after a few days I received a letter of several pages telling me, in simple language, that he understood my appeal and was anxious to respond to it to the best of his ability. The obvious sincerity of his letter was most touching: it was clear that he was anxious to help me as best he could to complete my picture of Noor, and to show that her wonderful bravery did not fail her at this time.

He explained that in the summer of 1944 he was commanded to take four Englishwomen from Karlsruhe prison to Dachau. (His Department of the Sicherheitspolizei of Karlsruhe had nothing to do with any aspect of the case except the transport.) The party went by rail—not in a prison carriage, but in a reserved compartment in an express train. Herr Wassmer gave the women the four window-seats. He does not know which one of them was Noor, as he had never seen any of them before that day. They had brought bread and sausages with them from the prison to eat on the journey, and two of them still had a few English cigarettes, which they shared round. When these were gone Wassmer gave them German ones. They talked together in a very lively and spirited fashion, and he did not feel that they were at all afraid; but as he speaks no English, he had no idea what they were discussing. Between Stuttgart and Augsburg there was an air-raid alarm and the train came to a standstill. The passengers stayed in the train, and the four prisoners continued their conversation and did not seem nervous. There was no actual air raid, and apart from the alarm the journey passed without incident.

When they reached Dachau Wassmer took the women, in accordance with his orders, to the part of the camp where prisoners were received. This is all he knows. Later, official information was received in Karlsruhe that the women had been shot.

APPENDIX I

CENTRAL CHANCERY OF THE ORDERS
OF KNIGHTHOOD

St. James' Palace, S. W. 1.
April 5th, 1949.

THE KING has been graciously pleased to approve the post-humous award of the GEORGE CROSS to Assistant Section Officer NORA INAYAT KHAN (9901), Women's Auxiliary Air Force.

Assistant Section Officer NORA INAYAT KHAN was the first woman operator to be infiltrated into enemy-occupied France, and was landed by Lysander aircraft on June 16th, 1943. During the weeks immediately following her arrival the Gestapo made mass arrests in the Paris Resistance groups to which she had been detailed. She refused, however, to abandon what had become the principal and most dangerous post in France, although given the opportunity to return to England, because she did not wish to leave her French comrades without communications, and she hoped also to rebuild her group. She remained at her post therefore and did the excellent work which earned her a post-humous Mention in Despatches.

The Gestapo had a full description of her, but knew only her code name 'Madeleine.' They deployed considerable forces in their effort to catch her and so break the last remaining link with London. After 3½ months she was betrayed to the Gestapo and taken to their HQ in the Avenue Foch. The Gestapo had found her codes and messages and were now in a position to work back to London. They asked her to co-operate, but she refused and gave them no information of any kind. She was imprisoned in one of the cells on the fifth floor of the Gestapo HQ, and remained there for several weeks, during which time she made two unsuccessful attempts at escape. She was asked to sign a declaration that she would make no further attempts but she refused, and the Chief of the Gestapo obtained permission from Berlin to send her to Germany for 'safe custody'. She was the first agent to be sent to Germany.

Assistant Section Officer INAYAT KHAN was sent to

250

Karlsruhe in November 1943 and then to Pforzheim, where her cell was apart from the main prison. She was considered to be a particularly dangerous and unco-operative prisoner. The Director of the prison has been interrogated and has confirmed that Assistant Section Officer INAYAT KHAN, when interrogated by the Karlsruhe Gestapo, refused to give any information whatsoever, either as to her work or her colleagues.

She was taken with three others to Dachau Camp on September 12th, 1944. On arrival she was taken to the crematorium and shot.

Assistant Section Officer INAYAT KHAN displayed the most conspicuous courage, both moral and physical, over a period of more than twelve months.

APPENDIX II

DECISION No. 13.

ON the proposition of the Minister of the ARMIES,
THE PRESIDENT OF THE PROVISIONAL GOVERNMENT
OF THE REPUBLIC
Chief of the Armies, Minister of National Defence,
CITES TO THE ORDER OF THE ARMY CORPS

A/S/O NORA INAYAT-KHAN, WAAF.

"Sent into FRANCE by Lysander on June 16th, 1943, as a wireless operator, with the mission of assuring transmissions between London and an organization of the Resistance in the Paris area. Shortly after her arrival a series of arrests broke up the organization. Obliged to fly, she nevertheless continued to fulfil her mission under the most difficult conditions. Falling into an ambush at GRIGNON, in July 1943, her comrades and she managed to escape after having killed or wounded the Germans who tried to stop them. She was finally arrested in October 1943 and deported to Germany.

This citation carries the award of the Croix de Guerre with Gold Star. [1]

PARIS, January 16th, 1946.
(Signed) DE GAULLE.

P. A. Lieutenant-Colonel PEDRON
Director of the Cabinet of the EMGDN.
(Signed) PEDRON.

[1] Literally **avec étoile de vermeil** (used of a medal, vermeil means 'gilded').

DREAMS OR INTIMATIONS

I cannot put a date to it, nearer than to say that it was after D Day and after the V.1.s, that I was moved, at the Censorship, to a new floor and a new table. Indeed, it was during the V.2.s, for it was at the new table that I put out my hand to stop a bottle of ink from sliding down the table as it rose a little at one end with the shock of a V.2 falling nearby. At this new table I had new companions. I knew that the moon-faced woman facing me had sung in grand opera, yet we had not talked much. We were not supposed to talk at all, at the tables, for our business was reading. I went out to the washroom, and as I was coming back, I encountered my new vis-à-vis on the staircase-landing. "Do you know the Inayat Khans?" she asked.

I was surprised, for we had never spoken of India, of Sufism, or of any subject which could lead the mind to the Inayat Khans. "Yes," I said, and asked her why she asked.

She had woken, she said, that morning with it in her mind that I would know them. She had known the whole family, had visited them at Gordon Square, when Noor-un-nisa was a tiny tot. She had lost touch with them for many years; but of late months they had been in her mind. More precisely, it was the two eldest children who had been in her mind. It had become fixed in her mind that Noor-un-nisa and Vilayat were on the continent, and that they were in danger. The idea had become lodged with her that because of their knowledge of France, they had been induced to undertake some form of secret work for this country.

The habit of saying little concerning people's possible service movements had been so instilled into us, for security reasons, that, taken by surprise, I said for a moment nothing at all.

Madame Nevada hastened to assure me that she was not questioning me as to what they might be doing. "I only want to know that they are all right," she said.

And this was precisely the assurance I could not give her. Vilayat came sometimes on leave, I told her, but he and their mother had received no letter from Noor-un-nisa for over a year. They were indeed concerned by the absence of news from or concerning her.

Was it a dream which had prompted her to ask me?

It was not a dream; or if she had dreamed she had forgotten the dream. It was simply that on waking this morning she had known that I was the person to ask.

We walked back to our table together. At my side sat a Mrs. Szabo. Mignon Nevada leaned across the table, and in a low voice

252

told her of our encounter and conversation on the staircase. She had the worst apprehensions concerning Noor-un-nisa.

Mrs. Szabo answered that she, also, had apprehensions concerning a girl. "I have a little niece," she said. And she described to us a pretty girl, who had been much away from home, and from whom nothing at all had been heard for a long time. It was as if she had vanished. She felt that she was in trouble. "When a pretty girl vanishes, one thinks usually of a certain sort of trouble, but I feel that it's not that sort of trouble." And she added, "I don't like to tell her parents what I think." What she thought was that as Violette was half-French, she had been sent to France on some kind of secret mission. She did not think they would ever see her again. "I think that she is dead."

When I looked back on it at a later time, it seemed to me strange that there had been this conjunction of persons connected with the only two girls to be awarded George Crosses after their death, Noor-un-nisa Inayat Khan and Violette Szabo.

But the uncertainty as to Noor's fate continued for a long time. It was while the Allied armies were sweeping across Germany, liberating Belsen and other camps that I had a dream. Babuly came towards me, wearing her FANY uniform, but surrounded by a blue light, her face radiant. "I'm free," she said.

When Vilayat came next on leave, I told him of this dream. He had dreamed the same, he said.

I supposed it meant she had been prisoner in a camp which had now been opened, and that she would soon be coming home.

He had interpreted it in exactly the opposite sense. "It means she is dead."

APPENDIX IV

OBSCURITIES CONCERNING THE CIRCUMSTANCES OF NOOR'S DEATH; THE NATZWEILER MYSTERY AND TWO DREADFUL LETTERS

On April 29th, 1946, a letter was sent from the War Office to Mrs. Inayat Khan, informing her that her daughter Noor had met her death by lethal injection at Natzweiler Concentration Camp on July 6th, 1944. The trial of the Natzweiler camp staff, began exactly a month later, at Wuppertal on May 29th, 1946.

The first I heard of it was when my doorbell rang unexpectedly, and I found Vilayat standing on the step. Still on the step, his eyes nearly standing out of his head, he said, "I've found out what happened to my sister. She was burned alive!" He had had advance notice of the trial, with some indication of what was likely to be said at it. In the next days, there was considerable publicity in the Press. It was alleged by one witness (though not proven) that the girls were not entirely dead when put into the incinerator and one newspaper carried headlines: *Four British women burned alive.* The names of the girls were not given in all the papers, but Mrs. Inayat Khan, having received this letter from the War Office, could not doubt that her daughter was one of the girls referred to, and collapsed into sobbing which Vilayat, sitting at her bedside, could do nothing to relieve.

I was therefore surprised and perplexed to read in the official citation for the posthumous award of the George Cross published on April 5th, 1949, that Noor had been shot at Dachau on September 12th, 1944, a difference in both the manner, place, and date of execution. I wrote to Colonel Buckmaster, whose name I now discovered for the first time in the newspapers, telling him that I had been a friend of Noor in private life and that I would like to see him to ask him more about what had happened. He replied saying he was just going abroad, but referred me to Miss Vera Atkins who, he assured me, could tell me as much as he could. One of the first questions which I asked Miss Atkins was, "Which is right, the letter from the War Office or the official citation?"

"The official citation," [1] she said simply.

Mrs. Inayat Khan died within about ten days of the publication of the award to her daughter. Vilayat, who feared that to have Press reporters ringing up to ask for details about her daughter would only renew her emotional distress, and indeed that if a reporter obtained her on the telephone she would cry, and say Noor should never have gone on this mission and blame those who sent her, took her away from London so that she could not be reached, but she died within a few days of his taking her back to their old home in Suresnes. She had never really recovered from the first announcement of her daughter's death, and now it seemed that she had lived only just long enough to hear of the honour which had been bestowed on her.

Some time later, when Vilayat and I saw Miss Atkins together, at her flat, on November 17th, 1949, she told us both, very frankly, how the first mistaken announcement came to be made. She had been retained by the War Office for about a year after the close-down of the Section, with the task of tracing the fate of its missing agents. She had discovered that in May 1944, a party of eight women were sent together by train from Paris to Karlsruhe, and seven of these eight she was able to identify as members of the French Section. On arrival at Karlsruhe the party had been split up; one, Odette, had been sent to Ravensbrück; and of the remaining seven, four, including the one unidentified, had been taken to Natzweiler for execution on July 6th, and the remaining

[1] She, in fact, composed it.

254

three to Dachau on September 13th. At this time she was ignorant
of Noor's fate, and so the thought not unnaturally occurred to her
that Noor might be the unidentified eighth girl in the party which
had travelled down together in May from Paris to Karlsruhe and
who subsequently perished at Natzweiler. She therefore showed
a photograph of Noor to Odette, the only survivor, and asked her
if she recognized in it the picture of their unidentified travelling
companion. Odette, doubtless in good faith, replied that she did.
It was on the strength of this mistaken identification that Miss
Atkins reported it as having been established that Noor was one
of the four girls[1] killed by lethal injection at Natzweiler.[2]

It was not until a letter was received from the French woman
Madame Yolande Lagrave, the sole survivor of the women prisoners held at Pforzheim, reporting that she had been in written and
continual contact with Noor until *the beginning of September*
that it was realized that she could not have been executed in July,
and that she must have been at Pforzheim. Reference to the records of Pforzheim prison revealed that Noor had in fact been held
there from November 27th, 1943 (six months before the transport
in May of the eight), until September 11th, 1944. The transport
official, Max Wassmer, then told her (as he later told me) that
he had in fact collected one woman from Pforzheim on the 11th,
whom he took, with three from Karlsruhe, to Dachau on the 12th.

With regard to the mysterious eighth woman of the party which
travelled together from Paris to Karlsruhe, subsequently the fourth
in the party taken from Karlsruhe to Natzweiler for execution,
her identity was discovered by Mrs. Elizabeth Nicholas, a journalist. She was a Polish girl, Sonia Olschanesky, who had acted as
courier to an agent, Jacques Weil. Curiously enough, her photograph shows her as a girl with dark hair and a face not altogether
unlike that of Noor, which makes Odette's mistake comprehen-
sible. Mrs. Nicholas has told her story in a book *Death Be Not
Proud* (Cresset Press, 1958) devoted to the six girls of this sad
party who died at Natzweiler and at Dachau, apart from Noor.
She left Noor out because I had already made Noor the subject
of a complete biography, whereas the others seemed neglected.

When I was writing the first edition of this book, I had to

[1] Miss Diana Rowden (Starr's courier), Miss Andrée Borrel ('Denise',
Prosper's courier), and Miss Vera Leigh were the three identified.
Diana Rowden was awarded a Croix de Guerre, Vera Leigh a King's
Commendation; Andrée Borrel, strangely, received no decoration at all;
yet her period of service in the field was one of the longest, the respon-
sibility of her work considerable, and there is testimony to her gallantry.

[2] Miss Atkins had discovered her mistake in time to avoid it when
giving evidence at the trial. Appearing for the prosecution, after giving
the names of the other three, she referred to "a fourth woman whose
identity I was and am unable to ascertain." The Natzweiler Trial ed.
Anthony M. Webb (Hodge, 1949), p. 39. Some lack of liaison must have
allowed Noor's family to receive uncorrected information.

consider whether I should end at the gates of Dachau, or continue on the basis of an account Miss Atkins gave me in 1949 of what Max Wassmer told her, when she interrogated him in 1946; according to this, the four girls had been put into cells for what remained of the night, and early in the morning (of the 12th) taken out and conducted to the crematorium, where they were required to kneel, in two pairs, one after the other, and shot through the back of the neck. My cause for hesitation was that Wassmer had not claimed to have seen this himself; on the contrary, he had said he learned of the execution from a teleprint received at Karlsruhe when he returned there in the morning. The details he had heard later, he had told Miss Atkins. I had no positive reason to doubt the account, but my reflection was this: what Miss Atkins told me Wassmer told her he had heard somewhere was not evidence; it would not be entertained in a court of law. It was hearsay, and I did not care to take the responsibility of giving it out on my own authority. When I wrote to Wassmer, he replied with the long letter, giving the details about the journey which I have quoted, but he said that after handing them over at Dachau he knew nothing more, excepting that official notification of their execution was received. In the circumstances, I decided to end the story with what was certain, that Wassmer took them to Dachau and left them there.

The original hard-cover edition of this book brought me many letters from the public but not one that touched the last chapter. After the paperback edition had given it a much wider circulation, I received still more letters, amongst them two which caused me the greatest distress.

One, posted from Canada, was from a Lieut. Col. H. J. Wickey, who said that for a short period just after the war he had been head of the Military Government in Wuppertal Eberfeld, and a member of the War Crimes Commission, and that while so employed he had, in Hamburg, in circumstances so unofficial he was unable to use it, obtained a word-of-mouth confession from a German, name withheld, who had been on the staff of Dachau Concentration Camp.

The other, posted from Gibraltar, came from a man who said he had been a prisoner at Dachau. He said he saw the four girls when they were brought in, and at close enough quarters to have looked into the eyes of the one he recognised in my frontispiece, which met his twice, but that then he went to his block and his

[1] Professor M. R. D. Foot, in his book SOE in France (H. M. Stationery Office, 1966, p. 429) follows Miss Atkins's account, that is to say an account in which I recognise what Miss Atkins told me Wassmer told her he had heard; for Professor Foot's source reference, given in a footnote to the page, "On interrogation, 27 May, 1946", specifies neither the name of the interrogator nor the person interrogated.

further account was furnished to him by another person in the camp (name given), who said he saw, and told him within hours. Had either of these communications been the only one, I might have disregarded it as perhaps based on imagination; there is a horrid concordance between the accounts, of different provenance, which forbids me to dismiss them.

Putting together the two, which I shall call, respectively, Hamburg and Gibraltar, the story which emerges is this: Noor (called by Hamburg "the Creole (Creolin)" was separated from the other three girls and worse treated. She was not, it appears, violated in the sense that a woman most fears, but was partially undressed (both accounts) and subjected to blows (both accounts, and according to Hamburg, by Hamburg himself, name or first name supplied by Gibraltar) which she received without crying out or speaking (Gibraltar). Gibraltar refers to her being at the time in chains. After this she was left for several hours in a cell, alone (Hamburg), and some time during the next day (the 12th), shot with a pistol (both accounts) through the back of the head (Gibraltar) (It could be that he should have said neck). Hamburg adds that it was within the cell where she had lain that she was shot, and Gibraltar that as she knelt to receive the bullet, she spoke one word, "Liberté".

APPENDIX V

SOE IN FRANCE, M. R. D. FOOT
(LONDON, HER MAJESTY'S STATIONERY OFFICE 1966)

I had not intended to refer specially to this book, but just as the present edition of my own went to the printer, I received a long letter from Mr. Wite Carp, containing passages he had copied from it, under the impression I did not know of it. The reverse is the case. I knew that it was to be, before the author.

It is perhaps good that a story behind this publication be set on record. *Madeleine* (the first edition of my biography of Noor) was followed by two other books which I wrote concerning mysteries of SOE which had come to my knowledge while engaged on the research for the first. In the second, *The Starr Affair* (Gollancz, 1954) I disclosed that certain of the radio sets belonging to those of our radio operators who were captured, were played back by the Germans, who transmitted asking for supplies of arms, which were parachuted to them, as were men and women, surprised to be received on the field by the *Sicherheitsdienst*. This had not been mentioned in a book by Maurice Buckmaster, and Victor Gollancz was so apprehensive lest in publishing it we should be breaking the *Offical Secrets Act*, that he delayed a year while the matter was examined. As he said in half-jest but half-earnest, his concern was not with libel, in the ordinary sense, but lest both author and publisher found themselves imprisoned in the Tower. I spent many hours in going through the *Offical Secrets Act* with his lawyer, whom I finally convinced that, as I had never served in S.O.E. and my information was acquired from a German, formely of the *Sicherheitsdienst,* who obviously had not signed the British *Official Secrets Act,* a publication by me could not be in breach of it. The publication, which was not denied from official quarters here, nevertheless caused considerable perturbation.

My third book, *Double Webs* (Putnam 1958), dealt with the even more disturbing case of the double agent, Déricourt, alias "Gilbert", and went, in addition, further into the case of the played-back radios. By this time, I had a friend in Dame Irene Ward, D.B.E., M.P., who made this book the subject of a Motion in the House of Commons on November 13th, 1958. Before doing this, she had also sent a copy of my book, itself, to Mr. Harold Macmillan, then Prime Minister, and she gave me, as a keepsake, the letter he wrote her in reply, saying he looked forward to reading it. She asked him the answers to certain question raised by the book, and suggested that there should be an official history written by a historian authorised to see the official files. Mr. Macmillan made an appointment for Dame Irene to see, at the Foreign Office, Lord Landsdowne, who answered the queries rising from my book as best he was able, and she passed the answers on to me. After careful consideration, Mr. Macmillan acted upon Dame Irene's suggestion that an official historian be appointed, and for a considerable time I was privileged to see a confidential correspondence.

On the morning, of July 31st, 1961, I received a telephone call from Dame Irene[1] to tell me she had just come from the Foreign Office, where somebody had been introduced to her. Would I join her and this person at the House of Commons for lunch, August 3rd. When I arrived, Dame Irene presented her companion to me, as "the historian." I asked him his name. We were standing within the House of Commons, and perhaps he feared the ear of persons passing, for instead of answering verbally, he pointed downwards, at the carpet, I first thought, or at the floor. I wondered if I should look for something lying on it: then I perceived that he was pointing at his own foot, and divined his name must be Foot. "My very existence is an Official Secret" he murmured.

When, almost five years later, in the spring of 1966 *SOE in France* appeared from Her Majesty's Stationery Office, I was, when I saw it, surprised to find that it contained no acknowledge-

[1] Afterwards created Baroness Ward of North Tyneside, C.H., O.B.E.

ment to Dame Irene Ward, and she, for her part, was sorry the story of how it came to be written had not been included, from the point of view that the telling would have constituted a personal tribute to Mr. Macmillan.

APPENDIX VI

NOOR'S HOROSCOPE

Noor, according to a note in her father's hand, was born in Moscow, at 10.15 in the evening of December 20th, 1913, according to the old Russian calendar. Adding the thirteen days needed to convert the Julian to the Gregorian, brings us to Friday, January 2nd, 1914, in terms of the calendar in general use over most of the world today. I have checked the birth data as given with a pre-natal epoch calculated for March 22nd, 1913, at London, when an appropriate interchange between the positions of the moon and the horizon will be found.

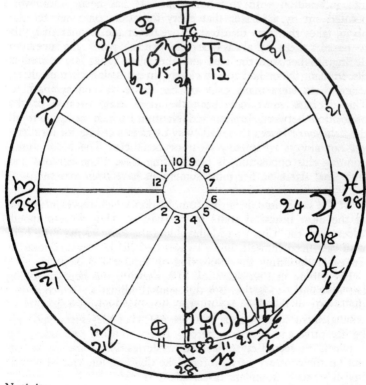

Nativity

In the nativity, it will be seen that the Ascendant falls in one of the latter degrees of Virgo, the Moon, in Pisces 24, being on the far side of the horizon, having just set. Virgo is Mutable Earth and Pisces is Mutable Water, and both signs have to do with purification and discernment. Virgo, the sieve, represents the principle of discrimination, Pisces of all embracing sympathy and compassion. Virgo is conscious of the need for purity; to Pisces, all things are pure. There is here at once suggested a tension between the solvent sympathy of Pisces, rendered even more fluid, and more powerful, as a tide, by the presence in Pisces of the Moon, and the need for a discerning vision shown by the rising Virgo. It is traditional that the very sympathetic nature of Pisces tends to be exploited. Pisces is idealistic, poetic, and renouncing; because it understands the needs of others, it tends to give way. Only, in order for Pisces not to be exploited, and to direct its gifts usefully, it is essential for the discernment represented by the opposite sign, Virgo, to be developed. It may be that this was the essential problem and test for the soul coming into incarnation with this horoscope. It has been, moreover, pointed out by a Master that every initiation, on whatever the plane, takes the form of a test, in whatever the manner that this is posed: there is always at the critical point the need to distinguish between the true and the false. What is required is discernment. Noor had to see clearly, in confusing circumstances, when there were many calls on her emotions and sympathies. This dilemma must have been the more acute because of the opposition between Jupiter and Neptune, which brings out all the liability of Pisces to be led away by causes calling for idealism, yet not always completely clear or beneficial. The Moon, mid-pointing this opposition, is highlighting it, and the nervous and emotional strain on her must sometimes have been extreme.

At the same time, it is this combination which represents some of the most beautiful traits in her nature. Her solvent poem 'Nocturne', the 'Chant au Madzub' and the story of the little hare who sacrificed himself, are all expressed in this liquid Moon in Pisces, midpointing the opposition of Jupiter and Neptune.

Everything that was mystical in her nature was here, including her attachment to fairies. But this same combination, which allows the beauty of the character to transpire, also permits a liability to entanglement with persons who are not what they seem, and may be deceptive and even treacherous. Every coin has two sides, and between the sacred mysteries and mysteries which are not sacred, but on the contrary very profane, the dividing line can be almost invisible, so that, unless discernment is very sharply developed, the person who should, by his or her sensibility and fineness, be concerned with the one, becomes sucked into the other. Should Noor's discernment have led her to refuse the terrible mission offered to her at the War Office? One cannot say, for it is not given us to know what may, in the end, forward the evolution of another. Nevertheless, I agree with Madame Hélène Bouvard that Noor was carried away by the idea that it was necessary to suffer, whereas "in reality she was made for joy, children and music." Noor believed she would gain through this work a self-discipline and practical efficiency which had previously been missing from her "dreamy" nature; also, as she confessed to me on the last evening, she had from childhood wished that destiny might offer her the occasion to face the test of a real martyrdom. So, do we sometimes draw to ourselves our fates. But certain it is that from the moment she stepped down from the aeroplane to be received by a man who had relations with the Gestapo as well as with London, she was in a world of deception, a shadow-world where everyone lived under false identities, where two "Canadians" were two Germans, and where she was treacherously sold to the Germans by a Frenchwoman. All this comes under the illusion- and snare-creating side of the opposition between Neptune and Jupiter, the two rulers of Pisces, swelled by the tide of her own Moon in Pisces. Against all this, her purity of motive shone so brightly as deeply to impress the interrogator who questioned her at the German Security Service Headquarters. She brought out the highest, the lowest, and again the highest of this planetary combination.

On the plane of natural woman's life, it should be observed that the Moon is on the 7th cusp, the cusp of the house of marriage. Therefore all questions affecting marriage are likewise affected by this Jupiter-Neptune configuration; and though she inspired men, each time that she gave her heart to a man, it was in one way or another unfortunate.

But the essential soul is always supposed to be represented by the Sun; and Mercury, in Saggitarius 28, Venus, in Capricorn 2, the Sun, in Capricorn 11 and Jupiter in Capricorn 25, are all in the 4th house, which represents the home, the parental influence and tradition, and everything belonging to the family ambience. Here one sees how important were her father and her mother to her, how her whole life was dominated by the awareness of them, and how deeply she integrated her family responsibilities. At the same time, one can see that the family life, just because it was so rich, threatened to become almost too engrossing to her, and one understands that at a certain moment she felt impelled to fling herself out from it, to the most removed point.

In and around the 10th house, which represents the most extraverted manifestation, are the three malefics, Saturn in Gemini 12, Pluto in Gemini 29 on the very cusp — the governor of the infernal regions on the Midheaven, — while Mars is close in Cancer 15 with Neptune 27. It can be said at once that Mars is not well placed in Cancer, the latter being an emotional and feminine sign, the special sign of the mother. Yet there is just one case in which the mother will always fight, and that is in the defence of her children, so that Noor has this maternally defensive Mars, elevated by mundane position, though weak by its containment in a feminine sign, urging her to fight in the cause of those she felt were under her protection. In the protection of her own mother, she was fierce; possibly because her mother's Capricorn Moon was close to her own Sun, Noor felt the protecting one, rather than, as a child usually feels, the protected. But this same emotional ferocity must have been with her when she clawed the air like a tiger when first arrested. There is a paradox in the fact that while the centre of gravity in Noor's map falls in the house of home and family, she had to go out from this and achieve a posthumous fame through the malefics gathered about her Midheaven, the point of honour. Pluto, situated here will represent the enemy she saw it as her duty to combat. This Pluto, which is opposite her own Mercury, falls exactly conjunct the Mars of Ernest, in Gemini 28, his Mercury being in Gemini 23, zo that one has here the indication of the intense mental strain of the long battle between them in which the only weapons were words (Mercury); the battle of the interrogator and the interrogated. One sees also in this position of her Pluto, why she impressed herself so indelibly on his mind. But his Moon, in Capricorn 10, was conjunct her Sun, and his 4th cusp Venus, Neptune and Sun, in Cancer 3, 5 and 6 opposite to her Venus and Sun, so that one sees at once that, the functions of office apart, there was more sympathy than enmity between the maps. Indeed, the horoscopic exchanges between these two nativities would have favoured quite a different relationship.

Referring to Vilayat's map, it strikes my eye at once that his Sun, in Gemini 28, was conjunct Noor's Midheaven and Pluto, which indicates the intensity of the relationship and her adoration of him. Also, this conjunction midpoints the trine between his Ascendant in Leo 28 and his Jupiter in Aries 28, so that one sees what support she felt his presence gave her; that his Saturn and Venus fall between her Mars and Neptune, perhaps suggests, on the other hand, the apprehension he so often felt on her account. His protective prudence (Saturn and Venus in Cancer) falling on her Mars, he would have liked to prevent her tendency to rush into dangerous situations.

With Hidayat's map, there is also a point of contact, in that his Moon is near to hers, in Pisces 27 (the common love of music), but this is in square to her Pluto, which perhaps explains his consciousness that Noor could be, in his phrase "strict" with the younger children. This may have been felt even more by Claire, since her Sun, in Gemini 11, fell beneath Noor's Saturn; but Claire's map, with its emphasis on the beginning of Gemini, takes more after their mother's — which might be expected in the case of the one whom their father called "Mother's Daughter."

In the horoscope of Inayat Khan, the Sun was in Cancer 13, conjunct the great star Sirius, and while this is nearly conjunct Noor's Mars, it is probably more important that it shines down very nearly on to her Sun, in the opposite sign, giving, so, an image of the manner in which the radiance of his personality almost overwhelmed her.

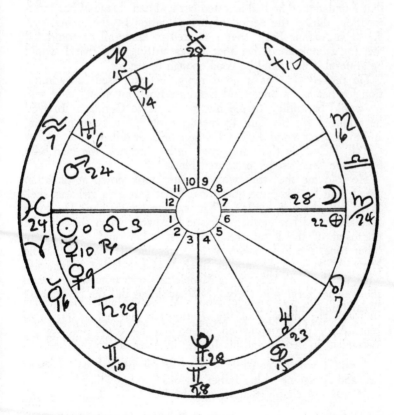

Pre-Natal Epoch

263

APPENDIX VII

IMMORTALITY

In order to write the story of Noor, I had to trace and to speak with those who had known her during the period of her mission and after she became a captive. This meant not only her colleagues in the Resistance, but the Germans; only they could tell me some things. Of the Germans, by far the most important was Ernest. After having been held for nearly five years in Allied hands for questioning, he had, when I began to look for him, just been discharged by the French authorities with a paper saying he was not wanted for any war crime, and it was an officer of the Tribunal Militaire Permanent de Paris who gave me the address in Germany which he had left. I wrote to him, explaining that I was a friend of 'Madeleine', Noor Inayat Khan, that I understood he had arrested her and had charge of her interrogation, during the period of her detention by the *Sicherheitsdienst* at Avenue Foch, that I wanted to know all he could tell me, for a book about her that I was writing, and that I would be grateful if he would be good enough to see me.

He replied. It was a good reply; he expressed his admiration for her as "a brave and steadfast Englishwoman", and said he would be willing to see me if I came to Germany. In fact, he arranged for his aunt to meet me on the railway platform, and to conduct me to the hotel, where he later called.

Tall, incredibly thin, grey-eyed, rather anxious, the man who had made her prisoner presented himself.

He told me the story which I later took down at dictation speed; and he asked me questions. What sort of a girl was she? What was she like, really? What was her family like? He knew that she loved her mother, for she had wept when she saw the photostat of the letter she had written her, and because, another time, she had spoken of her, weeping. It was all that he knew. What was her mother like? Was her father living, and what was he like? What were Madeleine's own occupations when she was not serving in the war? What things did she like doing? What things interested her?

As I answered him, he became more and more amazed and sad. "I suppose she is the best human being I have met in my life," he said.

I said I would send him a copy of the book I wrote about her, and also some of her father's books.[1]

It was not simply that he said he had been affected by her.

[1] In fact, I sent him **The Unity of Religious Ideals**, and of course, **Madeleine**, when it came out.

There was something else, which convinced me in an absolute manner. As he told me things she had said, he used turns of speech only she would have used. His voice even took on her intonation. It was as if I was hearing Noor speak, through his vocal chords.

"I feel you knew her as well as I did," I heard myself say. "It's like talking to a friend of hers."

Not yet used to freedom, Ernest was always anxious lest, if we met more than once in the same place, some secret service might have installed microphones to catch whatever he let fall. For this reason, he was really easiest when we were out of doors, and we spent much of our time walking. Thus, it was on a hillside, in the stillness of the following afternoon, that he broke a silence which had fallen, with words that surprised me. Recently, I set them in a poem. I did not write it for this book, but perhaps I may be forgiven for quoting from it:

We had climbed to a wooden seat above the town.
"Do you believe Madeleine is dead?" he asked.

"Oh yes, Wassmer took her to Dachau ..."

"It's not what I meant," he said. "I wondered
If you thought she was here now? She was so full
Of life. I still see her face and her eyes as she faced
Me. Her small clenched hands. I think she would join
Us, hearing us speak of her. You
Were a friend of hers, and I
Admired her in such a way that I would have liked
To have been her friend, if she had not been
My prisoner ...
                Why did she do it?" he burst out
Suddenly. "Why did she throw her beautiful
Life away? Why did she let herself be parachuted[1]
Where we were? I could be angry with her,
That she put herself where I had to arrest her ... If I
Had let her escape me, she might not be dead. You knew her. Why
Did she do it?"
                "To help liberate France from the Germans."
"To help liberate France from the Germans! I under-
Stand ... Her sacrifice was for nothing. We played her radio
Back to London, and used it to lure new English and Frenchmen
Into our hands. I never told her this. They died
In Buchenwald. Do you believe

[1] I leave his word uncorrected. Ernest did not know she had stepped to the ground from a Lysander.

265

In immortality?"
      He said that when he was young
He had almost been religious. But the Church said animals
Had no souls. This seemed to him unfair. He felt if they
Could have no afterlife, then we had none.
                              "Perhaps
They, too, survive", I said.
      He drew a breath:
"It's all of us or none of us!" he said. "She was so alive
I cannot believe she is no more. Because of her,
I believe in immortality . . ."

BIBLIOGRAPHY

A View of the Origin and Conduct of the War with Tippoo Sultaun, comprising a narrative of the operations of the Army under the command of Lieutenant-General George Harris, and of the Siege of Seringapatam, by Lieutenant-General Alexander Beatson, Late Aide-de-Camp to the Marquis of Wellesley, Governor-General of India; and Surveyor-General to the Army in the Field (London, W. Bullmer, Cleveland Row, St. James's, 1800)

Pages in the Life of a Sufi, Reflections and Reminiscences of Musharaff Moulamia Khan (London, Rider, 1930, Servire, 1975)

Confessions, Inayat Khan (London, Sufi Publishing Society, 1915)

Diwan, of Inayat Khan (Southampton, The Sufi Publishing Society, 1915)

The Way of Illumination, Inayat Khan (Southampton, The Sufi Movement, 1921)

The Unity of Religious Ideals, Inayat Khan (Southampton, The Sufi Movement, 1929)

The Gayan, Inayat Khan (Southampton, Sufi Order Society, 1923)

The Inner Life, Inayat Khan (Deventer, Holland, AE. E. Kluwer, 1923, East-West Publications (UK) Ltd, London, 1980)

Moral Culture, Inayat Khan (Deventer, Holland, AE. E. Kluwer, 1937)

Rassa Shastra, the Science of Life's Creative Forces, Inayat Khan (Deventer, Holland, AE. E. Kluwer, 1938)

Metaphysics, The Experience of the Soul through Different Planes of Existence, Inayat Khan (Deventer, Holland, AE. E. Kluwer, 1939)

Twenty Jataka Tales Retold, by Noor Inayat, Pictured by H. Willebeek Le Mair (London, Harrap, 1939, East-West Publications Fonds B.V., The Hague, 1977)

Concerning the life, mission, capture and captivity of Noor, there is no bibliography, for my only source was my field-research. Statements I took from my informants, whose names appear in the Acknowledgements which follow, my own typed resumés of what they had told me in conversation, returned to me with annotations in their hands, and letters from them to me are in my files.

SOURCES AND ACKNOWLEDGEMENTS

My grateful thanks are due to the informants whom I acknowledge below practically in the order in which their material has been used:[1]

The Master of the Household, Buckingham Palace, for permission to see the gold tiger's head and gold huma bird, from the throne of Tipu Sultan, kept in the Gold Pantry of Windsor Castle.

Mr. Ellis, the Superintendant, for receiving me at Windsor Castle and taking me into the Gold Pantry to see these relics of Tipu Sultan.

Mr. Owen Morshead, Librarian of Windsor Castle, for a note of the relics of Tipu Sultan in the Royal Library.

Mr. S. C. Sutton, Librarian of the India Office Library, and Mrs. C. M. McQuillan, for him, for showing me their relics of Tipu Sultan, and arranging for a photocopy of his manuscript record of his dreams to be made for me.

Pir Vilayat Inayat Khan, for the greater part of the family background, and for reading and checking the whole of Book I.

Hidayat Inayat Khan.

Claire Harper, née Khair-un-nisa Inayat Khan.

Noor's Uncle, Murshid Musharaff Moulamia Khan, and her cousin, Mahmood Maheboob Khan.

Dr. E. E. Van Tricht-Keesing

Madame Mignon Nevada.

Madame Raymonde Lacour, née Prénat; her mother, Madame Prénat, and her two sisters.

Mademoiselle Geneviève Vanlaère.

Madame R. Haas.

The Secretary-General of the Ecole Normale de Musique de Paris.

Mademoiselle Nadia Boulanger.

Mademoiselle Henriette Renié.

The Management of the Salle Erard.

Mr. Wite Carp, not only for producing this edition, but for collecting for it some of Noor's own compositions and early letters which did not appear in the original. (The English translations of these are by myself). I should like to make special mention of Mr. Carp's more than helpful secretary, Mrs. Tilly Muller.

Noor's first fiancé, who wishes to remain anonymous.

Dr. and Madame Jourdan and their daughter Françoise.

Madame Hélène Bouvard, whose testimony appears for the first time in this edition.

[1] I have preferred not to remove from this list some who have passed away.

The Baroness van Tuyll van Serooskerken, née Willebeek Le
Maire.

Professor Basil G. Mitchell, MA.

Dr. Theodore J. Cadoux, Ph. D.

Madame Magda Watteew, née Hoste, and her father.

Miss Wendela Wheating.

Squadron Officer B. G. Martin, The Air Ministry, for Noor's
record of service.

Mrs. Dorothy Ryman.

Mrs. Joan Wynne, née Clifton.

Mr. F. R. Archer.

Mr. Selwyn Jepson, who has himself written the chapter 'Interview at the War Office' from the beginning down to the
end of the inverted commas, and checked the footnotes to
that chapter.

Mr. Maurice Buckmaster, OBE.

Miss Vera M. Atkins, who gave me, in addition to her own
information, some help in tracing other members of SOE.

Mrs. Joan Sanderson.

Colonel Frank Spooner, whose testimony appears for the first
time in this edition.

The late Mr. Henri Eugène Alfred Déricourt, alias "Gilbert". As
I have mentioned in the text, I was at the time when the earlier
editions of this book appeared, wholly ignorant of the existence
and crucial role of this very important officer, the Air Movements Officer of S.O.E. "French Section". Doubtless, the sinis-
ter controversies of which his name was the centre had deterred
any of those whom I interviewed while writing *Madeleine* from
mentioning him to me. I had written two books on dramas of
this service, *Madeleine* and *The Starr Affair,* before chance, in
the shape of a German book, brought to my knowledge that
there had existed a "double" called "Gilbert". My third book
Double Webs was concerned with the steps by which I uncover-
ed his case, and my meeting with him. He had been tried and
acquitted by French Court Martial on a charge of intelligence
with the enemy on June 7th, 1948. Perhaps the testimony of
a "double" is always suspect; yet he dealt fairly with me, and
I believe what he told me of dealings with Madeleine to be
true. He remained in correspondence with me for two years
after the publication of my book about his case, and I much
regret that he has been killed in an air crash in The Far East.

Madame Marguerite Garry, née Nadaud. Madame Garry has
read very carefully all the passages in which she or her husband are mentioned. On the pages in the Avenue Foch section
which I wrote after her information, she re-wrote in her own
words three paragraphs, including that beginning, 'Madame
Garry adds . . .'

Madame Pinchon.

Professor and Madame Balachowsky. Madame Balachowsky has read and checked all the passages incorporating their information.

Madame Aigrain.

Madame Salmon, née Grutars.

Madame Grover Williams.

Miss Lise de Baissac, MBE.

Madame Jourdois.

Madame Peineau.

The gentlemen I have designated Maître Y, for an interview which he gave me at the side of Monsieur X, though I have made no use of the statement given me by X.

Monsieur P. Viennot. Monsieur Viennot offered, very gallantly I thought, to come with me to visit X, whom he had not seen since the war (but whom I had met before I met Viennot) to talk over the affair on the Avenue Mac-Mahon and decide, if possible with his consent, on the manner in which it should be presented. He asked Y, who was always in touch with X, to be so good as to tell him he would like to see him for this purpose; but Y informed him later by telephone that X refused. Faced with this impasse, we had to find a solution without him. Viennot then suggested, 'If you are willing to take my word that it happened as I say, I propose that you should call them both by letters of the alphabet.' He read and checked my draft of his part of the book.

Madame Simone Caillez, née Truffit.

Solange.

Mr. John A. R. Starr. Mr. Starr has been to very much trouble to enable me to prepare the long account which appears. He took me and Colonel Mercier (then Captain, of the Tribunal Militaire of Paris), back to 84 Avenue Foch and showed us over the building. Then we all three went on to 9 *bis* Square du Bois de Boulogne, where we made the discovery that the window broken by the three fugitives still remained unrepaired. With the permission of Madame Esmerian—who recognized Starr —we went up the stairs, first into the sitting-room where he and Madeleine had been recaptured, and then on to the roof, from where I could see the whole of the way by which they had come from the Avenue Foch, and where we found, mouldering it is true, even the little collection of flower-pots in which he had disposed of some notes. Starr composed with me the paragraphs from the beginning down to 'photographed and sent up to Berlin'; and the rest I wrote myself and sent to him to check. He permitted me to send a copy of the draft to Ernest for the interest of a check from the other side.

Madame Esmerian.

Ernest—whose surname is known both to the War Office and to the Sûreté. Ernest has been held for questioning by the Allies for the greater part of five years, having been examined and released by the American, British, German (De-Nazification), and French Authorities in that order. He was liberated by the last, after an eleven months' examination, in March 1950, with a *Non Lieu* (a paper stating they found no charge to bring against him) and another saying he was *Définitivement Relaché*, Definitely Released. At the same time, he was sent to the frontier and instructed to proceed to Baden-Baden, the centre of the French Military Government in Germany, where he was issued by the *Service des Crimes de Guerre* with a further paper certifying he was not a War Criminal. He showed me all these. We worked together for six days. The testimony he has given, though mainly in the third person, is entirely in his own words; he dictated it to me, phrase by phrase, and I took it down, only correcting the English when it was necessary, and left him with a copy of it. Afterwards I sent him the whole of the Avenue Foch section, and some pages from the Field section, on which he made the comments I have incorporated in the form of notes.

Herr Wilhelm Krauss. As Herr Krauss gave me his interview through an interpreter, I sent him afterwards a copy of his statement translated back into German by a third person, to be certain no errors had crept in.

Herr Neifeind—the present Governor of Pforzheim prison.

Herr Webber, District Attorney, for receiving me in the Staatsanwaltschaft, Pforzheim. Herr Webber gave me a man speaking a little English to conduct me to the prison and help me in my conversations with the staff if my German proved inadequate. He said I might ask any member of the staff what questions I liked. The guards conducted me through practically all the cells and courtyards; they offered to take me also into the cellars, kitchens, sick-bay, and other apartments, but I did not think this necessary.

Herr Anton Giller.

Herr Friedrich Fässer.

Mr. Dennis McFarlin, at one moment of UNRRA.

Madame Yolande Lagrave.

Herr Max Wassmer.

Baroness Ward of North Tyneside, CH., DBE.

M. Rémy Clément

Mr. Timothy d'Arch Smith, for his goodness in helping me to check both the galley and page proofs of this edition.

NOOR-UN-NISA INAYAT KHAN

by Jean Overton Fuller

INDEX

(compiled by Douglas Matthews)